HISTORICAL EXPLANATION
Re-enactment and Practical Inference

CONTEMPORARY PHILOSOPHY

General Editor
Max Black, Cornell University

Historical Explanation

RE-ENACTMENT AND
PRACTICAL INFERENCE

Rex Martin

Cornell University Press

ITHACA AND LONDON

First published 1977 by Cornell University Press.
Published in the United Kingdom by Cornell University Press Ltd.,
2–4 Brook Street, London W1Y 1AA.

International Standard Book Number 0-8014-1084-3
Library of Congress Catalog Card Number 77-3121
Printed in the United States of America by Vail-Ballou Press, Inc.
*Librarians: Library of Congress cataloging information
appears on last page of the book.*

Acknowledgments

I undertook my first serious study of philosophy of history in Charles Frankel's classes. I read Walsh's *Introduction to Philosophy of History* and discovered Collingwood's *Idea of History.* The stimulation of these classes and of the books I read then must have been powerful, for they set me on a course of study that I have pursued to this day and have found, in equal measure, endlessly fascinating and profoundly frustrating.

I have found Arthur Danto's books, especially his *Analytical Philosophy of History,* and several of his articles enormously helpful and have returned to them again and again. He has been, and not merely through his books, my teacher and counselor. It was at his suggestion that I began the task of writing what has now become this book.

A year in Edinburgh afforded opportunity to meet W. H. Walsh and to have the first of many discussions with him; these have continued, by mail and in person, over the years. I have appreciated his many acts of hospitality and kindness. He has undertaken on several occasions the laborious job of reading what I have written: I have benefited greatly from his advice and criticism and, especially, his encouragement.

In the fall of 1971 Georg Henrik von Wright's book *Explanation and Understanding* was published. It set me thinking along new lines;

Acknowledgments

in time, this thinking took shape in Chapters Nine and Ten of the present book. G. H. von Wright gave generously of his time and counsel during the year I spent in Helsinki. Our discussions of his book and other writings were of incalculable value. And I am grateful too for his many constructive criticisms of my work and, especially, for his thoughtfulness, his welcome friendship, and his supportive good will.

I am most indebted, though, to Donna Paul Martin. She has been a constant and benign influence on the development of my book: forcing me to think through problems, to weigh my words, to write as clearly as I could. I especially owe her thanks for helping me untangle the threads of argument in Chapter Seven and for suggesting some of the nuances of the particular historical example that I examine there. She has been my first and best critic.

I also want to thank friends and colleagues who have patiently listened to my arguments and responded with helpful comments and criticism of their own. Much of what they have contributed has found its way into the text; all of it has been considered. I am especially grateful in this regard to Jack Bricke, Allan Hanson, Deborah Johnson, Donald Marquis, and Raimo Tuomela. I have, in the bibliography, listed writings by each of them that I have found particularly helpful.

Several institutions have supported my work at its various stages: a grant from the Danforth Foundation and the Society for Religion in Higher Education made it possible for me to spend a year in Scotland; the Fulbright program provided a research scholarship to Finland; the National Endowment for the Humanities awarded a fellowship for independent study and research during the tenure of which I was able to complete the writing of this book. I am especially grateful to the University of Kansas for its generous support of my research efforts: with a Watkins summer research fellowship, with several General Research Fund grants (in particular, 3180–5038), with an international travel grant (jointly with the Philosophical Society of Finland) to attend a conference in Helsinki, and with a recent year's sabbatical leave. I am indebted too to my colleagues in Philosophy at the University of Kansas for the stimulation, the seriousness, the *esprit de corps* which is the backdrop of all philosophical work and indebted especially, for her encouragement and help, to Constance Ducey.

Acknowledgments

Marc L. B. Bloch. *Feudal Society.* Translated from the French by L. A. Manyon. By permission of Routledge & Kegan Paul (London, 1961) and the University of Chicago Press (Chicago, 1968). English translation © 1961 by Routledge & Kegan Paul Ltd.

R. G. Collingwood. *The Idea of History.* Edited with an introduction by T. M. Knox. By permission of the Oxford University Press (Oxford, 1946).

F. A. Hanson and R. Martin. "The Problem of Other Cultures," *Philosophy of the Social Sciences,* 3 (1973), 191–208. By permission of the Managing Editor, for use as a source, in particular, of Chapter Eleven.

R. Martin. "Explanation and Understanding in History," in J. Manninen and R. Tuomela, eds., *Essays on Explanation and Understanding* (Synthese Library 72), pp. 305–334. By permission of D. Reidel Publishing Company (Dordrecht, Holland, 1976), for use as a source, in particular, of Chapter Five.

R. Martin. "The Problem of the 'Tie' in von Wright's Schema of Practical Inference: A Wittgensteinian Solution," in J. Hintikka, ed., *Essays on Wittgenstein in Honour of G. H. von Wright. Acta Philosophica Fennica,* 28 (1976), 326–363. By permission of the Secretary of the Philosophical Society of Finland, for use as a source, in particular, of Chapters Nine and Ten.

W. H. Walsh. *An Introduction to Philosophy of History.* 3d ed. By permission of the Hutchinson Publishing Group (London, 1967, in the Hutchinson University Library series; currently the third edition is being reprinted in Great Britain by Harvester Press and in the United States by Humanities Press).

REX MARTIN

Contents

HISTORICAL EXPLANATION

Re-enactment and Practical Inference

One

Introduction

The expression "the philosophy of history" has come to have various associations. By some it may be regarded as signifying a submarine monster, dredged from the deep waters of nineteenth-century metaphysics, its jaws occasionally opening to emit prophecies in a dead (or at any rate a foreign) tongue—the language of Hegelian dialectic. By some it is thought to be a mysterious subject, not quite philosophy, and yet again, not quite history, but a kind of vaguely disreputable amalgam of both. [p. ix]

These words, apologetic and somewhat wary, introduced Patrick Gardiner's monograph on *The Nature of Historical Explanation* (1952). Much the same note was struck by W. H. Walsh in the opening pages of his *Introduction to Philosophy of History* (1951). Walsh even went so far as to note, in a section called "Current Suspicion of the Subject" (pp. 9–12, 1st ed.), that "a writer on philosophy of history, in Great Britain at least, must begin by justifying the very existence of his subject." He added that nineteenth-century philosophy of history, in attempting to provide a "speculative treatment of the whole course of history," had quite early taken on a rather bad reputation among British philosophers and that, as a result of this bias, "philosophy of history has been, until recent years, virtually non-existent" in Britain.

13

Historical Explanation

Such defensive statements would hardly find expression today. Indeed, interest in philosophy of history, among both philosophers and historians, has revived dramatically, largely as a result of the analytic turn which recent philosophy of history has taken. This new, analytic approach marks a sharp break with the older style to which Gardiner and Walsh made allusion. The main feature of this older or metaphysical style was its concentration on the actual course of history to divine the basic purpose or meaning and thereby exhibit the essential rationality of historical events by seeing in them some overall plan or pattern. Philosophy of history, conceived as treating of the course of history as a whole, was best done in the grand manner of an Augustine or a Hegel. Not even sober Victorian gentlemen like Mill and Marx were wholly immune to its charm.

The analytic style, in contrast, is not involved with the event side of history at all; rather, its chief concern has been to elucidate the concept and structure of historical inquiry. Its object has been the analytic study of history as a discipline and form of knowledge; accordingly, it has amounted to systematic reflection on the presuppositions, the character, and the implications of historical knowledge.

Such questions as the following come under consideration in the analytic type of philosophy of history: How does history relate to other forms of knowledge? Is history a science? What is historical "truth"? How are historical facts located and established? What is our idea of the historical past? What sort of objectivity, if any, is possible for historians? How do historians explain or understand? Are there any laws that historians formulate or use in their explanations? [1]

The last of these, the question of historical explanation or understanding, tended to become and has remained the principal focus of attention; and it provides the topic of the present book. The term *historical explanation* is not as clear as one would like and a brief cautionary note seems called for accordingly. For what I intend to discuss under this heading is only *one* of the main types of historical explanation, that whereby we explain actions by referring deeds to the

---

1. I have given a composite list. It draws on Walsh (*Introduction to Philosophy of History*, pp. 17–26), Gardiner (*Nature of Historical Explanation*, pp. x–xi), and Dray (*Philosophy of History*, pp. 2–3). See also the more recent standard texts in the subject: Gardiner, ed., *Philosophy of History* (esp. pp. 1–15, 218–222) and Atkinson, *Knowledge and Explanation in History: An Introduction* (introd. and ch. 1, esp. sec. 1–3).

Introduction

"thoughts" of individual agents (to their purposes, situation-conceptions, means/end beliefs, and so on).

Now, clearly, there are other types of explanations offered by historians. Sometimes they are concerned to explain the "thoughts" or even the world view of historical agents, sometimes the institutional setting in which these deeds and beliefs have substance. Sometimes, indeed, we can even find, in works of history, explanations of physical events (such as the desolation of a city or the gradual wasting away of a countryside) in which deeds and beliefs played some part but by no means the whole or even the most important causal role. We must take care then not to overemphasize the place of "intentionalistic" explanations in history: there are connections within the world view of a people, just as there are happenings in its social institutions or in its ecosystem, of which individual persons are largely, perhaps wholly, unconscious; and these can hardly be explained on an intentionalistic model.

Equally, we find the thing I have described as historical explanation in many other places than history: in courts of law, in journalistic accounts, in the various social sciences. Historical explanation, in the rather limited sense of an action accounted for by referring to the agent's purpose and the like, is not limited to historians.

Nonetheless, what I have designated, and what is conventionally called up, by that name is central to the concerns of historians and characteristic of much of what they do. And it is, strangely, since such explanations are so common, precisely this type of explanation which has proven peculiarly recalcitrant to philosophical analysis.

We might do well to note another odd fact: history is the least developed of the social sciences (if it even is one); yet analytic philosophy of history is generally more sophisticated than the philosophy of social science. There are surely reasons for this, though it may well be that the strikingly problematic character of historical explanation is mainly responsible for this curious state of affairs. In any event, philosophy of history by taking the analytic turn has moved from being suspect and "vaguely disreputable" to become at least as solid as the discipline of history, if not the social sciences themselves. We are now able to make out the character of what has emerged.

The present-day trend in philosophy of history can be traced back to the 1940s, to three seminal treatises: Hempel's "Function of General

Laws in History" (1942), Collingwood's *Idea of History* (1946), and Ryle's *Concept of Mind* (1949).[2] But the book by Collingwood probably deserves pride of place. And that book, a prime mover in the revival of philosophy of history, has remained one of its continuing formative influences. Collingwood was able to raise a number of philosophical issues important to historical inquiry and to suggest solutions to these issues, solutions that his younger contemporaries have felt worth considering.

Collingwood's ideas have been singularly influential among practicing historians; indeed it may well be true that "historians have read *The Idea of History* who have not opened another philosophical book since they were undergraduates" (Mink, *Mind, History, and Dialectic*, p. 1). I myself have met historians who practically glowed at the mention of Collingwood's name. There seems to be a peculiar sense, on the part of many working historians, that Collingwood is *their* philosopher of history. Yet I find it interesting that of the major studies on Collingwood that have appeared, most of them only recently, not one has made *The Idea of History* central.[3]

Donagan sees in *The New Leviathan* (1942) the key to Collingwood's "later philosophy." Mink regards *Speculum Mentis* (1924) as the fundamental work in Collingwood's "system" and even goes so far as to assert that the substantive chapters of *The Idea of History* are "largely unintelligible unless they are interpreted in the light of Collingwood's dialectical theory of mind as we have reconstructed it" (Mink, p. 157; see also pp. 3, 80). Rubinoff, if anything, outdoes Mink in his emphasis on *Speculum Mentis*; indeed much of Rubinoff's discussion of history is focused on that work, and not really on *The Idea of History* at all. And, finally, the most interesting single feature of the volume of *Critical Essays*, to my mind at least, is the al-

2. *The Idea of History* was published in 1946—after Collingwood's death—under the editorship of T. M. Knox. Although the book came out in 1946 and the effective influence of Collingwood dates from that year, the *content* of the book is of somewhat earlier vintage, 1935 to 1940 but primarily 1935 to 1936 (see "Editor's Preface"). Throughout, Collingwood's *Idea of History* has been cited in the form: *IH*, 213, where that means p. 213 of the book.

3. I am referring to Alan H. Donagan, *Later Philosophy of Collingwood* (1962); L. O. Mink, *Mind, History, and Dialectic: The Philosophy of R. G. Collingwood* (1969); Lionel Rubinoff, *Collingwood and the Reform of Metaphysics: A Study in the Philosophy of Mind* (1970); and Michael Krausz, ed., *Critical Essays on the Philosophy of R. G. Collingwood* (1972). The Rubinoff and Krausz volumes have extensive and useful bibliographies.

Introduction

most total absence of any sustained discussion of *The Idea of History*. Indeed, the only essay that takes up the themes of *The Idea of History* at any length, Mink's essay on "Collingwood's Historicism," is principally devoted to substantiating the claim, already noted, that this book of Collingwood's must be seen as "a part of a more comprehensive philosophy the understanding of which greatly illuminates and partially modifies it but which cannot be reconstructed from the text of *The Idea of History* itself" (in Krausz, *Critical Essays*, p. 155).

I am not, of course, suggesting that Collingwood's *Idea of History* has been ignored—far from it. For there have been many studies, in books and dissertations and articles, that touch on it or that take up one or another of its themes. Yet nowhere has *The Idea of History* received the extended treatment that it warrants.

Furthermore, virtually none of the literature that touches on Collingwood's philosophy of history has said much of value about the essential link Collingwood saw between historical judgment or understanding, on the one hand, and such notions as "historical process" and "human nature," on the other. There has been considerable discussion about Collingwood's peculiar conception of historical judgment; we are told that Collingwood denied generalization in history in the interests of something called variously "empathy" or "intuition" or "re-enactment." But there seems to be little awareness of the grounds of Collingwood's peculiar conception, of what lies behind his arguments respecting the nature of historical explanation.

The difficulty in the attempt to get at Collingwood's views is not simply that his underlying conception (of mind–process–human nature, if I may call it that) has largely been ignored. The problem is compounded by the fact that those few discussions we do find have not been particularly helpful.[4]

---

4. The only notable exception to my remarks is found in the writing of W. H. Walsh, whose treatment of Collingwood at this point is sound but has the disadvantage—to be expected in any introductory work—of being too compressed and rather unsystematic.

Morton White has also discussed the important role that the idea of "transcultural principles of human nature" has played, especially in the writing of Hume and Mill, in the development of our conception of a science of man. White's discussion is very sophisticated and he even notes the connection of that idea with Collingwood's own philosophical predispositions; but he notes it only in passing, with a remark. (See *Foundations of Historical Knowledge*, pp. 6, 38, 52–53, 216–217, and esp. p. 217.) Rubinoff has devoted an entire appendix of his book to the suggestive topic of "Positivism, Historicism, and the Idea of a Science of Human Nature" (*Collingwood and the Reform of*

Historical Explanation

Indeed, some of the discussions have been positively misleading. Thus, we find Hodges saying, in the course of summing up similarities and differences between Dilthey and Collingwood, "The experience of seeking and finding in the sphere of history is a fundamental experience for them both, and they accept without doubt the presuppositions which seem necessary to account for it, viz. the fundamental invariance of the structure of human nature and especially of the ideals of thought and action." [5] But in my opinion, the idea of an "identity in nature" between different men at different times and of the "fundamental invariance" of the "structure of human nature" was the very thing that Collingwood meant to *deny*. If this is so, then one can hardly allege that the presumption of an invariant and uniform "human nature" lies behind Collingwood's re-enactment theory of historical understanding.

I want to begin my study of historical explanation by attempting to restore Collingwood's doctrine of re-enactment archeologically, by returning it to its original site, to its grounds. Let us conceive Collingwood's position as a two-part structured theory: we can call these two parts, respectively, (a) the methodological—Collingwood's dicta on the nature of historical understanding—and (b) the anthropological—Collingwood's process view of mind. Logically, the anthropological part is the presupposition and foundation of the methodological part. Now corresponding to this let us conceive a similar theory belonging to what we can call the "philosophy of human nature"; and its two parts can be summarized as: (a) methodology—the idea of general laws of social science—and (b) anthropology—the notion of universal regularities.

The "dialectical" relationship between these two positions, that of Collingwood and that of the "philosophy of human nature," can be described in a series of moves.

(1) Behind Collingwood's distinctive views on historical understanding lies a theory of human activity which we might call the "process view of mind."

Metaphysics, pp. 338–363); but surprisingly little of what he says is directed to Collingwood specifically (see here pp. 5–6, 338–339, 354–356) and that little, to my mind at least, is of no great philosophic interest.

5. H. A. Hodges, *The Philosophy of Wilhelm Dilthey*, p. 357. Very similar views, as regards Collingwood, have been expressed by Nathan Rotenstreich; see his "History and Time: a Critical Examination of R. G. Collingwood's Doctrine," esp. pp. 54–56.

Introduction

(2) This theory was developed as a critical reaction and reasoned alternative to the conception of an invariant and uniform human nature (as we find it, for example, in the philosophy of Hume or Mill) and, in particular, to the assertion of universal regularities in mind and in behavior.

(3) Collingwood's countertheory, the process view of mind, was advanced as a ground for denying this notion of universal regularities in principle, as systematically impossible.

(4) Collingwood's strategy was to undercut general law methodology in history and the social sciences by ruling out what he took to be its logical prerequisite, the idea of universal regularities.

(5) Finally, Collingwood attempted to replace this general law methodology with an alternative theory of explanatory judgments which did not, he claimed, logically require general laws or rest on any presumption of universal regularities and which was, at the same time, consonant with the principles of his process view of mind.

This rather intricate relationship of theory and countertheory represents, in my opinion, the main *argument structure* of Collingwood's philosophy of history—as we find it expounded, primarily, in *The Idea of History*. I would not claim, in saying this, that the argument structure I have outlined encompasses every feature of Collingwood's idea of history. But I do think that this structure, if elaborated, delineates one of the fundamental and characteristic themes of *The Idea of History* and that it makes explicit a widely held opinion about the nature and subject matter of social science inquiry.[6]

Accordingly, if we are to understand the internal logic of *The Idea of History*, and in particular the notion of re-enactment, we need to work out this argument structure with some care. And since no work on Collingwood has laid out this structure and developed its interior logic, it is to this task that I would like to turn.

The issue Collingswood has raised in his critique of the idea of a science of human nature, the issue of universal regularities in mind and behavior and of the grounds on which they hold, is of substantial importance in the philosophy of history and the social sciences. For it is widely believed that to accept or to reject the notion of universal regularities marks out a sort of continental divide between differing interpretations of the character and presuppositions of social science in-

6. As a shorthand device, I have usually referred to this argument structure as Collingwood's critique of the idea of a science of human nature.

Historical Explanation

quiry. If we take naturalism (sometimes called positivism) and antinaturalism (sometimes called historicism or idealism) as the polar positions, then the basic dichotomy goes somewhat as follows. Those who hold to a naturalistic view of social science, wanting to approximate it to the model of natural sciences like physics, and who propound a general law methodology, also subscribe to the notion of universal regularities. On the other hand, those who are antinaturalistic and who propound radical alternatives to the general law methodology also tend to deny the notion of universal regularities.

Whether there is a logical and necessary relationship between one's philosophical views on methodology and the position one takes on universal regularities is the obvious and crucial question to raise. But, without either begging or prejudging the question, I would suggest the following consideration: it seems that any argument that (a) requires or postulates "universal hypotheses" or "general laws" among the premises of explanations in history or in social science and (b) states that these general propositions have transhistorical *application* would have, *prima facie*, a logical commitment to the notion of universal regularities.

What I have said here would hold as much of Hempel as it does of Hume. My point is that, whether the "universal hypothesis" in question is a general law (Hempel) or what can loosely be called a "general principle" (Hume), the stipulation of unlimited scope in formulation *and* of transhistorical application in explanatory use would appear to involve, logically, a commitment to some notion of universal recurrences. Both men, I would add, are aware of such a commitment and endorse the idea of universal recurrences explicitly. For instance, Hempel asserts that his general laws amount to "an explicit statement" of "general regularities" (p. 349). And he specifically ties his argument into the Humean idea of "reference to similar cases and to general regularities" ("Function of General Laws in History," p. 354 n. 7; see also pp. 345–346).

In any event, if there is a plausible case for what I have just outlined, then there is good reason to consider an argument that attempts to discount general law methodology by ruling out the notion of universal regularities in principle and, conversely, that supports its case for an alternative methodology on the systematic impossibility of general recurrences. Such an argument—and it is, of course, the one in Collingwood's critique—rests, as I have indicated, on a premise that may be questionable: the premise that the formulation and use of "universal explanatory hypotheses" *necessarily* requires the notion of universal regularities as a presupposition. But we can determine the acceptability of this premise only by considering Collingwood's argument.

One of my principal concerns in this study, then, is to determine whether universal hypotheses are logically required by the explanations which historians and other social scientists give of human actions, and whether their use would commit us to accepting *some* version of universal regularities in mind and behavior—in particular, that version provided in the uniformity conception of human nature.

At the same time I do not want to lose track of the peculiar bearing that Collingwood's overall view has on the issue of explanation in history and the social sciences. According to his account of historical understanding, our true objective is to understand the actions of others by recreating or re-enacting their deeds in our own minds. But here the question naturally arises: how can we have any basis for believing that the thought-connections we entertain in order to re-enact these actions are in fact those of the persons we are studying?

The usual way of solving this problem has been to bridge the gap with an assumption of *similarity* between the investigator and his object. Thus we find Dilthey saying "the fact that the investigator of history is the same as the one who makes it is the first condition which makes scientific history possible." Berlin is in agreement: "The modes of thought of the ancients or of any culture remote from our own are comprehensible to us only in the degree to which we share some, at any rate, of their basic categories." [7] But these passages serve merely to remind us that the move to similarity will not work in the case at hand, for one of Collingwood's primary assumptions is transhistorical, or cross-cultural, *difference*. This implies, precisely, that the thoughts we attribute to the persons of another period or culture are probably not their own, for the assumption of basic difference makes it highly unlikely that we actually could share ideas, concepts, and beliefs of a culture or period significantly different from our own.

This, then, is the other crucial issue with which my study is concerned: is the process view of mind which Collingwood developed

---

7. W. Dilthey, *Pattern and Meaning in History*, p. 67 (see also p. 123) and I. Berlin, *Historical Inevitability*, p. 61. Berlin has elaborated his viewpoint at greater length in his essay "The Concept of Scientific History," esp. pp. 43–51.

compatible with his own theory of explanatory re-enactment or, for that matter, with any theory of historical explanation? This is perhaps the most acute problem raised by the argument of Collingwood's critique of the idea of a science of human nature.

My study of historical explanation is intended to raise an important set of philosophical issues, to treat these issues in a contemporary philosophical idiom as well as in Collingwood's own, and to use the distinctions and analyses propounded in more recent philosophy of history as a way of getting a purchase on the issues. The point of my study is to provide a philosophical criticism both of Collingwood and of the development of philosophy of history since his time. For I think that, just as the literature on Collingwood has tended to ignore or misconstrue his critique of the science of human nature, so also has the literature of philosophy of history failed to take adequate account of his theory of re-enactment.

In the final analysis my study, though it does assign an important place to that theory, is not principally about Collingwood's book or his ideas. It could more accurately be described as a series of meditations on themes raised by *The Idea of History*. For I found as I worked that, while Collingwood's views did represent to some extent the working assumptions and the methods of the practicing historian, his appreciation of the logical problems involved in the notion of re-enactment, like his reponse to them, was defective. I had in my thinking about re-enactment to go well beyond the point at which I started, indeed beyond Collingwood. I found it necessary to consider a widening circle of thinkers, as further aspects of the logic of explanation by re-enactment were disclosed. And I have attempted to take some measure of the considerable refinement in the *theory* of historical explanation which has occurred since the time of Collingwood's book: in the work of Walsh and Dray and Donagan, of Hempel and Danto and Morton White, of Paul Churchland and, especially, of G. H. von Wright.

My study has become a philosophical history of the philosophy of history during the time since that crucial formative decade of the 1940s. The theory of historical explanation I ultimately propound and defend in the course of this book can be regarded as a radically modified version of Collingwood's original theory, transformed under the pressure of more recent philosophical materials. But it can equally well be taken as an attempt to integrate the notion of re-enactment

Introduction

into a more comprehensive theory of my own regarding the nature of historical explanation.

Here then is the only expedient, from which we can hope for success in our philosophical researches, to leave the tedious lingring method, which we have hitherto followed, and instead of taking now and then a castle or village on the frontier, to march up directly to the capital or center of these sciences, to human nature itself. [Hume, *Treatise*, p. xx.]

The uniformity conception of human nature is perhaps best known in the English-speaking world from the writings of David Hume; certainly his formulation of it has been among the most influential. And it is chiefly Hume's conception and that of his follower J. S. Mill which Collingwood undertook to attack in his critique of the idea of a science of human nature (see *IH*, 206). In the concluding part of this chapter, then, I would like to provide a brief summary, and I think a rather standard account, of Hume's views in this matter.[8]

There is in Hume's writings an unmistakable air of originality. He regarded himself as an innovator in an exceedingly difficult and complex field. Hume developed his conception of mental phenomena on the model of physical phenomena. His attitude was shaped by several considerations, but most important was his belief, part dogma and part hypothesis, that "our thoughts and conceptions [go on] in the same train with other works of nature" (*Inquiry*, p. 68). The mind is a system of nature: "the secret springs and principles by which the human mind is actuated in its operations" are not unlike "the laws and forces by which the revolutions of the planets are governed and directed" (*Inquiry*, p. 24). The originality of Hume lies in his conception of a *human* nature, of a system of mental phenomena structurally like the physical world.

For Hume the mind of man, conceived as simply and as fundamentally as possible, was analogous to the world of corpuscular matter envisioned by Newtonian physics in that it was composed of "particular perceptions," the atoms of the mental world. (See "Abstract," p. 194; and also *Treatise*, pp. 253, 634–635.) In the continual occurrence of perceptions, i.e., impressions and ideas, one perception follows an-

8. On the notion of a "standard interpretation," see Wertz, "Hume, History, and Human Nature," p. 483 (and esp. n. 7). Wertz thinks, and I agree, that Collingwood (among many others) could be listed as holding such an interpretation.

23

other, but the striking fact about this succession is the regularity with which certain perceptions are followed by certain other ones. This constant conjunction, holding between kinds of perceptions, Hume traced to certain universal associative operations which were themselves highly regular and which could, on the analogy of gravity, account for the regularities he had observed.[9]

These operations (or, as Hume often called them, "laws of association") are fundamental in the mental world; they are the principles of regular succession among "particular perceptions," the basic stuff of mind. They are the foundation of the regular successions observed in the understanding, in the imagination and the various passions, and, finally, in the actions of men.[10]

Let us take Hume's analysis a step further by seeing precisely how he worked human action into this conceptual apparatus. "There is," he said, "a general course of nature in human actions, as well as in the operations of the sun and the climate" (*Treatise*, pp. 402–403). This uniformity Hume attributed to the passions, which he said were "naturally alike in every individual" and were "the regular springs of human action and behavior." (See *Inquiry*, pp. 90 and 93, respectively.) Hume's idea seemed to be that the various passions were the crucial intermediary between the fundamental associative operations and the actions of men. Thus, by treating the passions as the motives or springs of action Hume was able to bring human action into his conception of a uniform system of nature. The peculiar force of Hume's conception of "a general course of nature in human actions," then, was that a wide variety of patterns could be detected in human behavior—a host of recurrent actions and passions constantly conjoined "in all times and places"—and that these patterns were all traceable to a single source, the fundamental constitution of the human mind.

9. The analogy with gravity occupies an important place in Hume's analysis: "Here is a kind of ATTRACTION, which in the mental world will be found to have as extraordinary effects as in the natural, and to show itself in as many and as various forms" (*Treatise*, pp. 12–13).

10. "These principles I allow to be neither the *infallible* nor the *sole* causes of an union among ideas; . . . yet I assert that the only *general* principles, which associate ideas, are resemblance, contiguity, and causation" (*Treatise*, pp. 92–93). At a later point he adds that "impressions" (that is, "impressions of reflection" or passions) are associated "only by resemblance" (see *Treatise*, p. 283).

Introduction

It is universally acknowledged that there is a great uniformity among the actions of men, in all nations and ages, and that human nature remains still the same in its principles and operations. The same motives always produce the same actions; the same events follow from the same causes. Ambition, avarice, self-love, vanity, friendship, generosity, public spirit—these passions, mixed in various degrees and distributed through society, have been, from the beginning of the world, and still are, the source of all the actions and enterprises which have been observed among mankind. [*Inquiry*, pp. 92–93]

The architectonic principle of Hume's "science of man" is provided by his conception of the uniformity of human nature. The notion of such a science begins with the assertion that human mental and behavioral activities are organized by certain universal and all but invariant associative operations, which belong to what he called the "original" or "primary" or fundamental "constitution of the mind." [11] This assertion, when systematically worked out as a conception of human nature, was meant to provide a rationale justifying the employment of a certain method in the scientific investigation of human affairs. And this was clearly stated by Hume when he said that "in pretending therefore to explain the principles of human nature, we in effect propose a compleat system of sciences, built on a foundation almost entirely new and the only one upon which they can stand with any security" (*Treatise*, p. xx).

Moreover, we have a warrant for saying that the methods for studying physical nature are also appropriate for the study of human activities. Since human activities constitute a type of natural system, the study of human affairs, according to Hume, is to be conducted in the same way as the study of the physical world: the methods and aims of social science should be those of natural science. The methods are those Hume called "experimental": observation, classification, and the framing and use of general laws. (See *Treatise*, p. xx; and *Inquiry*, p. 24.)

We can readily conceive of laws at each of three levels: (a) laws that describe the "original" associative operations of mind; (b) laws that describe the regular generation of each of the human passions (or

---

11. See *Treatise*, pp. 286, 368, for his use of the term "primary"; in his "Abstract" (p. 186) Hume used the term "original." By "primary" Hume did not mean primary in time; he meant ontologically primary, fundamental. I think the phrase "fundamental constitution of the mind" most accurately describes what he meant.

emotions, as we would call them) out of associative operations, and that describe the regular relationship of the various passions to one another; and, finally, (c) laws that describe the constant conjunction of actions and passions.[12]

In order to frame these general laws it is necessary only to observe the activities of present-day men and to see the relationships which obtain there. From these observations we can generalize to include men at other times. In each case, we move from observations to laws by way of generalization. This procedure, wholly consistent with Hume's postulate of uniformity, is one about which he was quite explicit:

> Would you know the sentiments, inclinations, and course of life of the Greeks and Romans? Study well the temper and actions of the French and English: you cannot be much mistaken in transferring to the former *most* of the observations which you have made with regard to the latter. Mankind are so much the same, in all times and places, that history informs us of nothing new or strange in this particular.[13]

And most of what Hume had to say in his discussion of the science of man was directed—often in a rather sketchy, programmatic way—to the special case of framing the general laws of human activity, especially those at the first two levels (laws we would call laws of psychology). But he allowed, of course, that there would be laws at the third level as well (framed, he suggested, by such sciences as economics and politics).

Hume thought that his conception of a uniform human nature and his maxim of following experience made possible an objective knowledge of human affairs. His idea of the laws of human nature held out the promise of an objective science of man, which would be analogous in subject-matter and method to the sciences of nature. This

12. Hume cites *two* associative laws concerned with the passions (for both: see *Treatise*, pp. 283–284). One of them is the law of association for "impressions" mentioned in n. 10 above; the other combines this law with the three associative laws for "ideas." What I have called laws for the generation of the various passions might better be described as *applications* of this combinatory law—with a different set of impressions and ideas involved for each of the kinds of passion. There are a variety of other laws which "assist" the application of the combinatory law in a given case. A full and helpful account is provided in two papers by Bricke: "Emotion and Thought in Hume's *Treatise*" and esp. "Hume's Associationist Psychology," pp. 397–402 and 408–409 in particular.

13. *Inquiry*, p. 93. Hume added, "Nor are the earth, water, and other elements examined by Aristotle and Hippocrates more like to those which at present lie under our observation than the men described by Polybius and Tacitus are to those who now govern the world."

Introduction

belief is expressed in his aphorism that "Human Nature is the only science of man" (*Treatise*, p. 273).

It is a remarkable proposition. And in the next chapter we will have occasion to examine an equally remarkable one, Collingwood's claim that "the science of human nature resolves itself into history" (*IH*, 220).

Two

History as the Science
of Human Nature

Hume's idea of a uniform system of human nature provides the rationale for his general law analysis, which was the central notion in his theory of the social sciences. Although Hume envisioned a set of constituent sciences within this general program for the science of man, he did not delineate these substantive sciences in any great detail. The one exception is his elaborate treatment of "mental geography," the basic science in his program, which would frame the laws of mind, beginning with the laws of its fundamental constitution.[1] Mill, on the other hand, did give a more exacting and systematic delineation of the various substantive sciences and their relationships; and whereas Hume's basic science was largely suppositional, Mill was able to identify that science with one actually existing in his own day, the science of empirical psychology.

The social science philosophies of Hume and Mill differ in detail and in emphasis but not in fundamental conception. Hume's emphasis was on the concept of a system of human nature, on the phenom-

1. What Hume called "mental geography" (*Inquiry*, p. 22), despite its curious name, is recognizable as the theoretical or law-producing science of psychology. Note also his use of the term "accurate anatomy" (*Treatise*, p. 263) to describe his conception of this enterprise.

enology of the human mind and of action; his argument focused on the postulate of uniformity. Mill's emphasis was on the concept of a science of human nature, on the idea of a system of substantive social sciences; his argument focused on the primacy of the laws of mind, as formulated by empirical psychology, and on the principle that all the other laws of social science can, ultimately, be deductively subsumed under these psychological laws.

Both men, in arguing for a natural science of human affairs based on the uniformity conception of human nature, put forward the thesis that general laws—regularity generalizations having universal scope and validity—can be framed and used in the study of human activities. It was the view of each philosopher that general recurrences in human action could be accounted for by reference to a limited set of psychological traits (called "passions" by Hume) which must be predicated of all men at all times. Both men believed, in consequence, that the general laws of human behavior could be brought under laws describing the universal and regular workings of the mind. And, for each man, the ultimate and fixed point of reference in any mental science was said to be the fundamental constitution of the mind.[2] No better summary of the program for a science of man, based on the uniformity conception of human nature, can be provided than Mill's own brief description of it: "In other words, the science of Human Nature may be said to exist in proportion as the approximate truths which compose a practical knowledge of man can be exhibited as corollaries from the universal laws of human nature on which they rest" (*Logic*, pp. 554–555).

For Collingwood the issue posed by the idea of a science of human nature, especially the character and status ascribed to psychology, was precisely that of transhistorical generalization. The essence of his criticism of the science of human nature was that, due to the development and increasing differentiation of mind in historical process, there are no universally recurrent phenomena. What we do have is a transhistorical heterogeneity in the phenomena of human thought and action. Since there is no long-term recurrence or regular connection in human phenomena, Collingwood argued, we do not have that degree of likeness in the thoughts and deeds of agents at various times in his-

2. For Mill's discussion of the "ultimate" uniformities, see *Logic*, p. 557; he specifically related the universal laws of psychology to the "constitution of the human mind" on p. 612.

tory sufficient to allow for any universal laws: accordingly the transhistorical generalization which we find in general laws is in principle impossible. (See *IH*, 239–240.)

Collingwood's position is not clearly understood even by persons who have a detailed familiarity with his work. W. H. Walsh, for example, correctly interprets Collingwood as having said that "there are no 'eternal truths' about human nature, only truths about the way in which human beings behaved at this epoch or that. There are no eternal truths about human nature . . . because human nature is constantly changing." Walsh is willing to grant that this is an "apparently plausible assertion." But he immediately casts doubt on the assertion by asking, "When it is said that human nature changes from age to age, are we meant to conclude that there is *no* identity between past and present, no continuous development from one to the other, but that the two are sheerly different?" (*Introduction to Philosophy of History*, p. 68).

Walsh's question is meant to undercut Collingwood's "plausible assertion" by suggesting that on his view the historical career of human nature, like the flight of Zeno's Eleatic arrow, is marked by a series of cessations with no movement from point to point. But Walsh has ignored the principal idea of Collingwood's analysis: the notion that a process of thoughts exists as a changing continuity.

Collingwood would be the first to insist that there is a "continuous development" from one point in historical time to another. Walsh's suggested criticism is not quite fair. In fact, it recapitulates Collingwood's own criticism of Toynbee. The author of A *Study of History* is, according to Collingwood, in error because he sees historical time as divided into "mutually exclusive parts" and thereby "denies the continuity of the process in virtue of which every part overlaps and interpenetrates others." As a result, Collingwood charged, we are not allowed to say that one part "shades off into the next." (See *IH*, 162–164.)

But there is, I think, a kernel of substantial insight in Walsh's question which needs to be brought out. Instead of asking whether Collingwood meant to deny continuous development, we can ask whether the historical process as Collingwood conceived it is such that development and differentiation over time would lead to the profound difference between past and present which Walsh suggested. If this is our question, I think the answer to it should be *yes*: a process of historical development and differentiation would, in the historical long run, lead to a "sheer difference" between widely separated points in the continuum. The implication of Collingwood's position is that, in a process of development, there will be some short-term carryover from one age to the next but no "identity" in the long run between past and present.

The main thrust of Collingwood's criticism of the philosophy of human nature was directed, not against the notion of uniformities as such, but against the assertion that recurrences in human thought and behavior are universal and that a given set of qualitatively similar actions and thoughts can be found in all times and places. Collingwood's position was not that human phenomena are unique and hence, strictly speaking, nonrecurrent, but rather that the recurrence of like phenomena is limited in scope. The historian's world is "a world of change, a world where things come to be and cease to be" (IH, 20). In history we confront the fact of radical change leading to profound difference over time.

Human nature, the nature of the mind-as-thought, has a historical being and is wholly involved in processes of historical differentiation and development. At the root of Collingwood's criticism of the notion of a uniformity in human nature is his belief that nothing historical is unchanging.

In the philosophy of human nature of Hume and Mill, the activities of men were organized by reference to a "constitution of the mind," which was conceived as common to and constant in all men. But Collingwood denied that there is any such fundamental constitution of mind. Rather, the mind-as-thought has no primary and enduring ground upon which a process of cumulative development is grafted, no unchanging core implicated in but not altered by that process. Hence, neither the ground of any determinate cultural nature—its corporate inheritance of thought—nor any set of widely exhibited constancies in behavior dependent on that inheritance can be considered exempt from changes over time. The order and structures that we do find in any phase of human life are not immutable, or eternal, or in existence from the beginning; they are produced in process. (See IH, 223, 248; Metaphysics, pp. 74–75; New Leviathan, p. 285, sec. 34.63.)

The basic category of Collingwood's analysis of the mind-as-thought is change. And the implications of this idea are radical, as I have tried

to indicate. There is no absolute constancy in determinate human natures: no pattern of thought and behavior is invariant over historical
time. Rather, we have a coming into being and a passing out of being
of determinate human natures; one set turns into another and wholly
different set. Thus, in a process of historical development and differentiation, the conduct and conceptions of men will vary widely at
widely separated times. This difference is not a function of the mere
passage of time but of the pervasive and unceasing changes which, according to Collingwood, do take place in the historical life of man.
Such changes are gradual but they proceed in the direction of increasing differentiation; their long-term result is a total dissimilarity between men at one time and men at a later time. And this is the case
even with men who stand in roughly the same historical continuum,
for example, the Europeans of today and of the early Middle Ages.[3]

But this analysis of Collingwood's was strictly delimited. It was
meant to apply exclusively to the mind-as-thought. For unlike the philosophers of human nature, Collingwood started from the notion that
there is a radical contrast between thinking and feeling.[4]

The philosophically interesting thing about Collingwood's idea is
that he used this contrast to divide the entire range of activities designated "mind" into two types, thought and feeling. And, since he included actions in what he called "mind," he read this division into
human actions. Not only did Collingwood regard thought as sharply
distinct from feeling but he also considered it proper to speak of some
actions as "determined by thought" and of others as determined by
"mere impulse and appetite." (See *IH*, 216.)

Those actions in which the thought of the agent plays an essential
and causative role Collingwood called "reflective" or "rational" actions. The class of such actions is quite large and embraces, in Collingwood's opinion, most of what he and others would call human action. (For Collingwood's list see *IH*, 309–315.) The thinking exhibited
in reflective action includes, in Collingwood's analysis, several ele-

3. My account is specifically intended to challenge Rotenstreich's comment that
"Collingwood is a unique example of a philosopher of history who did not 'take time
seriously' " ("History and Time," p. 69). Rotenstreich bases his comment on his view
that "the common sense meaning of history *qua* process" does not represent the "main
trend" in Collingwood's "system" (p. 78).
4. This contrast is drawn in all of Collingwood's later writings, from *The Idea of History* on. For an extended statement of the contrast, see his *Principles of Art*,
pp. 157–160, 163.

ments: the agent's situational awareness, which provides his motives for acting, his purposes, his scruples and values, his dispositions, his know-how, his weighing of practical means and consequences. "Clearly," Dray says, "the kinds of thoughts which Collingwood's theory requires are those which could enter the practical deliberations of an agent trying to decide what his line of action should be" (*Philosophy of History*, p. 11). Such thoughts provide a reason for the agent's doing what he does. And insofar as the agent's deed can be referred to these thought-factors collectively, as a set of causal conditions for what he does, his action can be said to be "determined by thought."

Collingwood was not, of course, oblivious to theories that treat feelings as a proper subject for consideration in a discussion of motives or even of purposes. In his own theory Collingwood treated feelings as a usual element in what he called a state of affairs, the context of an action. An agent, in acting, takes account of this state of affairs; accordingly, feelings are often included in an agent's situation-conception. We can say then that when an action exhibits situational thinking, feeling affects that action as an element in the agent's situation-conception. (See *IH*, 214–216; and for an example, *IH*, 315–316.)

It should be recalled that Collingwood also conceived of feelings as, sometimes, direct determinants of action. On occasion an agent performs an action without taking any account of the state of affairs in the context of which he acts. Here feeling is not an element in a situation-conception; the action can be said to stem directly from feeling. In Collingwood's analysis, only when feeling is an unadulterated or direct determinant of action and not a conceptual element can an action be said to be determined by feeling. All determinants of conduct are, accordingly, arranged by Collingwood under one of two headings, either thought or mere feeling.

It is thus plausible to conceive of mind as thought and actions determined by thought, on the one hand, and as feelings and actions determined by feeling, on the other. It is only a short step from this to speaking elliptically about mind simply as a complex of thoughts or, alternatively, as a complex of feelings. Collingwood took this step; for example, in his frequent contrasts of mind to nature he meant by mind simply a complex of thoughts and of thought-determined actions. Ultimately, it was Collingwood's thesis that mind conceived of as thought is radically different from mind conceived of as feeling and that accounts of mind under each of these headings must be set up according to wholly different principles. What, then, are we to make of those mental activities that do not come under the heading of "thought"?

There are, according to Collingwood, in mind "elements that are not rational. They are not body; they are mind, but not rational mind or thought. . . . These irrational elements are . . . the blind forces in us which are part of human life as it consciously experiences itself, but are not parts of the historical process: sensations as distinct from thought, feelings as distinct from conceptions, appetite as distinct from will" (IH, 231). These irrational elements are all included by Collingwood under the general heading of "feeling." They constitute man's psychological or "animal nature" and "the process of these activities," Collingwood noted significantly, "is a natural process" (IH, 216).[5] By this he meant that man's psychological life, his experience at the level of feeling, can be regarded as a sum of activities characterized by universal regularity. The life of feeling—sensation, emotion, appetite or desire—is common to all men and its basic patterns are constant, unchanging over time.

Here there is no evolution of man's animal nature into something different, no new configuration of feelings within new limits. Rather, in each new generation the same old patterns of feeling are repeated within the same old physiological limitations. As with the growth of the kitten into the cat or of the acorn into the oak, we have change but not evolution, different stages but not transformation. Such change is not the cumulative and species-modifying development associated with both natural-evolutionary and historical process. Old men and young boys are not different species, even though they may both think so, and the changes, for example in desires, from youth to old age do not represent differentiations into new species but only stages in the growth of a single species. The life of feeling here does not exhibit that cumulative development peculiar to historical process.

The fundamental constitution of the mind-as-feeling is grounded in human anatomy and physiology. Man's "animal nature" comprises a fixed repertory of specific patterns of feeling, within fixed biological limits. Each pattern exhibits regularity and the change from one pattern to the next is also regular. Changes from one psychological stage

5. Collingwood habitually used the word "psychological" in reference, not to mind, but to the mind-as-feeling (see IH, 230–231).

to another are not correlated with historical changes. Rather, they are correlated with changes in human physiological functions, such as those involved in growing old. Relative to man's thinking or historical nature, which has developed cumulatively, man's animal nature has stayed constant, for within the period of human historical development, the human body has not evolved biologically.

This observation does not, of course, preclude the possibility that man's "animal nature" might evolve into something different. But if it does evolve it will be because of organic and structural changes in the human body. If there are modifications in the regularities that characterize human psychological life, it will be because of evolutionary changes in human anatomy and physiological makeup. The nature of the mind-as-feeling is in either case, evolving or not, "part of the process of nature, not of history" (IH, 330).

At this point I want to turn from Collingwood's conception of mind to the implications he saw in it for the study of human affairs. At the core of Collingwood's doctrine of mind is his separation of human mental and behavioral activities into two subclasses, thought and feeling; his program for the social sciences took this separation as its point of departure. In Collingwood's analysis, any social science will study thinking activities and actions "determined by thought" or it will study feeling and actions determined by "mere impulse and appetite." His principal thesis, then, is that two different types of subject matter imply two different types of social science, and hence two models for social science inquiry. Collingwood's dualistic conception of human nature ("determinate human nature" appropriate to thought and "animal nature" appropriate to feeling) is mirrored in his idea of two types of social science and is a rationale for this idea. But in Collingwood's dualistic program the two types of social science were certainly not equal in importance.

The first type of social science, the naturalistic, is appropriate to the study of feeling. The idea that there can be general laws of feeling is strongly suggested by Collingwood's analysis (see IH, 302–303; also 29–30); it follows from his claim that there are "permanent conditions of human life" at the level of man's "animal nature" (see IH, 92, 224–225). In Collingwood's analysis, such a "positive mental science" as Mill's psychology, if delimited to certain mental and behavioral activities, is plausible: although it cannot formulate the general laws of mind, there is good reason to expect that it can formulate the general laws of feeling and of activities "determined" by feeling.[6]

For both Collingwood and Mill psychology was the archetype of a naturalistic social science. (See *IH*, 173, 186; also 231.) In this particular, a common ground is marked out between their two positions: each man thought that psychology is a law-framing science. But the direction in which each took this claim marks out the difference in their positions. For Mill, psychology provided the foundation for a complete science of human behavior: it formulates laws of mental process that would have application in any study of human affairs. Psychology was the basic science of the social sciences. For Collingwood, psychology was, once we grant its generalizing character, capable of dealing only with a restricted subject matter; it could be only a science of feeling. And it was thus unable to serve as the basis for any of the other social sciences—with the possible exception of physical anthropology. The fact that psychology was a typical naturalistic science led, in the case of Mill and Collingwood, to radically different conclusions: for Mill theoretical psychology was the basis for all social science inquiry; for Collingwood it was, due to its peculiar methods and subject matter, a kind of isolate.

A suitably conceived psychology will, according to Collingwood, renounce "interference with what is properly the subject-matter of history" (thought); at the same time, it will not renounce all claim to being a science of *mind*. Rather, psychologists should devote themselves exclusively to an investigation of the nonrational elements in mind, to feeling or "psyche" as Collingwood called it, i.e., to sensation, emotion, desire, and to actions determined by mere impulse and appetite. (See esp. *IH*, 230–231.) [7] But for Collingwood, the work

6. Donagan says, "Collingwood claimed that no system of laws of human behavior in any department of life would hold good in all periods of human history" (*Later Philosophy of Collingwood*, p. 234). This statement is not true insofar as the human behavior in question belongs to that "department of life" which Collingwood called "feeling."

7. For the idea that "feeling," in Collingwood's sense, is the proper subject matter of psychology, see also *IH*, 186, 305; *Principles of Art*, p. 171n; *Metaphysics*, p. 117; and *Autobiography*, p. 95. Collingwood buttressed his assertions about the subject matter of psychology with certain etymological and historical references. He asserted that the Greek word *psyche* referred to lower mental functions, i.e., "such functions as sensation and appetite" (*Autobiography*, p. 94; see also *Metaphysics*, p. 110). He also asserted that the men in the sixteenth century, such as Melancthon, who first used the word "psychology" used it to refer to the study of feeling as distinct from both body and thought. (See *Metaphysics*, pp. 106, 109, 110, and *Autobiography*, p. 94.)

done by historians, economists, and others who have "thought" as their proper subject matter will not presuppose at any point the general laws of feeling and action that these psychologists propound.

Directly contrary to the program of Hume and Mill, Collingwood's interest was in asserting the autonomy of history and of the traditional social sciences, first, from the principles and methods of the natural sciences and, second, from the data of any theoretical social science, such as Mill's science of empirical psychology, which claims to formulate universal laws of human thought and action. And this, I think, is the main point of Collingwood's antinaturalism and of his attack on the uniformity conception of human nature.

In his rejection of naturalism Collingwood turned to history, for it was his conviction that modern historical study is ideally suited to serve as the prototype in the investigation of human thinking and actions "determined by thought." The discipline of history is accorded special status in Collingwood's program, not as a basic science in the manner of Mill's psychology, but as a model.

The type of social science appropriate to the study of thought, then, is the historical. Parallel to psychology as the archetype of a naturalistic social science is history as the archetype of a nonnaturalistic social science. This is the sense in which "historical thought, attaining at last its proper shape and stature, is able to make good the claims long ago put forward on behalf of the science of human nature" (IH, 229).

Collingwood regarded the traditional social sciences as engaged in a study of thought, in the special sense of rational human actions, as their exclusive subject matter. For Collingwood, these disciplines would include—besides history—economics, political science, cultural anthropology, and probably sociology. (See IH, 224; and also Metaphysics, p. 142, together with IH, 309.) Accordingly, his conception of the role of history was intended to have far-reaching implications.

Thus when Collingwood said, "The so-called science of human nature . . . resolves itself into history" (IH, 220), I take him to be contrasting two forms of social science, the naturalistic and the historicist, and to be asserting that in the study of human actions, insofar as these are thought-determined, historical presuppositions and methods should replace scientific ones. Donagan has put the matter well: "[Collingwood's] sole intention was to show that all the social sciences, so far as they have been fruitful, have employed the same methods as history, and that those methods are neither applications nor anticipations of a putative natural science of human behavior" (*Later Philosophy of Collingwood*, p. 170).

But Collingwood's historicism was not intended as an account of the social sciences in general. His idea of the separation of thought from feeling was meant to preclude the possibility of a unity in principles and methods among the social sciences and, hence, to rule out the notion of a single, comprehensive scheme for the study of human affairs. What Collingwood desired instead was to establish the principle of a division of labor within the social science disciplines between naturalism and historicism.

Historicism represents the main line in Collingwood's conception of social science, based on dispensing with the science of human nature and its presupposition of a universal and unchangeable constitution of the mind. But psychology, as a science of feeling, was specifically excluded from it. So, when I refer subsequently to the "social sciences," I will mean only those disciplines which describe and attempt to explain rational actions.

At the very outset it should be made clear that Collingwood in his historicism never worked out an exhaustive theoretical account of these social sciences and their interrelationship. Rather, his historicism can be described much more modestly as an attempt to identify certain generic traits of any systematic study of rational action. The basic and defining thesis in his analysis, and my reason for using the term "historicism," is his contention that social science disciplines which investigate rational action and which claim to render such actions intelligible are all properly placed under the category of history; this much at least seems to be implied in his statement that "historical knowledge is the only knowledge that the human mind [i.e., the mind-as-thought] can have of itself" (*IH*, 220). This statement not only establishes the focus of our inquiry in the latter half of this chapter but also sets the problem of determining precisely what his historicist thesis was meant to assert.[8]

8. The term "historicism" does have a rather general currency in philosophy; accordingly, some mention should be made of its larger profile. Kluback says, "The dominating assumption of historicism . . . holds that the methods of the sciences of nature [do] not apply to the study of human society and culture" (*Dilthey's Philosophy of History*, p. 20). Popper identifies as the central proposition of what he calls "historicism" the statement that "social science is nothing but history" (*Poverty of Historicism*, p. 45). I will use the term "historicism" to designate a philosophical conception, specifically a conception of the nature of explanatory judgment in social science.

The Science of Human Nature

Near the beginning of his essay "Human Nature and Human History" Collingwood set down concisely the principal contention which he wished to defend:

The thesis which I shall maintain is that the science of human nature was a false attempt—falsified by the analogy of natural science—to understand the mind itself, and that, whereas the right way of investigating nature is by the methods called scientific, the right way of investigating mind is by the methods of history. I shall contend that the work which was to be done by the science of human nature is actually done, and can only be done, by history: that history is what the science of human nature proposed to be, and that Locke was right when he said (however little he understood what he was saying) that the right method for such an inquiry is the historical, plain method. [IH, 209; see also 220]

In this turn to history, I do not think that Collingwood was interested in historical methods in any narrowly procedural sense. His statement about these "methods" has to do, not with the practices of historians, but with the logic of explanatory statements in history. What he wanted to assert is that the criterion of intelligibility presupposed and employed in statements of historical explanation is generic to the study of rational action. And in this way it is proper to all the social sciences.

The heart of Collingwood's theory of the explanation of rational actions by historians, and presumably by other social scientists, is his rather complicated discussion of what he usually called "re-enactment." In Collingwood's theory the very statement of what the historian is trying to explain gives the clue to what will count as an explanation. "The historian is not concerned with events as such but with actions, i.e., events brought about by the will and expressing the thought of a free and intelligent agent." Collingwood reasoned that, if the event "expresses" the thought of the agent, then the way to understand the agent's performance is to discern his thought; this is accomplished, in the historian's case, "by rethinking it in his own mind" (IH, 178). The historian performs the action in imagination, re-enacts it, by rethinking the thought that lies behind the deed.

Nothing in what has been said so far would limit Collingwood's notion of re-enactment to the study of actions in the past; accordingly, there is no barrier to extending the notion, as Collingwood apparently desired to do, into all systematic investigations of actions "determined by thought." Re-enactment cuts across the conceptual distinctions between history and the other social sciences; it cuts across the distinction between actions imputed from documentary evidence and actions described on the basis of direct observation and it involves no distinction between actions done in the past and those done in the present. Collingwood expressed this in an oblique and rather awkward way: "If it is by historical thinking that we rethink and so rediscover the thought of Hammurabi or Solon, it is in the same way that we discover the thought of a friend who writes us a letter, or a stranger who crosses the street" (IH, 219). The "historical thinking" to which Collingwood referred is simply re-enactment, and it is on this point that Collingwood intended to effect the *rapprochement* of history and the other social sciences.

But if the notion of re-enactment is indeed a generic principle applicable in all the various social science disciplines, why is it repeatedly called up by Collingwood under the name of history? Several possible reasons for this might be advanced.

Collingwood certainly seemed to think that historians, and archeologists, in particular, had a clearer and more mature grasp of the re-enactment principle than other social scientists. History may have been singled out, as a sort of model, because it was thought to be the best developed member of a certain genus. Second, Collingwood seemed to believe that history was the first social science to be reconstructed along the lines he was suggesting or, even, that it was the only one where the re-enactment thesis had been accepted in both theory and practice.[9]

Whatever the reason Collingwood had for according a priority to history, it is clear that Collingwood's historicism was not an attempt to commit the social sciences to the "idea" of history in any wholesale way. As Collingwood noted, history as a science of the past is "a science of a special kind. It is a science whose business is to study events not accessible to our observation, and to study these events inferentially, arguing to them from something else which is accessible to

9. Donagan lists two "chief reasons" Collingwood had for "preferring the name 'history.'" One of these was presented as a curiously indirect one: "By saying that the various sciences of human action must be historical [Collingwood] implied that they presuppose methodological individualism" (*Later Philosophy of Collingwood*, p. 171). But it seems to me that Donagan has things turned around. Collingwood may have used the point about methodological individualism, although I find very little evidence that he did, as a feature in an argument designed to show that the social sciences were "historical" in their logic of inquiry; but he certainly did not call them "historical" in order to assert their commitment to the postulate of methodological individualism.

our observation and which the historian calls 'evidence' for the events in which he is interested" (*IH*, 251–252). Collingwood's contention about the historicity of social science does not cover those aspects in which history, considered as a discipline, is peculiar.

We can put this point positively by saying that Collingwood's historicism is restricted to certain generic features of social science inquiry. History and the other social sciences have a subject matter—rational action—in common even though the distinction remains between actions "in the past" and in the present. Consequently, they can be said to have a structure of inquiry in common, even though, again, we allow for a distinction between procedures which rely on documentary evidence exclusively and those that do not. This idea of a generic structure of inquiry, as formulated in his theory of explanation by re-enactment, is the substance of Collingwood's historicism.

Since most of what Collingwood had to say about re-enactment is framed by reference to the work of historians and since he repeatedly directed our attention to the "methods of history" as exemplifications of the re-enactment thesis, we must turn to his account of historical knowledge or "understanding." But we shall be concerned with this account only to the extent that it bears on the logic of studying and explaining rational actions.

We have already established that rethinking is the essential component of re-enactment; the investigator "performs" the action in imagination by rethinking the thought that is expressed in the deed. This relatively straightforward conclusion is sometimes stated paradoxically. In one of his best known passages, Collingwood stated his point by drawing a distinction between the "outside" of an event and its "inside," using actions in the career of Caesar as an example. Insofar as we describe "the passage of Caesar, accompanied by certain men, across a river called the Rubicon at one date, or the spilling of his blood on the floor of the senate-house at another," we are describing the outside of certain events. But to understand these events, we must look at the reasons for these deeds, at the thoughts involved in this conduct; here we are concerned with the insides of these same events, with "Caesar's defiance of Republican law, or the clash of constitutional policy between himself and his assassins." (See *IH*, 213.) "Outside" and "inside" refer not to two planes on which events go on but to two different ways of looking at the same event.

We can factor out what an agent does, including descriptions of certain movements that he made, from the reasons that lie behind his doing it; but a full account of any action will include both kinds of factors. This is the force of Collingwood's dictum that "an action is the unity of the outside and inside of an event" (IH, 213). Collingwood's point was that accounts of action consist of inseparably connected statements: those that describe events as the movements of bodies and those that describe the same events in the language of motives, purposes, and so forth. An action discussed solely in the language of bodily motions is being talked about as a "mere event." To describe an action as an action means including, if only obliquely, statements about the agent's thought. And by making reference to the thought of the agent, we render what he has done intelligible.

The work of the historian "may begin by discovering the outside of an event, but it can never end there; he must always remember that the event was an action, and that his main task is to think himself into this action, to discern the thought of its agent" (IH, 213). Logically, discernment can be subdivided as follows: (a) discerning the thought by establishing its components—the agent's situational awareness, his goals, his scruples and values, his dispositions and skills, his knowledge of means available, his weighing of practical consequences, and so on—and (b) discerning the thought by establishing its relevance to the deed performed. Under (a) the investigator formulates for himself, and in his own words, what he takes to be the pertinent elements in the agent's thought. But the investigator must also be able to see the event in question as "determined" by this specific set of factors. He must, in Collingwood's language, "think himself into this action." Only when he can do this can he be said to have re-enacted the agent's action.

If he cannot accomplish both these dimensions of rethinking then he cannot claim to have discerned the thought side or "inner side" of the event; there is, in short, no re-enactment. But when the investigator has performed this re-enactment in both dimensions, moving from the elements of thought to its enactment, then and only then can he be said to have understood the agent's action. Explanation is the further business of making this re-enactment explicit, in the form of a narrative account, so that the investigator's understanding can be communicated to others.

Re-enactment is the principle of explanation in historical science. Re-enactment, in Collingwood's analysis, amounts to providing an explanatory statement of the form "he did *x* because *y*" under the condition that *y* is a formulation in words of the agent's "thought." When Collingwood said that the historian is interested in thoughts *alone*, he was not delimiting the historian's subject matter; rather, he was indicating the kind of terms that would figure in the "because . . ." part of a historical explanation.

One critic, Danto, has professed to see a distinction in Collingwood between "understanding" and "explaining." The distinction is that scientists "explain" but historians "understand." The distinction to which Danto points is that (scientific) explanations logically involve reference to general laws whereas historical "understanding" does not. I am not sure that Danto's way of putting the matter is wholly satisfactory. Danto suggests that Collingwood made a conscious terminological discrimination between "understanding" and "explaining" but, so far as I can tell, Collingwood treated the words as virtual synonyms. (See Danto, *Analytical Philosophy of History*, pp. 205–206, 218.) In any case, the issue between historicism and naturalism is not over terms. The point for Collingwood was not that scientists explain and historians do not but that scientific explanation is different from historical.

In natural science, we provide the explanation "*x* because *y*" by classifying and then by bringing these classified phenomena under a general law or set of such laws. What we assert when we explain, or predict, an event (E) by reference to certain other events (C_1, etc.) is that the class of which E is an instance can be connected, by means of some formula of universal and fixed relationship, to certain other classes of which C_1, etc. are the instances respectively. In such a case, reference to a general law is said to be the principle on which we explain. We can summarize this by saying that explanation in science involves subsuming an event under a general law.

For the historian, whose object is a rational action, an event is rendered intelligible when he can "think himself" into it by "discerning" the thought of the agent. Hence, "the historian need not and cannot (without ceasing to be an historian) emulate the scientist in searching for the . . . laws of events (*IH*, 214).

What we call intelligibility in science is appropriate to events that have no thought side. "Instead of conceiving the event as an action and attempting to rediscover the thought of its agent, . . . the scientist goes beyond the event, observes its relation to others, and thus brings it under a general formula or law of nature" (*IH*, 214). Collingwood's point was that a natural event can be rendered intelligible only by assigning it to a class and determining, where possible, the general law relationship between that class and others. Natural phenomena are, Collingwood asserted, unintelligible in the individual case. "It is therefore a genuine advance in knowledge to discover something intelligible in the relations between general types of them" (*IH*, 222).

Collingwood did emphasize two features which are generally conceded to be intrinsic to scientific explanation—the classification of instances and the use of general laws. And it is in contradistinction to these two features, I think, that Collingwood's account of re-enactment must be placed.[10]

That the historian *cannot* use, or formulate, general laws in his explanation of rational actions is a point with which we are familiar from my exposition of Collingwood's ideas earlier in this chapter. For Collingwood believed, on the basis of his conception of historical processes of differentiation and development, that generalizations having universal scope and validity are impossible in principle.

That some sort of general law principle is not even needed by historians, a point central to our present discussion, represents Collingwood's conviction that the human sciences can, in fact, operate with an entirely different principle. Where the scientific move, in explanation, is in the direction of classification and the use of general laws, the historical move, in explanation, is in the direction of "penetrating to the inside of events and detecting the thought which they express" (*IH*, 214; see also 228). The historian's move is not in the direction of generalization at all, even where generalization might be restricted to a nonuniversal scope.

Dray, in a brief discussion of Collingwood, puts the basic contrast clearly: "The kind of understanding thus achieved . . . is different in *concept* from that sought on the scientific model. For the latter endeavors to make clear, in the light of circumstances, the *inevitability* (or, at least, the high probability) of what was done. The former—which we might perhaps call 'rational' explanation—tries to make clear its *point* or *rationale*" (*Philosophy of History*, p. 12). Another way of pointing up the contrast, and one which I would emphasize, is to indicate a difference in structure, a difference in the role played by

10. Collingwood explicitly identified as a "positivist misconception" the notion that "events [in history are] to be understood as the scientist understands natural events, by classifying them and establishing relations between the classes thus defined" (*IH*, 228).

generalizations. For the essence of Collingwood's position was to conceive a logical discontinuity between explanation by re-enactment and explanation by generalization.

In one of his most widely discussed passages, Collingwood laid down his idea of a logical discontinuity succinctly: "For history, the object to be discovered is not the mere event, but the thought expressed in it. To discover that thought is already to understand it [i.e., the event]. After the historian has ascertained the facts, there is no further process of inquiring into their causes. When he knows what happened, he already knows why it happened" (*IH*, 214). The exact meaning of this passage has been widely disputed but when it is read in conjunction with another, less cited passage, Collingwood's point becomes, I think, unmistakable. "There is no such thing as the supposed further stage of . . . scientific history which discovers their causes or laws or in general explains them, because an historical fact once genuinely ascertained, grasped by the historian's re-enactment of the agent's thought in his mind, is already explained" (*IH*, 176–177).[11]

What is striking in both these passages is Collingwood's assertion that once we have "ascertained" the facts (identified the event and rethought its "inside") there is no need for the additional step of classifying them with other similar instances and then relating class to class by reference to some connective generalization. An individual action is understood when the investigator discerns (rethinks) the particular thought expressed in it. The use of generalizations, as we find it in the case of classification and of subsumption under a general hypothetical statement, is neither intrinsic nor logically necessary to historical inquiry.

In history, what is treated as a datum for generalization must already have been understood "from within"; otherwise, Collingwood asserted, "the fact is being used as a datum for generalization before it has been properly 'ascertained.'" Once the historian is ready to generalize, there is, from the point of view of understanding, "nothing of value . . . left for the generalization to do" (*IH*, 223). In this sense, generalizations are extrinsic to historical inquiry. Thus, "if, by historical thinking, we already understand how and why Napoleon established his ascendancy in revolutionary France, nothing is added to

11. Collingwood concluded, "For the historian there is no difference between discovering what happened and discovering why it happened" (*IH*, 177).

our understanding of that process by the statement (however true) that similar things have happened elsewhere" (*IH*, 223).

Collingwood's position on the character and role of generalization in what he called the "historical plain method" is easily and frequently misconstrued. As we have seen, he was not committed to asserting that there can be no generalizations in a historical science but, rather, that there could be no universal laws formulated from the data of thought. He did believe, however, that historically localized generalizations, delimited statements about the thought and action of agents at a given stage in historical process, could be framed. I think it is fairly clear that Collingwood regarded generalization as possible where there was a more or less common historical inheritance of thought. But Collingwood wanted to replace the idea of universal generalizations with the idea of historical generalizations. (See *IH*, 223–226, in particular.) Collingwood's position, then, was that all generalizations are delimited, in scope and validity, to a definite period of time.[12]

Collingwood was willing, moreover, to endorse the idea that a science of rational action, such as economics, can and does generalize from the presently observable data of thought and action.[13] But the point which he made, if we take his account of re-enactment explanation in history as the standard case, is that these generalizations play no explanatory or predictive role in such inquiries. (See esp. *IH*, 220.) Collingwood's intention was not to repudiate generalization in the social sciences; rather it was to define their structure of inquiry without reference to generalization.

Generalizations in history and the other social sciences are, in Collingwood's analysis, primarily summative. They are, said Collingwood, "only inventories of the wealth achieved by the human mind at a certain stage in its history" (*IH*, 229). The generalizations one does find in a historical science are the results, not the explanatory premises, of inquiry. Such inventories, valid so far as they go, hold only for some men and for some time, and not for men at all times. In the

12. Popper identifies as "historicist" the contention that "in the social sciences the validity of all generalizations . . . is confined to the concrete historical period in which the relevant observations were made" (*Poverty of Historicism*, p. 98).

13. "Such a science (as we have lately been taught with regard to what is called classical economics) can . . . describe in a general way certain characteristics of the historical age in which it is constructed" (*IH*, 224).

normal case, they merely supervene on explanations in order to summarize what has already been explained.

The account which I have given of Collingwood's position can be said to represent his version of the paradigmatic or logically normal case of historical explanation, explanation by re-enactment. Collingwood did allow that generalizations might sometimes be required in an overtly explanatory role, but he hedged this admission by pointing out that "it is only when the particular fact cannot be understood by itself that such statements [i.e., generalizations] are of value." Collingwood was talking here not about generalization as an element in re-enactment explanations but about generalization as replacing re-enactment. When an investigator is unable to think himself into an action, when he cannot re-enact the deed by rethinking its thought side, he may then find it helpful to fall back on the generalization that "similar things have happened elsewhere" as a second-best expedient. (See *IH*, 223.) But we are still left with the thesis that explanation by re-enactment is logically distinct from explanation by generalization. Further, explanations by generalization do not, in Collingwood's analysis, render rational actions fully intelligible, for they fall below the standard of what is to count as intelligibility in cases of actions "determined by thought." They represent an imperfect understanding at best and, in a sense, a failure to understand at all.

Collingwood's historicism, then, would comprise three points: (1) There are no general laws of mind and behavior, either formulated or used, in the social sciences. (2) Rational actions, the objects of social science investigation, are understood and explained by re-enactment, specifically by rethinking the thought of the agent, without reference to generalizations of any sort. (3) Restricted or historical generalizations, generalizations limited in scope, are normally used only as inventories or summarizations of data which have been previously "ascertained" through re-enactment. These three features are, I think, what Collingwood meant when he said that "the right way of investigating mind is by the methods of history."

Three

Re-enactment

The singular feature in Collingwood's theory is that the investigator need not subsume his explanatory statement, "*x* because *y*," in which he connects deed with thought, under a general law or, indeed, under a generalization of any sort. But the question naturally arises: what then is the nature of the discursive or connective reasoning by which the investigator warrants his connection of deed with thought?

This question is a perplexing one. In answering it, one must begin by admitting that the logical structure of explanation by re-enactment, at least in its positive aspects, was not brought out clearly by Collingwood's discussion. There seems to be a lacuna in Collingwood's theory, left by his denial of any role to generalization, which has tempted some critics of his work to try to provide an answer for Collingwood. In this vein, Walsh says, "Collingwood makes the negative point that . . . historical understanding does not depend on knowledge of general laws, but says little or nothing about what it does consist in. The inference that he thought it must be immediate [i. e., non-discursive] is entirely natural" (*Introduction to Philosophy of History*, p. 71). Since Collingwood's text is opaque on the subject of an explanatory warrant and since many of his passages seem to indicate the kind of answer Walsh has provided, this answer has been widely accepted and must arrest the attention of any serious student of Collingwood's work.

Walsh and many others have contended that Collingwood was an intuitionist. The version of Collingwood as an intuitionist stems from his remark that the investigator proceeds by "penetrating to the inside of events and detecting the thought which they express" (*IH*, 214). Then it is alleged that the investigator reconstitutes the detected thought in his own mind; in so doing, he repeats or rethinks it for himself and understands it as if it were a piece of his own thinking. So, since the investigator can be directly acquainted with the thought of the agent and can repeat it in his own mind, the investigator is able to short-circuit the whole problem of explanatory connection. He simply has a nondiscursive realization that a certain thought lies "behind" a certain deed, and this is all the connecting he has to do.

Sometimes this bare outline of the intuitionist version of Collingwood is fleshed out in an elaboration of further details. Gardiner, for example, says that Collingwood's passage "suggests that historians are in possession of an additional power of knowing which allows them to 'penetrate into' the minds of the subjects of their study and take, as it were, psychological X-ray photographs." The X-ray photograph is then somehow revitalized by the investigator. According to Gardiner the investigator's "own experience is in some way transformed into the experience of the person whose motives [he is] examining. . . . [W]hen, for example, an historian is said to understand why Caesar crossed the Rubicon he becomes Caesar and intuitively rethinks in his own mind thoughts which are literally identical with Caesar's thoughts on the occasion in question." The investigator introduces the X-ray photograph into his own stream of consciousness, as a way of developing the negative, no doubt, and there relives the experience and rethinks the thoughts of the agent: he becomes the agent. Collingwood thus avoids the question of an explanatory warrant, contends Gardiner, by suggesting that "we can know *why* somebody did something just as directly as we can know *what* it was that he did." [1] It would be pointless to prolong this matter; I have included it only to show the sort of thing that dominated the initial phase in the discussion of Collingwood's *Idea of History*.

I think that some of Gardiner's critical reaction against Collingwood

1. For the passages quoted, see Gardiner, *Nature of Historical Explanation*, pp. 128, 135, 117, respectively. Similar points are made on pp. 131–132. An even more extreme version of Collingwood's position is developed by Gardiner in his essay "The 'Objects' of Historical Knowledge."

rests on an honest mistake in interpreting Collingwood. Gardiner takes Collingwood's inside-outside metaphor, which Collingwood applied to *action*, and uses it as evidence for saying that, according to Collingwood, the "thought" must be "inside" the agent, and, further, interprets this to mean exclusively *private* to the agent. It follows on this interpretation, which ultimately derives from Ryle's *Concept of Mind* (see pp. 56–58), that the investigator would have to use some sort of X-ray technique to get at the agent's thought. There is, however, almost nothing in Collingwood's texts to warrant this interpretation of thought as absolutely private: as exclusively inward and radically unexpressible.

The intuitionist interpretation raises more questions than it resolves. And if we turn to Collingwood's own remarks, in which he tried to expound and clarify his conception of re-enactment, we find that his own description can be interpreted as pointing in a substantially different direction.

When Collingwood said, for example, that the investigator should "penetrate" to the "inside" of an event, he was not hinting at some sort of anti-inductive procedure to get at a peculiarly inaccessible thing. He was stating, metaphorically, the aim of a science of human action: that it should go to the heart of the matter, to the "thought" of the agent. Collingwood's remark was concerned with what the investigator should be up to, not with how he should proceed to do it. "Penetration" is not the name of a peculiar technique whereby one can perceive "invisible microbes" or "mysterious agencies." [2] Insofar as we do have a question of procedure here, Collingwood's answer is clear-cut. The investigator "penetrates" to the thought expressed in a deed, not by some queer kind of X-ray perception, but by Baconian questioning of the information he has about the deeds and sayings of an agent.

We know that the character of his information will differ, depending on whether the investigator is a historian or not. If he is a historian, he can never be an eyewitness of the deeds and sayings of agents; his information about these things will necessarily be refracted through

2. The phrases are Gardiner's. It is only fair to note that Gardiner adopts a less patronizing attitude toward Collingwood in his brief introduction to an anthology selection of Collingwood's writings. (See Gardiner, ed., *Theories of History*, pp. 250–251.) Indeed, in his more recent writings Gardiner has become increasingly sympathetic toward what he now takes to be Collingwood's position; see for example, his "Historical Understanding and the Empiricist Tradition," pp. 274–280.

Re-enactment

the medium of what collectively is called "evidence," reports, documents, artifacts. If he is an investigator from one of the other social sciences, his information will often be based on direct acquaintance with the deeds and sayings of agents. But whether we are talking about history or about one of the other disciplines, Collingwood's point remains the same: the investigator "detects" the "inside" of an event by reflecting on and reasoning from the data available to him. Collingwood put this simply and clearly when he said that we "recreate" an agent's thought "in our own minds by interpretation of . . . evidence" (*IH*, 296; see also 9–10, 234, 252). The work of detecting thought is a species of induction; no faculty of intuition is required in such a procedure.

The inductive reconstruction of the agent's thought through the interpretation of evidence is only the first stage in re-enactment. The second is that the investigator must ascertain that the deed performed is the "expression" of the reconstituted thought; he must demonstrate that the deed is "determined" by that thought. It is in this second stage that Collingwood conceived of rethinking under the category of empathy. This empathetic dimension of Collingwood's theory of re-enactment is easily misunderstood and has been misinterpreted in the version of Collingwood as an intuitionist.

Collingwood cited, in a discussion of his concept of rethinking, the example of a historian who is trying to understand the issuing of one of the edicts of the Theodosian Code. In order to do this, Collingwood said, the historian "must envisage the situation with which the emperor was trying to deal and he must envisage it as that emperor envisaged it." In short, the historian must "re-create" the emperor's thought, in particular, the element of situational awareness in it, through interpreting evidence; this I have called the first stage of rethinking. "Then he must see for himself, just as if the emperor's situation were his own, how such a situation might be dealt with." He must imagine the alternative courses of action possible and calculate for himself "the reasons for choosing one rather than another; and thus he must go through the process which the emperor went through in deciding on this particular course." (*IH*, 283; see 215 for a similar example.)

Collingwood was suggesting, I take it, that the deed under consideration, the issuing of an edict, is explained if and only if the investigator can establish that the deed is plausible, given his own reconstruction of the agent's thought, and also that it was the one, among the several conceivable alternatives, that seems *most* plausible in the light of this reconstruction. The investigator completes his re-enactment by means of a practical deliberation, in which the emperor's action is revealed as the plausible thing to do relative to the thought—the situational awareness, purposes, scruples, and so on—which the investigator has attributed to the emperor on the basis of evidence. This is the second stage, or empathetic dimension, of Collingwood's re-enactment theory of explanation.

Perhaps no point is more problematic in Collingwood's account than his apparent insistence that the investigator must put himself, imaginatively, in the agent's place. The temptation to regard Collingwood as suggesting that this is the investigator's way of stumbling onto the agent's actual thought has proven strong indeed. It is largely Collingwood's use of these examples of empathy—together with his battery of favored metaphors (inside-outside, penetration, rethinking) —that has given rise to the version that his position is intuitionist. But such an interpretation, I think, misses the point of these examples.

The investigator does not take, in his imagination, the role of the agent in order to find out facts about him. Empathy is not a kind of research; accordingly, it is not an alternative to inductive inquiry. The investigator's use of empathetic imagination is not a substitute for the interpretation of evidence. It is not a way of disclosing something that cannot be gotten at through evidence, nor a device for uncovering facts that on principle can only be found out through an act of imaginative identification. Rather, insofar as our question bears on the acquisition of information, Collingwood's answer is clear: the investigator utilizes evidence, records and reports of what the agent did and said and, presumably, thought. To regard empathy as a way of discovering peculiarly inaccessible facts or as a method of self-certifying verification is a category mistake; it confuses the dimension in which empathy does operate, that of explanatory deliberation, with the logically distinct stage of investigation and reconstruction from evidence.[3]

3. An account of empathy along the lines I have just been criticizing can be found in Walsh, *Introduction to Philosophy of History*, pp. 52, 57–58. The same view is apparently held by Danto. When he speaks of "empathetic apprehension of the inner workings of another mind" and, again, of "empathetic projection" to "verify" facts,

Re-enactment

Another version of empathy alleges that the historian puts himself, imaginatively, into the role of the agent, not to acquire information otherwise inaccessible, but to determine what reasons he himself would have for doing what the agent did in the situation described. Then, once he has determined his own reasons for such an action, the investigator extrapolates them to the agent. Now this is certainly nearer to what Collingwood seemed to have in mind, but it still misstates his point. The historian, in Collingwood's account, is not concerned with what his own reasons for acting in a certain set of circumstances would be; rather, he is concerned with determining how certain courses of action would fit in with the mental configuration that evidence has led him to attribute to the agent. And these are two very different things. The fault of this version of empathy is not that it confuses empathy with inductive inquiry but that it rests on a substantial misunderstanding of the aim of empathetic identification: the goal is not to imagine reasons for a course of action; rather it is to imagine alternative courses of action and to measure these against the reasons which the agent presumably had, as indicated by the evidence.[4]

The point of empathy, as we find it in Collingwood's theory, is simply to put the investigator into a position where he can understand what the agent did, given his reconstruction of the agent's thought. The function of empathy is to suggest alternative courses of action, by considering the situation in which the agent stood, and to select one of these, by means of a calculation of plausibility, as the most plausible relative to what the agent thought. It is the essence of empathy to take the point of view of the agent, by regarding his situation and the elements of his thought, and to deliberate on possible courses of action from that point of view.

William Dray, a careful student of Collingwood's work, put his finger on the principle involved in the empathetic or deliberative dimension of Collingwood's re-enactment theory of explanation when he said that "in so far as we can say an action is [rational] at all, no

---

Danto's language suggests that empathy is a counterinductive way of perceiving or of certifying "unobservable occurrences in the agent's mind." (See Danto, *Analytical Philosophy of History*, pp. 205, 232.)

4. The version of empathy which I have disputed in this paragraph has been suggested, by Gardiner, as a possible way of interpreting Collingwood. (See Gardiner, ed., *Theories of History*, p. 250.)

matter at what level of conscious deliberation, there is a calculation which could be constructed for it. . . . And it is by eliciting some such calculation that we explain the action" (*Laws and Explanation*, p. 123).

The virtue of Dray's way of putting Collingwood's empathetic principle is that it allows the social scientist to utilize the device of deliberation, in order to account for the performance of a deed, without committing him to the belief that the agent must have propositionally rehearsed alternative courses of action or reasons for acting to himself. The notion of practical deliberation belongs, as Dray rightly points out, to the *logic* of re-enactment explanation; it is necessarily an investigator's device even though it does not imply or require a biographical interlude of explicit, deliberate calculation by the agent.

An explanation by re-enactment is complete, and satisfactory, when the investigator assembles the elements of the agent's thought through the "interpretation of evidence" and then, in Dray's phrase, "displays the *rationale* of what was done" by showing the performance in question to be, on balance, the most plausible course of action relative to these elements. Inductive reconstruction and empathetic deliberation are the two logical dimensions of Collingwood's theory of explanation by re-enactment. We might say that inductive reconstruction provides the element of *chronicle* in the historian's account and that empathetic deliberation provides the element of *narrative*. Empathy completes reconstruction by showing the plausibility of what has happened, but an explanation, though plausible, cannot be correct unless the inductive component is true. The ideal in history is to provide a narrative connecting facts.

Collingwood's answer to the question of an explanatory warrant has now emerged. The principle of explanatory connection between the agent's thought, conceived as a set of factors, and his deed is the investigator's calculation of what is appropriate: the historian's assertion of connection, Collingwood said, is established when his "picture of the past to which the evidence leads him is a coherent and continuous picture, one which makes sense" (*IH*, 245). The principle of explanatory connection in history and the other social sciences is ultimately one with that of literary or dramatic inevitability. The historian, like the novelist, "makes it his business to construct a picture which is partly a narrative of events, partly a description of situations, exhibi-

Re-enactment

tion of motives, analysis of characters. [He] aims at making his picture a coherent whole, where . . . this character in this situation cannot but act this way, and we cannot imagine him as acting otherwise" (*IH*, 245).

The notion of "coherence," as Collingwood called it, supplies the need for an explanatory warrant in re-enactment; the principle of maximum appropriateness is the principle of the explanatory connection of thought and deed. When an investigator says of an agent that "he did *x* because *y*," the explanatory force of the "because . . ." part of his statement is derived from the claim that the deed *x*, in respect of the agent's thought *y*, is the most appropriate course of action. The investigator's explanation is justified when he can calculate the plausibility with regard to the agent's thought of a number of possible courses of action and show through systematic elimination that *x*, the deed performed, was the most plausible among them.[5]

To accept the proposition that "*x* is the most appropriate course of action relative to *y*" enjoins the assertion "*x* because *y*" where *x* is, in fact, the deed performed. The explanation of a rational action by re-enactment carries a presumptive claim to adequacy and to acceptance in this case. But, in saying that we explain a rational action by showing that it "makes sense," Collingwood was not committed to the proposition that one can always make sense of an action "determined by thought." The crucial contention in Collingwood's analysis, as I see it, is that the "right way," and hence the preferred way, to explain a rational action is by re-enactment. Collingwood nevertheless maintained that in some cases an investigator will fail to re-enact an action even though he has reason to believe that the action was "determined by thought." Note, for example, his remark: "And if it has to be said of a certain man that he doubtless had a policy but that we cannot discover what it was (and one sometimes feels inclined to say this of, for example, certain early Roman emperors), this is as much as to say that

5. Dray says, "Rational explanation may be regarded as an attempt to reach a kind of logical equilibrium at which point an action is *matched* with a calculation" (*Laws and Explanation*, p. 125). I have found this remark very helpful in my efforts to understand Collingwood. My interpretation of Collingwood's theory of re-enactment, especially of its deliberative dimension, is indebted to the two books on philosophy of history written by William Dray—in particular, to ch. 5 ("The Rationale of Actions") of his *Laws and Explanation*, pp. 118–155, and to ch. 2 ("Historical Understanding") of his *Philosophy of History*, pp. 4–20.

one's attempts to reconstruct the political history of his actions have failed" (*IH*, 310).

Any such failure to explain, it would appear from Collingwood's analysis, could occur at either of two points. The investigator might be unable to reconstruct the agent's thought—because the data for it were contradictory, or inadequate, or because he simply could not interpret these data. He just could not get together an adequate description of what the agent had thought. Here we would have a failure at the inductive level of re-enactment. Or the investigator might, even though he was working with a relatively adequate inductive reconstruction of the agent's thought, fail in his calculation of plausibilities—either because the deed actually performed could not be calculated as the *most* plausible or because it simply could not be included at all among the investigator's supposal of alternative courses of action. Here we would have a failure at the deliberative level of re-enactment.

Finally, even when an investigator can exhibit the coherence of thought and deed in an action, this in no way guarantees the correctness or the indefeasibility of his explanation in respect of its inductive premise. The fact that the investigator can go through the required steps of a deliberative calculation successfully proves only that he can, given a reconstruction of the agent's thought and of the deed performed, "make sense" of the agent's action *as described.* But the establishment of an explanatory equilibrium does not rule out the possibility that the equilibrium is based on mistaken interpretation of data or on inadequate information, nor does it rule out the possibility of a different interpretation or of new information which, when taken into account, could upset the calculated "fit" of the agent's deed with his thought (see *IH*, 248–249).

The thought of the agent, like the deed he performed, is something that must be reconstructed on the basis of available evidence. All the ingredients of the historian's story stand in this respect on the same footing. There is no way in which re-enactment can ever verify, in the sense of make true infallibly or beyond doubt, the facts that the investigator has adduced in his explanation. On the other hand, if the data have been assembled as completely and carefully as possible on a basis of extensive evidence and if the investigator has formulated in his own words that composite of factors called the "thought" of the agent and if an explanatory continuity between deed and thought has been achieved through calculation, then we have the paradigm case of an adequate re-enactment, one which we could consider the correct explanation of the action under study.

Collingwood's analysis was not designed to show that a particular explanatory re-enactment could ever be beyond doubt or conclusive in any final sense. Rather, it was designed to show, on the assumption that re-enactment is the "right way of investigating mind," what is involved in the concept of explanatory re-enactment. Collingwood's primary concern was with developing a theory of explanation on the principle that an action is rendered intelligible by "the discerning of the thought which is the inner side of the event" (*IH*, 222). He was trying to analyze the logical structure of social science inquiry insofar as it was directed towards actions "determined by thought" and, in particular, to characterize the proper type of explanation for such actions.

It has been my contention throughout that Collingwood, although he regarded generalizations as having no logically necessary role to play in re-enactment explanations, did not fall back on intuition in order to provide the principle of explanatory connection. With this contention in mind, let us return to the interpretation of Collingwood as an intuitionist. It was alleged that in re-enactment, as described by Collingwood, there is no deliberative process of conjoining deeds with thoughts at all. Rather "it is suggested that it is possible to have the same thought as another person. . . . We can know *why* somebody did something just as 'directly' as we can know what it was that he did" (Gardiner, *Nature of Historical Explanation*, p. 117; see also p. 135).

The claim made by the critics is that Collingwood argued for a nondiscursive explanatory warrant; the investigator just "sees" the connection directly or immediately. They contend that, for Collingwood, the explanatory warrant is a "literal identity" between the investigator's reconstruction of thought and the thought which lies "behind" the agent's deed and that the investigator appeals to this alleged identity, as the sole and sufficient ground, in certifying his explanation. It follows in this interpretation that, since literal identity is the explanatory warrant in re-enactment, the establishment of identity is the precondition of any such explanation. And this implies, it is further alleged, that identity can be indefeasibly established in some noninductive and infallible way. In their interpretation, then, justifying an explanatory re-enactment depends, in Collingwood's theory, on the investigator's ability to guarantee identity procedurally.[6]

Indeed, it is precisely because these critics have interpreted Collingwood in this way that they claim his theory of re-enactment presupposes a mode of direct acquaintance on the historian's part with the thought of the agent. For if re-enactment really does require, as they have contended, a "literal identity" between the thought of the agent and that of the investigator, then there must be some sort of direct "penetration" or imaginative projection whereby the investigator can "detect" the actual thought of the agent and rethink it in his own mind.

Now all this implies a radically different interpretation of Collingwood's re-enactment theory of explanation from that which I have put forward in this chapter. I would say that, if Collingwood had been an intuitionist, there would be no need for the deliberative dimension of re-enactment in his theory at all. Collingwood's idea that the investigator "makes sense" of an action by showing the peculiar appropriateness of the deed performed, with respect to his reconstruction of the agent's thought, would be a logical excrescence in an intuitionist theory. It seems that we cannot have it both ways. Either understanding by re-enactment derives its explanatory force from an appeal to identity, as its premise, or it derives it from the investigator's calculation, from his supposal of alternative courses of action and his deliberative consideration of plausibilities. Contrary to the interpretation of Collingwood as an intuitionist, I do not think that, for Collingwood, an explanation of an action is ever warranted by appealing to a "literal identity" between the agent's thought and the investigator's interpretative re-creation of that thought. Hence, the question of a procedural guarantee is not even raised.

How can we resolve the point in dispute between these two interpretations? The claim that Collingwood's principle of explanatory connection, in re-enactment, is intuitionist rests on a peculiar reading of one chapter of his *Idea of History*, specifically of the chapter entitled "History as Re-enactment of Past Experience." In this chapter Coll-

6. Walsh implies this when he argues against Collingwood that "all we can claim is to have a point of contact with past events, enabling us perhaps to divine their true shape in some degree, but not such that we can check our reconstructions by comparing them with [the thoughts of agents] to see how far they are correct" (*Introduction to Philosophy of History*, p. 92).

ingwood took up the question of "literal identity." The way to resolve the issue, then, is to turn to this chapter and to see precisely what Collingwood was saying.

Collingwood believed that an investigator engaged in rethinking the thought of an agent is involved in an attempt to repeat that thought; he believed, in other words, that, when "x because y" is asserted as the explanation of an action, the interpretative re-creation of thought designated by y should be identical with the thought of the agent.[7] Now it follows from this, Collingwood reasoned, that, if identity defines an ideal to be achieved in any inductive reconstruction of thought, then some sort of identity between the agent's thought and the thought attributed to him by the investigator must be possible. In short, the issue presented to Collingwood by his own analysis was whether there *can* be an identity between two thoughts, and he attempted to resolve this issue in the affirmative through a discussion of identity.

The critics of Collingwood's alleged intuitionism think that Collingwood, in asking how such a thing is possible, intended to discuss some self-certifying procedure for attaining a "literal identity" between the thoughts of agent and investigator; they think that he was preparing to outline some infallible test whereby literal identity could be definitely established.[8] But, when we turn to the text of the chapter, we find nothing of the sort. Rather, we find Collingwood attempting (a) to state the sense in which two different thoughts *must* be the same for us to assert that the one counts as a repetition of the other and (b) to show that, in the sense stated, two different thoughts *can* be the same. The whole point of Collingwood's chapter is to show that two thoughts can be the same in the crucial sense in which they must be the same.

It is important to note the dialectical character of Collingwood's argument. By "dialectical" I mean that Collingwood stated and revised his position by reference to points raised by an "imaginary objector"

7. See *IH*, 288; note especially Collingwood's dictum that "to know another's act of thought involves repeating it for oneself." Part of what Collingwood meant by "repetition" can be replaced in paraphrase by the notion of *formulation in words*, as is clearly pointed out in the context; but something more than this is obviously intended insofar as Collingwood's remarks had to do with the *accuracy* of a formulation.

8. Cebik interprets Collingwood, in his chapter on re-enactment, to be raising precisely this theme. Accordingly, says Cebik, he arrived "at a position which asks *how* we can re-think what someone (historical figure or even ourselves) has thought" ("Collingwood: Action, Re-enactment, and Evidence," p. 81). There is no doubt why Cebik says earlier that Collingwood's "doctrine of re-enactment makes little if any sense" (p. 68) and suggests that it would require a "logical impossibility" (p. 69).

Historical Explanation

(see *IH*, 283). This objector is, no doubt, Collingwood himself. He "objects," I would surmise, because he was uneasy about the precise meaning and abstract possibility of an "identity" between two different thoughts and because he wanted to clarify these matters. And he "objects"—a good lecture room tactic, and not uncommon when a lecturer is dealing in argument rather than exposition—because he wanted to work out his ideas in front of his auditors, the better that they might grasp them. For it should be noted that the "chapter" was actually a part of Collingwood's lectures, which would account for its dialectical quality, and it was not written up in finished form for publication. The fact that the chapter is dialectical should, moreover, alert us to two points. Collingwood's principal theses come at the end of the argument and not at the beginning. His initial position, the notion of a "literal identity" between two different thoughts, is a dialectical starting point and is substantially revised in the course of his argument.

By the end of the chapter Collingwood was no longer asking whether two thoughts can be "literally identical" but instead had accepted a revision to the effect that "the question is how exactly two [thoughts] are the same, and how exactly they differ" (*IH*, 301). His answer was that so long as two thoughts are the same in their content, so long as two "arguments" are the same in their "logical structure," then the crucial sense in which they must be the same is preserved. A good bit of Collingwood's argument is taken up with showing that two thoughts, or "acts of thought" as he sometimes called them, can be the same in their thought content and that such differences as differences in time, or in the immediate mental context in which they occur, or in the personal identity of the men who think them do not make the so-called identity of thoughts impossible. It follows in a limited and specific sense that "an act of thought, in addition to actually happening, is capable of . . . being revived or repeated without loss of its identity" (*IH*, 300). [9]

This conclusion satisfied Collingwood on the point into which he was inquiring. He had shown that if a thought could be inductively reconstructed on the basis of evidence there is no *logical* barrier to saying that this is the agent's thought: it *could be* the thought of the agent.

9. Points made in this paragraph can be found in *IH*, 288, 296–297, 301–303. See also *Autobiography*, pp. 111–112.

Re-enactment

The suggested correspondence is not, in the nature of things, impossible.

But what bearing does all this have, it might be asked, on how we can establish identity? Very little. What Collingwood has to say on this head is said incidentally and indirectly. Insofar as there is a question of establishing identity procedurally, Collingwood's answer seems to be the following: if the investigator can reconstruct a thought for the agent through interpretation of the data and if he can "make sense" of the deed performed by reference to this thought, then he has a *prima facie* ground for saying that the agent's thought and his reconstruction of it are the same. (See *IH*, 296, 301.)

We have reached a conclusion that is markedly at variance with the interpretation of Collingwood as an intuitionist. The critical point of divergence is that, as I see Collingwood's theory of explanation by re-enactment, the notion of identity has no methodological function at all. The procedural "establishment" of identity is a consequence of re-enactment and not something involved in or presupposed by it. In short, we "establish" identity by appeal to understanding and not *vice versa* as the intuitionist version of Collingwood's position would have it; we do not argue *from* identity but, rather, *to* it.

It will, no doubt, be retorted that in my exposition of Collingwood's position his notion of identity appears to be of no practical consequence. For identity is wholly parasitical on re-enactment. There is no way in which we can "check our reconstructions" directly against the thought of an agent and no way in which we can establish identity independently of re-enactment. And, even though the thought reconstructed *could be* the thought of the agent, there is no way we can be absolutely sure of this identity. The notion of identity is dispensable methodologically. But this is precisely the point which I think needs to be made. Collingwood simply was not discussing peculiar "methods" of detecting thoughts and guaranteeing identity in his chapter on re-enactment.

The critics may reply that if the notion of identity is dispensable for all practical purposes then it is not an ideal at all. This is true. The notion of identity is not an ideal except for purposes of clarifying what it is, in Collingwood's opinion, that investigators are trying to do. Collingwood contended that the adequacy of a reconstruction of thought, with respect to its accuracy, is defined ideally by the identity

61

of that reconstruction with the thought of the agent. And, contending this, he wanted to show that this ideal was not an impossible one. But he also wanted to argue that the attainment of identity can be handled procedurally only by reference to the available data and to the investigator's calculation of plausibilities.

Perhaps Collingwood can be accused of raising a spurious issue; perhaps his line of reasoning can be scored as tortuous and unrewarding. But to expose the many flaws in his discussion of identity does not weaken Collingwood's case for re-enactment explanation. For Collingwood did not rest his case for re-enactment on the possibility of a direct, prior attainment by the investigator of a thought identical to that of the agent. Collingwood did not define re-enactment as thinking the *same* thought as the agent nor did he make it depend on the establishment of identity, as a precondition. Collingwood did not claim that an explanation by re-enactment could be warranted by appeal to identity.

The conclusion I reach is not that Collingwood's account of explanatory re-enactment was diluted or controverted by his discussion of identity, but that there is no good reason provided in his chapter on re-enactment for interpreting Collingwood as an intuitionist. There is in Collingwood's theory of explanation by re-enactment no place for the mechanisms of intuition: no noninductive penetrations or imaginative projections, no direct and indefeasible acquaintance with the thoughts of agents, no self-validating procedures for achieving or guaranteeing the identity of the investigator's interpretative reconstruction with the thought of the agent. Collingwood argued for no shortcuts; he provided no way of bypassing either the inductive reconstruction of thought or the deliberative calculation of a "coherence" between thought and deed as the principle of explanatory connection in re-enactment.

Collingwood's rejection of generalization as an explanatory principle did not lead him then to take an intuitionist position; as we have seen, he conceived of re-enactment as a peculiar mode of explanatory reasoning which depended neither on intuitive penetration nor on subsumption under generalizations. Although I do not think Collingwood's conception of explanation by re-enactment is open to the objections of the critics of his alleged intuitionism, I do feel that his position is vulnerable from another direction.

The peculiar claim put forward in Collingwood's historicist thesis is that explanation by rethinking is different in type from explanation by subsumption under a generalization. Re-enactment explanation, it is alleged, does not logically require any move to put actions under classificatory concepts, or any reference to generalizations, or regularity analysis of any sort. These steps are neither taken nor presupposed; rather, for the historian, "the object to be discovered is not the mere event, but the thought expressed in it. To discover that thought is already to understand it [the event]" (IH, 214). Generalization is wholly extrinsic to the logic of re-enactment; and, by the extension we find in Collingwood's historicist argument, generalization is extrinsic to the logic of explanation in all the "sciences of mind," in economics and cultural anthropology as well as in history. When an investigator explains re-enactively, he simply establishes the coherence of the performance or event-side and the thought-side of an action by showing that the deed "makes sense" or is "appropriate" in reference to the particular situation and thought of the agent.

But Collingwood did not attempt to analyze these explanatory categories; he did not attempt to go behind the claim that a certain connection "makes sense" to show the logical basis on which this claim would be made. He neither considered what was presupposed in his use of this particular battery of explanatory terms nor tried to determine what is logically involved in explanations under the category of plausibility. His analysis simply stopped with the claim that we can assert that a given connection "makes sense" and that such an assertion carries a *prima facie* explanatory force. The assertion of plausibility, while it does involve certain calculative moves, is in Collingwood's theory a sort of irreducible, unanalyzed datum.

To be strictly accurate, however, I would have to acknowledge that Collingwood did indicate one way in which we could interpret an assertion of plausibility; he suggested that we should treat the assertion that a connective account "makes sense" as a psychological datum about the historian. In the final analysis, we can take him as saying that what warrants any explanatory connection by re-enactment is the investigator's judgment as to what makes sense: the historian's "criterion" is "simply himself" (see IH, 139; and also 138–140, 236–238, 249).

Collingwood's failure to analyze the "criterion" of re-enactment further than the investigator's psychological makeup would appear to leave explanation wholly dependent on the idiosyncrasies of the investigator. If this reading were accepted as the final word, many explanations would lack any force at all for persons other than the one advancing the explanation. For by this criterion, any account would qualify as an adequate explanation so long as the investigator is able, through his deliberations about plausibility, to "see" the connection he is asserting. This is objectionable because it imposes an end-stop at the very point where the serious questions about a putative explanation would be raised.

Moreover, we have no way to check out these subjective appraisals. We have no recognizable way to confirm or disconfirm an explanation put forward in accordance with this criterion, for the appraisal behind such an explanation is not arguable. In short, we have no way to develop discriminations between more or less adequate explanations or, what is worse, between explanations and pseudo-explanations.

What is disconcerting about Collingwood's suggested criterion is its note of radical subjectivism. If there can be no appeal beyond the investigator's subjective appraisal, then we have subtly shifted the focus of our account of explanation from the apparently objective connection of deed with thought, which is what was originally meant by the statement that this deed *makes sense* in the light of that thought, to the psychology of the investigator when he asserts a connection of plausibility.

Any such shift to subjectivism is, I think, self-defeating. Collingwood intended to establish the autonomy of the "sciences of mind." For by treating this autonomy not simply as freedom from the principles of natural science but also as an apparent freedom from any clear-cut principle at all, he has moved these sciences dangerously close to anarchy. If we take the criterion of mere subjective appraisal as the final word, all of the social sciences would seem to constitute an elaborate system of questionable explanatory judgments.

Even were we to free Collingwood's criterion from this charge of subjectivism, by close attention to his text, the line he has taken would still be unsatisfactory as it stands—because it is begging the question. It may be true that deliberative or empathetic rethinking necessarily involves subjective appraisal and that the investigator "works" his material in accordance with his own appraisals of appropriateness, but this does not dispose of any need to consider the logical side of explanation by re-enactment. I would suggest that the logic of giving explanations under the category of plausibility, even if we take re-enactment to be a correct form of such explanation, has not adequately been worked out by Collingwood and that we must pursue the implications of his re-enactment theory beyond the confines of the account he has given.

Four

A Schema for
Action-Explanations

In order to indicate the logical, as distinct from the psychological, character of re-enactment, I want to review the main points of Collingwood's account and to provide a reconstructive analysis of the notion of re-enactment. The object of this analysis is not to paraphrase Collingwood's ideas but, rather, to map out the logical structure of those explanations in which re-enactment plays a constitutive role and to show the criteria involved in explaining deeds by reference to thoughts under the category of plausibility.

According to Collingwood, the place to begin a re-enactment explanation is with the agent's situation. We must, he asserted, consider the situation the agent faced and how he conceived it and how he was inclined to deal with it. In delineating this complex situation, we are, in effect, stating the agent's *motive* for action, what Collingwood called the agent's *causa quod*.[1] From this statement of the situation, of the agent's *causa quod*, the investigator generates a set of alternative courses of action open to the agent. Collingwood laid this principle

1. See Collingwood, *Metaphysics*, pp. 292–293. Collingwood went on to refine this notion of a situational "cause" of action. "The *causa quod* is not a mere situation or state of affairs, it is a situation or state of affairs known or believed by the agent in question to exist" (p. 292).

66

A *Schema* for Action-Explanations

down succinctly when he said that "the historian of politics or warfare, presented with an account of certain actions done by Julius Caesar, tries to understand these actions. . . . This implies envisaging for himself the situation in which Caesar stood, and thinking for himself what Caesar thought about the situation and the possible ways of dealing with it" (*IH*, 215).

Collingwood's own attempt to explain "Caesar's invasion of Britain" is an instructive example of the application of this principle. In a chapter of his history of Roman Britain, Collingwood posed for himself and his readers the problem of an explanation of an event under the following description: Caesar went into Britain from Gaul with troops in 54 B.C. This description of Caesar's deed we can call the *explanandum*; it states what is to be explained.[2]

This problem is set by Collingwood in the first paragraph of his chapter. The resolution to the problem, he wrote, consists in finding answers to two questions: What motives induced Caesar to go into Britain? What did he intend to bring about there by his expedition? These "are questions to which [Caesar] has given us no answer." And yet "we cannot help asking them; and unless we can find some sort of answer, . . . the mere narrative of his campaigns must remain unintelligible."

How then did Collingwood propose to "make sense" of Caesar's deed? Immediately after telling us what Caesar had done, Collingwood turned in his narrative to a description of Caesar's situation. The crucial fact in this situation, as Collingwood saw it, was that Caesar, who had recently completed the conquest of Gaul, was faced with hostile interventions in Gaul by the British tribes. The British tribes were a continuing source of unrest in the Gaulish world. It was fairly clear to Collingwood that Caesar would curb these hostile interventions if he could, for he had become, Collingwood said, "more and more preoccupied with the problem of keeping the peace, and forestalling or repressing movements of rebellion among the fiercely independent tribes he had conquered." There is, Collingwood added, "little room for doubt that the same motives played a part in determining the enterprise [against the Britons]. . . . So long as Gaul was restless, Britain, a refuge and reservoir of disaffection within a few hours'

---

2. I want to emphasize that the *what* which is to be explained is never a deed *per se* but, always, that deed *under some particular description*. (The point is Danto's; see *Analytical Philosophy of History*, pp. 218–219.)

sail, was an added danger: for the sake of Gaulish security, therefore, Britain must be made harmless." [3] From this account of Caesar's situation, we could generate a set of alternative courses of action open to Caesar: he could curb these interventions by taking diplomatic initiatives or by a mere showing of the flag or by leveling some sort of forcible sanction (e.g., an invasion).

The job of the historian, Collingwood has told us, is to assess the plausibility of each of these supposed alternatives as it relates to the case at hand. On the evidence that Caesar apparently felt that these hostile interventions could be curbed only if the British tribes were inhibited by force, an impression consistent with his successful use of force against the Gauls, and on the evidence that Caesar was in no way averse to using force, Collingwood's explanatory argument proceeds by showing that one of these alternative courses of action (leveling a sanction of force) is appropriate to what Caesar was thinking.

Now it is easy enough to see that whatever forcible sanction Caesar was going to employ would involve an invasion of Britain. This brings us to the really problematic part of the matter, the question which Collingwood's explanatory account was principally designed to answer: What did Caesar intend to bring about there by his expedition?

Collingwood felt, given the evidence he had, that one of two possible aims lay behind Caesar's invasion: either Caesar wanted to conduct a punitive expedition, a large-scale raid, against the British or he was attempting to conquer the tribes forcibly. By a rather complicated, perhaps tenuous, line of reasoning, Collingwood argued that the latter intention was the more likely, insofar as he was able to reconstruct Caesar's thought. (See Collingwood, *Roman Britain and the English Settlements*, pp. 32–33.)

Although Collingwood's treatment of the historical materials at his disposal may be open to question, there is little question about the conceptual apparatus which he employed in his explanation of Caesar's invasion of Britain. What he tried to do, if I may put the matter in its simplest form, was to establish two features of Caesar's thought in particular, his situational motivation (*causa quod*) and his intention

---

3. See R. G. Collingwood and J. N. L. Myres, *Roman Britain and the English Settlements*, Vol. I of *The Oxford History of England* (2d ed.; Oxford: Oxford University Press, 1937), p. 32 for the passages quoted. (Note: Collingwood wrote the chapters on Roman Britain and Myres those on the English Settlements; I am referring to chapter 3, "Caesar's Invasion," pp. 32–53.)

A *Schema* for Action-Explanations

(*causa ut*), and to indicate that these two features are coherently aligned (i. e., to show that the agent's intention is responsive to his situational motivation).[4]

In the case of Caesar's invasion of Britain, Collingwood's re-enactive explanation of Caesar's deed is largely constituted by building a kind of bridge between Caesar's situational motivation and his intention. As we move along we have a progressive determination of the "causes" of Caesar's deed. Beginning with the agent's situational awareness, we have, at first, a relatively indeterminate causal matrix; but its description becomes more determinate as we take in more of the agent's thought: we move from "curbing hostile interventions" to "trying a sanction of force" and, finally, to "attempting to conquer." This process is completed when we have a summary description of the agent's thought that serves to align what Collingwood regarded as the crucial explanatory features of the agent's thought, his situational motive with his purpose or end in view.

Collingwood's explanation goes through when he is able to assert that a particular course of action, an invasion in this case, is appropriate to this particular alignment of elements and is, among the imagined alternatives, the most appropriate one. I would not, of course, want to suggest that a consideration of other elements of the agent's thought—his scruples, relevant know-how, etc.—plays no part in the explanatory assessment. But these other elements are used principally to help show that one of these particular ways of acting does line up in a sort of triangulation with the key elements of the agent's thought: his situational motivation and his intention. We can use the image of a triangle to exhibit the crucial features of a re-enactment explanation.

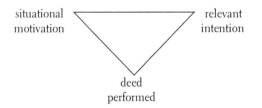

situational motivation   relevant intention

deed
performed

4. See Collingwood, *Metaphysics*, pp. 292–293. There Collingwood suggested that the cause of an action is "made up of two elements, a *causa quod* or efficient cause and a *causa ut* or final cause. The *causa quod* is a situation or state of affairs existing; the *causa ut* is a purpose or state of affairs to be brought about. Neither of these could be a

Historical Explanation

This "selection" of one deed from among the alternative courses of action, although an important and indispensable move, is logically subordinate to the claim that the deed performed does match up with the thought of the agent, in particular with his situational motivation and intention. It is the "coherence," as Collingwood called it (see *IH*, 245), of a deed, as described, with these particular thoughts that is at the heart of the matter.

Of course, in any given explanation, which element is emphasized will depend on what the investigator finds problematic, generally because he is having difficulties in his work of inductive reconstruction or, much less frequently, because he cannot "think himself into" (*IH*, 213) the action with the inductive reconstruction he has achieved. Usually, as I have indicated, it is the agent's situation-conception or his intention that will be the focus of the investigator's extended attention. In general, then, we can say that the principal task of any re-enactment explanation is to find the situational motivation and relevant purpose to which the deed performed properly connects.

In the case of Caesar's going into Britain, the difficulty Collingwood encountered was to determine, on the basis of available evidence, what in particular Caesar had intended. Once he had solved this problem to his satisfaction, Collingwood was able to integrate the explanandum (which we can refer to as "Caesar's invasion of Britain") into a "completed picture" with the crucial components of Caesar's thought, his situational motivation and his relevant intention. Caesar's going into Britain was an invasion and we can say, in explanation, "He was invading in an attempt to pacify the tribes through conquest so as to curb their hostile incursions."

Collingwood's explanation of Caesar's invasion looks adequate enough, but it could be subjected to a rather straightforward challenge. Let us suppose that someone wanted to challenge his explanation, not with respect to the facts Collingwood cited or the way he employed his evidence, but, rather, with respect to the explanatory force of accounting for a deed by reference to the agent's thought.

He might say, for instance, "Why bring in the situation as Caesar conceived it?" Or he might ask why Caesar's purpose, of conquering the tribes, was adduced as relevant. His question is, what gives a re-

cause if the other were absent" (p. 292). He continued by noting that "the *causa ut* is not a mere desire or wish, it is an intention. The *causa ut* of a man's acting in a certain way is not his wanting to act in that way, but his meaning to act in that way" (p. 293).

A *Schema* for Action-Explanations

enactment explanatory force? How would one go about meeting this sort of challenge?

I think Collingwood, or, better, someone who had followed the development of his argument to this point, could retort that these things are brought in because they are features of a general schema which tells us what sorts of things are involved in giving a satisfactory action-explanation of a certain type. The claim on Collingwood's behalf is that we provide an explanation of anyone's action when we can show that (1) he did perceive himself to be in a certain situation, (2) where he might do some such deed, and (3) he had a purpose relevant to dealing with his situation and (4) could be taken as seeing that that particular deed would accomplish this end.

I am suggesting here that some fairly definite general conditions of explanatory adequacy govern all explanations by re-enactment. It would follow that a nondefective explanation by re-enactment must represent the fulfilling of these conditions. We want to see, though, the ground for thinking that the explanatory practices of re-enactment are, as Collingwood thought them to be, definitive and satisfactory. We need to determine what particular general explanatory form is presupposed by these practices.

My program is to elicit the criteria of a nondefective re-enactment explanation by noting the conditions Collingwood himself tried to satisfy, or said that he did, and by noting what any person would consider in *following* such an explanation. It might prove valuable as well to consider what sorts of objections, beyond objections to the use of particular pieces of evidence or to the factual conclusions drawn, could be advanced to disqualify an explanation and would need to be overcome for any re-enactment to be regarded as a successful one. I am concerned to exhibit the "structural details" of our capacity to make and follow nondefective explanations by re-enactment.[5] I have already indicated the most important of these details. Principally, then, what remains to be spelled out?

The most obvious point of puzzlement, I would think, is where Collingwood's emphasis on conjectured alternative courses of action is going to fit in. Now it is clear enough that Collingwood regarded this

5. I am much indebted, for my program in this and the previous paragraph and for the basic idea of explanatory adequacy, to the important essay by Churchland, "The Logical Character of Action-Explanations." The terms "structural details" and "capacity" are taken from this article. (See p. 215.)

71

supposal of alternatives as a constituent feature of re-enactment. Are we to regard it as another condition of explanatory adequacy? I think it could be claimed either that it is such a condition or, alternatively, that it figures crucially in the proper statement of these conditions.

There is a solid core, I think, to Collingwood's contention that the agent could and the investigator must consider the alternative courses of action that the agent's situational awareness might give rise to. In my earlier image of a triangle of explanation, one of the sides of the triangle is the line that connects what "moved" the agent to act (i.e., his situational motivation) with the act that he performed. It is difficult to see how the investigator could show that the deed performed was situationally responsive, that it was a deed the agent might do in the situation, without a consideration of alternatives.

One might say in support of this contention that the seeing of any one action as possible in its situational setting involves seeing alternatives as well. Even so, the argument lacks force: since it rests on saying that we *can* see action A as situationally responsive, it is not clear why we *must* see other courses of action, say B and C, that way as well.

Hence, we need to find a better reason for bringing in the investigator's supposal of alternatives. Earlier I indicated in the schema that, presumptively, the agent must believe or see that acting that way (the deed performed) is a means to his end or part of accomplishing it. But surely this alone is not enough. For we must also be implying, where we say "the agent performed a particular action because he intended such-and-so," that given the situation he was in and how he proposed to deal with it, there was no other action he preferred or even considered equal as a means to his goal. This is the point of the supposal of alternatives: it provides the indispensable conceptual framework for stating the condition of preference, which *is* necessary for explanatory adequacy. The crucial role played by supposing alternative courses of action is that it helps to complete another of the sides of the triangle, the line that connects the agent's intention with the deed performed.

There seems to be something intuitively satisfying in an explanation that can select one course of action and eliminate the others. Such explanations have a peculiar force. Our intuition represents the natural rhythm of explanation: we believe the agent's situational motivation generates alternative possibilities for acting; so there must be some way—on the intention side—of cutting them out. It is by reference to the condition of preference, together with the agent's purpose, that the

A *Schema* for Action-Explanations

investigator is able to do this cutting out, to select the one course of action and to eliminate the others. A kind of symmetry results, as we have it in the triangle of explanation.

Let me add parenthetically that the condition of preference can actually be stated in diluted form. Consider the following example. (1) I am typing a letter. Why? (2) In order to get an extra bookcase. Surely there is a sense in which (2) may be said to explain (1), even though there is no evident elimination of alternatives to typing such as dictating the letter, making a phone call, or presenting the request in person. Nonetheless, I think the explanatory force of "(1) because (2)" does depend on the satisfaction of the condition of preference. It is not so much that we can positively show the preferred status of letter-typing over these alternatives but, rather, that we have no reason to believe, or evidence to show, that one of the alternatives was preferred. This is, admittedly, a very weak version of the condition (nonevidence for nonpreference); still the condition does operate, as would become clear if we actually did have the pertinent reasons or evidence.

Sometimes we rule out those competing alternative courses of action that the agent might have taken simply in the way we describe the deed actually done. Or, to put the matter squarely, we eliminate any *real* need to consider them. Hence, when Collingwood described Caesar's expedition as an *invasion*, he ruled out, by that very fact, the competing alternative description of it as a diplomatic mission. The justification of letting this and other alternatives go by default, as it were, is that the condition of preference, in its weak form, is satisfied here (in that no evidence exists to show a preference on Caesar's part for any of the alternatives to invasion).

The condition of preference is also involved in talk about scruples and know-how. For where one was trying to see whether this condition was actually fulfilled in a given case, he would bring in such things as a man's moral principles or his skills. These things constitute a relevant consideration since the agent's course of action is not determined solely by his end in view. Accordingly they indicate what, besides the agent's intention itself, the investigator might call upon to help him select that one course of action as the preferred one from among the set of imagined alternatives.

We have now gone through the major points that Collingwood emphasized in his account of re-enactment, developing a list of necessary conditions of explanatory adequacy which could be generated, dialectically, out of his account. One would find on reflection, however, that the list is incomplete, since explanations that *merely* satisfied these conditions would not be thought adequate. We can return to the metaphor of a triangle of explanation in order to see this point more clearly.

I stated that the agent must have a "purpose relevant to dealing with his situation." Part of what is involved in calling a purpose "relevant" is simple enough; the purpose or end in view must be responsive to the agent's situational motivation. A purpose is "relevant" in this sense when it would satisfy, if acted upon, the situational motivation we have ascribed to the agent—or so he believes. This provides the side that would complete the explanatory triangle, the line that connects the agent's perception of his situation with one of his purposes.

The problem, of course, is that it is only one of his purposes. What if the agent had an end in view which was relevant in the sense just described but which was also canceled out by another of his purposes? (As was the case when John Kennedy's relevant "purpose" of bombing the Cuban missile sites was suppressed by his prudent goal of avoiding a nuclear war with the Soviet Union.)

It seems that the notion of a relevant purpose must be richer than we have allowed. For we must establish not only that such a purpose was responsive to the agent's situational motivation but also that no other goal, in that situation and with the supposedly available alternatives for action, overrode it. I am not saying that the agent's designated purpose is absolutely the overriding one (for very few of our resolves are resolves "at any cost") but only that, whatever his other purposes are, none of them is thought to override this particular one at this particular point.

I have been assuming for the sake of simplicity that there is only one proper intention for a given explanation by re-enactment. I have treated as a paradigm the case that involves finding just a single purpose for what the agent did. But, of course, the relevant purpose might often be complex rather than simple, as the example about Caesar probably is in truth. No doubt his intent to conquer Britain was itself in concatenation with certain ambitions he had and with his conception of Roman imperial policy, and so on. The point is, though, that none of these overrode his purpose, if it was his purpose, to conquer Britain. Hence that purpose serves as the revelatory focal point for what the agent intended.

A *Schema* for Action-Explanations

Of course, a historian might want to explain Caesar's relevant purpose: he might want to explain why Caesar was attempting to conquer Britain. And here these further features of Caesar's "purpose" might be called in as the explanatory "thoughts" behind Caesar's wanting or intending conquest. But this is a different matter from explaining Caesar's expedition into Britain, which is what Collingwood wanted to explain. Indeed, the subsequent explanation of Caesar's intention actually presupposes the truth of the explanation of Caesar's action that Collingwood gave.

Moreover, it would not matter if the deed could not be ascribed to just one intention. For example, a man might want to go to a particular opera in another city but only if he could manage to be there at the time on other business. Re-enacting this deed would surely become more complicated, but it would not be essentially different from the simplified example I have been considering.

Let us suppose now that all the conditions which I have spelled out were satisfied in a given case. Would this yield the material for an explanation? Consider a well-known action: Columbus sailed into the New World in 1492. Could we explain this deed by reference to what was surely efficacious in this event, the thought-factors of Columbus and his crew? That is, could we explain it solely by reference to such things as Columbus' situation-conception ("the world is round and an unbroken ocean stretches from Spain to the Orient"), his motivation ("great wealth could be gotten, and economically, too, on the ocean route"), and his means/ends purposive thinking ("by sailing west we can reach the East")? I think the answer is clear enough; Columbus' deed, under the description which the interested historian would give it, cannot be explained simply by reference to these thought-factors. And the reason for this failure is ready to hand. It is that a disparity exists between Columbus' conception of his situation and the actual facts of his situation. This brings us to a criticism of Collingwood.

It has been alleged by certain of Collingwood's critics that there is a problem in his contention that "the explanation of actions is to be given *entirely* by reference to the thought of the agent"; specifically the problem is the claim that "it is the agent's *conception* of his situation, not his *actual* situation, that explains his doing what he did." This introduces, it is said, a "*lacuna*" in his account: for the action to happen, as opposed to being merely intended, the situation "must cooperate."

75

Historical Explanation

Dray, the critic I am quoting, goes on to point the moral. "[E]very thought explanation, if it is to yield strict deduction of an overt action, requies a premiss about the actual situation." Moreover, Dray continues,

if the agent's control over his own body, at least, is a generally necessary condition of action in the historically interesting sense, then clearly we can *never* (as a matter of mere logic) deduce individual actions from statements about the agent's thought alone; we can never, as Collingwood has generally been thought to use the term, deduce the "outside" from the "inside." We shall always need an "efficacy" premiss, asserting something about the agent's powers and opportunities.[6]

Although there is merit to these criticisms, I believe Collingwood's position is less vulnerable than his critics think. Even when we turn to the most notorious of the passages they have cited (for example, *IH*, 200, 315–317), we find that Collingwood does draw an explicit distinction between the agent's *actual* situation and his situation as he perceives it. The point of Collingwood's distinction can, I think, be put simply: what moves an agent to act is always his perception of a situation but what determines whether his action is successful or not, or whether it can even occur, is the *facts* of the actual situation. Sometimes the actual situation is describable by reference to what other people are thinking and doing and sometimes by reference to certain physical facts of nature. But, in either case, the actual situation is *there*; it is a "raw material" for the agent's action and has its "effect" (see *IH*, 200; also 316).

Indeed, we can find many passages in Collingwood's *Idea of History* that suggest considerations which would satisfy Dray's idea of an "efficacy premiss" in the explanation of human actions. Historians are, sometimes but rarely, concerned with the question of an agent's sheer physical ability or inability to do a certain thing (see *IH*, 239). Again,

6. Dray, "Singular Hypotheticals and Historical Explanation," pp. 195–196. The reason Dray used such un-Collingwoodian terms as "deduction" and "deduce" is that he was principally addressing himself to Donagan, who had used these terms. Indeed, Dray was endorsing a criticism that Donagan had once made of Collingwood. (For Donagan's criticisms of Collingwood, see *Later Philosophy of Collingwood*, pp. 202–206.) Leach also has criticized Collingwood on this point (see "The Logic of the Situation," p. 271 and, also, 260, 261–264). Donald Marquis has remarked that these criticisms represent an objection of principle, since they tend to undercut Collingwood's maxim that "all history is the history of thought" (*IH*, 215). They do, I grant, raise a serious question about the explanatory adequacy of Collingwood's re-enactment model.

76

A *Schema* for Action-Explanations

Collingwood says that an agent could not perform some actions unless he had the know-how to do so (see *IH*, 266, 270, where this issue is raised). Finally, it should be noted that Collingwood drew a long and explicit analogy between legal methods (those of the detective and the law court) and historical method (*IH*, 266–282; esp. 268–271), thus endorsing a consideration in history of such matters as the agent's opportunity, his "control over his own body" (in Dray's phrase), his normal abilities, and so on.

Additionally, I think some defense can be offered of Collingwood's relative neglect of situational matters and "efficacy premises" in favor of such things as situational motivations and relevant purposes. According to Donagan,

> Dray has overlooked that historians, by introducing historical agents as men or women, as kings, ministers, generals, party leaders, and the like, implicitly provide most of the efficacy premises he demands. Just as a natural scientist, describing an experiment in which a metal rod was heated in a Bunsen burner, need not mention that the supply of gas did not fail, so an historian writing of somebody whom he has introduced as a man, need not mention that that person has the control over his body that is normal to men. . . . When historians do not find such impairments or interferences, they show it by not mentioning them. ["Alternative Historical Explanations and Their Verification," p. 79]

Similarly, the historian mentions the *actual* situation, as opposed to the situation presumably envisioned by the agent, only when the two are so decidedly out of phase as to abort the agent's contemplated deed. (As happened when, unbeknown to Columbus, the American continental landmass lay athwart his course, thereby preventing his sailing to Asia.)

With this point about "efficacy premises" made, I think we have assembled the material for a conclusion to the question of criteria for explanatory adequacy. A statement on the model of "an agent did A (e.g., Caesar invaded) because he intended such-and-so state of affairs to be brought about in response to this or that situation" is satisfactory as an explanation if and only if certain conditions are fulfilled.

These conditions are that the investigator can explicitly show or can in effect judge that:
(1) The agent perceived himself to be in a certain situation and was disposed to act toward it in some definite way (e.g., as Caesar was disposed to curb the hostile incursions of the Britons).

(2) There were a number of alternative courses of action (designated as A—e.g., invading—B, C, and so on) open to the agent who had the situational motivation described in (1).

(3) The agent did want to achieve or accomplish such-and-so end (e.g., conquest), which he believed would satisfy his situational motivation.

(4) He believed that doing A was, in the circumstances already described, a means to accomplishing his stated purpose or a part of achieving it.

(5) There was no action other than A believed or seen by the agent to be a means to his goal which he preferred or even regarded as about equal.

(6) The agent had no other purpose which overrode that of accomplishing such-and-so.

And we might add, although Collingwood gave little attention to it, that (7) the agent knew how to do A, was physically able to do it, would be able to do it in the situation as given, had the opportunity, etc.

We could, perhaps, expand this list of conditions further. But the point is that some such set of criteria provides the basic operating sketch of the necessary conditions for explanatory adequacy in a reenactment. And the list we have, especially when written down in a general and summary way, does seem altogether obvious. For surely an explanatory statement of the sort we have been considering, such as the one Collingwood gave of Caesar's invasion of Britain, would not be followed or accepted by the person who thought any one of these conditions to be unfulfilled in the case at hand.

Of course, we are concerned that the statements of fact offered in fulfillment are true ones and this requires, minimally, that they be consistent with the available evidence. But whether a statement is true and whether it is the filling of an explanatory form are two different questions. It is important that we separate these issues: I am asking here what conditions for explanatory adequacy must be fulfilled by an explanation. This is different from asking a question of evidence, from asking whether these conditions, which must be fulfilled, are fulfilled in a particular case by true statements.

I would contend, additionally, that the question of the truth or falsity of particular statements in a particular explanation is logically subordinate to the prior question of what constitutes explanatory adequacy in an explanation of that sort. The question, then, is why we would reject an explanatory statement if we believed one of these conditions to be instantiated by a false statement or, alternatively, why we would tend to accept such a statement in which all the conditions are thought to be fulfilled by true statements. The answer, I believe, is that we do regard an explanation as nondefective or adequate where something, presumably true on other grounds, e.g., evidential, is offered in fulfillment of each of these conditions.

So, where an investigator says "the agent did A because T" (where T is an expanded statement of the "thought" of the agent of the sort we are familiar with), the explanatory adequacy or force is provided by the fulfilling of the conditions expressed in the formula, subject always to the proviso that the fulfilling statements are consistent with the body of available evidence. We could, accordingly, rewrite any such explanation to exhibit the point more clearly: "the agent did A because" and here we would have a long conjunctive list of statements each one of which satisfied a necessary condition of adequacy, (1)–(7). Each statement would be prefaced by a "because" and each one would assert some singular state of affairs that satisfies, or would satisfy if true, one of the criteria.

I am contending that the formula we have been discussing states, more or less accurately and completely, the necessary conditions of adequacy of a certain kind of explanation, the kind Collingwood called re-enactment. Those conditions, when fulfilled, conjointly warrant explanatory statements of the form "A (action done) because T (thoughts of the agent)." My point, then, is that these conditions, or something substantially like them, are necessary and conjointly are sufficient to provide the warrant of explanatory connection whereby one moves from asserting certain facts about the agent's "thought" to asserting that the agent performed a certain action because of these thoughts.

The schema I have produced, or something very like it, is the principle of adequacy of any explanation by re-enactment. Let us designate it then as R (R standing here for "re-enactment"). I think it could be argued that the principle is in no way eccentric. Indeed, I am sure that most people would regard it as setting forth an unobjectionable set of conditions and would regard it as the sort of formula that governs not only re-enactment but also many of the explanations of human behavior offered in literature and in everyday life.

Historical Explanation

I think we can summarize this amiable consensus by saying that my formula, "the agent did A because (1)–(7)," does provide an operative sketch of the principle of connection for explanations of actions. It does give us the set of necessary conditions which conjunctively are sufficient to warrant the adequacy of explanations of the form "A because T" or, alternatively, "A is appropriate in the light of T." We might describe this formula as representing the "theoretical commitment" of explanations by re-enactment.

Once this point has been made, it would be useful to note that the formula is susceptible of a certain philosophically interesting restatement. Instead of saying R, "he did A because (1)–(7)," we could say "If (1)–(7) then the agent does A." This way of putting the formula, which we could designate as R', is not necessarily clearer or intuitively more obvious than it was in the form of a principle of explanatory adequacy. But it does represent the logical point that where we explain "q because p" we are equally committed to "if p then q." Additionally, the associated "if . . . then . . ." form does have the virtue of indicating that the conditions (1)–(7) are conjunctively sufficient for saying that "the agent does A." [7]

On this analysis what I have called the schema for action-explanations is simply one way of stating these conditions, and the "if . . . then . . ." form another. It would be pointless to regard either of these two forms (the explanation sketch or the associated hypothetical inference) as *the* groundform; rather, the use of either is a license to use the other (see the argument of Ryle's paper " 'If,' 'So,' 'Because' ").

We have said, then, that the conditions which conjunctively warrant or license an explanation are the same as the conditions that warrant a connection, of the "if . . . then . . ." sort, between an action and the thought of the agent. But, surely, this would be a relatively uninteresting point unless we were willing to specify these conditions, as in R or as in its associated hypothetical form R', and to recognize these unrestricted, universal formulas as informative with respect to our capacity for making and following explanations of human action

7. I am not claiming, by the way, that the associated hypothetical statement here is an exact transcription of R, for it is not. The exact translation would go something like this: "If (1)–(7) and (8) the agent does A, then the agent does A *because* (1)–(7)." To mark this difference, I would call the formula in this footnote the "translation" of R into hypothetical form and I would call the "If . . . then . . ." formula in the text the hypothetical statement "associated" with R.

and as in some sense true. My contention, then, respecting the *logic* of explanations by re-enactment is that the practices of such explanations presuppose and are controlled by a particular principle of explanatory adequacy. And I have indicated roughly what this principle is by developing R. [8]

It would seem from this that an adequate or nondefective explanatory re-enactment is, in effect, an instantiation of this general formula. At the risk of oversimplification, we can say that the logical structure of explanation by re-enactment has these two levels: (a) the abstract general schema R and (b) particular re-enactments, each of which can be construed simply as a detailed application of the principle of inference R.

This way of treating re-enactments provides for an interesting reconstruction of Collingwood's oft-quoted remark, "To discover that thought is already to understand [the event]. . . . When [the investigator] knows what happened, he already knows why it happened" (*IH*, 214). For we can interpret him as saying that reference to the agent's thought has explanatory value insofar as these references do represent a full-fledged filling in of R in a particular set of behavioral circumstances; the investigator just states certain facts—he locates what the agent did and what his situation was and his intention and so on—and in this way he gives an adequate explanation. He does not go beyond the facts to classify or to subsume under general laws. Once the principle has been instantiated in that case, there is nothing further to determine or to do; for the investigator already understands why the agent acted as he did. Indeed I would suggest that many of Collingwood's puzzling dicta about historical explanation, in particular his claim that there is something a priori involved (see esp. *IH*, 245–246), could be translated into the two-level structure I have been describing.

Moreover, it does seem that if someone were to accept the various interpretations that the investigator has put on the material—agreeing that the agent did a particular action in a concrete situation to ac-

8. My analysis and presentation of the formulas R and R' have been influenced by Churchland and by von Wright in particular. (See "The Logical Character of Action-Explanations," esp. pp. 221–222, for the analogous formulas as developed by Churchland; and von Wright, *Explanation and Understanding*, esp. pp. 96–101 and 106–107.) I should add that my formulas also bear an affinity to one that Donagan has developed (see "Popper-Hempel Reconsidered," p. 150). Perhaps all of these formulations can be traced back ultimately to Popper's "logic of the situation" in his *Open Society*.

complish a definite aim such-and-so, etc.—then he would be compelled to accept the investigator's re-enactive explanation, so long, that is, as both accepted R as the ultimate principle of explanatory connection for actions. This latter point seems to occasion no difficulty since the principle of inference employed is, in the instance, so far from "subjective" that it would probably be widely regarded as unexceptionable.

We have in the contention that re-enactments can be construed as the filling in of a rather exacting explanatory form a way out of the radical subjectivism that underlay, to all appearances, Collingwood's use of appraisal terms like "makes sense" or "is appropriate." That is, we do if we take these terms, not as the substantial stuff of explanatory connection, but rather as indicators that a given explanation satisfies the conditions of the formula R. This is to suggest that a given re-enactment "makes sense" and is acceptable *as a whole* if the facts it cites can be taken, in effect, as substitution instances for the "variables" of R—under the condition, of course, that these substitutions are consistent (or "univocal") throughout the re-enactment and are supported, as true, by the available evidence.

Even so, I do not think this answer can dispose of the issue of subjectivism altogether. For there is still a question as to what is involved, logically, in "interpreting" something as a motive, something else as an intention, and so on. It would seem that the claim that a given statement of fact "fulfills" or "satisfies" one of the necessary conditions of explanatory adequacy in the formula R is itself susceptible of further analysis. And it is to this problem that I will turn in the next chapter.

There I want to show why adherence to the rule of univocal substitution is not enough and to indicate that there is a logic to appraisals of appropriateness that requires us to go beyond the principles discussed so far in this chapter. I intend after that to explore more fully the philosophical bearings of these judgments of appropriateness.

Five

Explanation and
Understanding in History

There is something problematic about the concept of explanations by re-enactment which remains even after we have adduced their ground of explanatory force—the basic sketch or schema—and shown how individual re-enactments can be regarded as instantiations of this schema. How can the investigator vindicate his selection of particular facts where these are said to operate, in effect, as the filling in of the corresponding "place" in the schema for action-explanations? The schema is wholly formal; all it can do is exhibit the way talk about actions relates to talk of beliefs, intentions, etc. The schema justifies our treating particular intentions, beliefs, scruples, and so on as explanatory of particular actions; it does not tell us, however, what specific facts to include but only what kinds of facts would satisfy the formula.

Let us suppose we were trying to explain a particular action, say, a man's throwing a bomb at a bank. We might say simply that he had done it because he wanted to. But this, though an explanation of sorts, would be a trivial one—much like saying the chicken crossed the road to get to the other side.

For a nontrivial explanation we could look to the situation of the bomber, to those circumstances in his life that might have moved him to this course of action. We find that he was a poor man, a man who

83

worked for little and whose children were always hungry. We find in addition that he had come, albeit vaguely, to conceive socialism as an end to be achieved. So now we have a motivational background—hunger and poverty—and an end in view—socialism.[1] Citing these things does seem relevant to explaining his action and the triviality disappears, for these things do seem genuinely informative. They add to the deed, as it has been described. A deed is explained nontrivially, then, when it can be referred to something different, to things that have a significantly different description from the action taken.

It is not yet clear, though, how being hungry and wanting a socialist system of property can explain throwing a bomb at a bank. We seem to have gained in explanatory capacity but at the same time to have lost the sense of connection that existed—in the earlier, trivial explanation—between the agent's intention and the deed he performed. How can we have both the significantly different descriptions needed to avoid triviality and the connective capacity to hold these together in an explanation?

The problem is not one of evidence. Rather, it has to do with what is involved when we say that a particular purpose (described one way), e.g., wanting to achieve socialism, provides a reason for the doing of a certain action (described in a wholly different way), e.g., throwing a bomb at a bank. A reason is not just something to be cited, presumably on the basis of evidence; it must be *seen* to be a reason as well. Evidence can provide the basis for attributing a particular purpose to the agent but not the basis on which we can claim, justifiably, to see a connection between that purpose or end in view and the deed we are trying to explain.

In short, we are not yet clear on what is involved, logically, in applying the basic formula for action-explanations. How can we say, justifiably, that a particular insertion of facts does instantiate the schema so as to provide a full-bodied, nontrivial explanation of the action performed?

It could be replied, though, that the answer is ready at hand. We simply take the agent's *beliefs* about means to the end he intends (insofar, of course, as we have evidence for these), and this means/end relationship *in the context of the agent's belief* underwrites our judgment that certain particular facts (the man's throwing the bomb, his

---

1. The example is an elaboration of one suggested by Collingwood (see *IH*, 315–316).

socialist goal) can justifiably be inserted into the relevant "places" under the formula. Once this point is made, what remains of the logic of action-explanations is a matter of simple consistency. So long as we consistently substitute the same facts throughout the explanation, in the places where they belong, then we have satisfied the formula and produced the explanation called for.

This answer to the problem I have posed is persuasive and has, in fact, been advanced on a number of sides. Von Wright has, in my opinion, put the reply particularly cogently:

> The [belief] premise can be said to "mediate" between the primary intention of the first premise and . . . the conclusion. One can also speak of a transfer or *transmission of intention.* The "will" to attain an end is being transmitted to (use of) the means deemed necessary for its attainment [i.e., to an action]. This principle of "transmission of intention from ends to means" is basically identical, it seems, with a principle which Kant thought analytically (logically) true and which he expressed in the following words: "Who wills the end, wills (so far as reason has decisive influence on his actions) also the means which are indispensably necessary and in his power." ["Practical Inference," p. 45] [2]

The logic of von Wright's point is clear enough. Relying on the idea that the basic feature in an action-explanation is the means (action)/end (intention) relationship, he argues that the agent's *belief* that action A is a means to his end in view E "transmits" his intention to include the action. Hence the agent can be said to intend A as well. Thus the agent's means/end belief serves as a sort of glue to hold the agent's end in view and his action together. Furthermore, we also know it to be the case that where the agent does intend A then, normally, he *does* A. In fine, the agent's means/end belief binds his action (i.e., the will to do A) to his intention (that he pursues E as an end) and, in the normal case, leads him to do A. (See "Practical Inference," pp. 47–48.) [3]

---

2. Von Wright is quoting Kant's *Groundwork of the Metaphysic of Morals* (tr. H. J. Paton; London, 1948), pp. 84–85. He quoted the same passage in *Varieties of Goodness*, p. 170n (there the passage is quoted in German; see the Prussian Academy edition, IV, 417). Interestingly, Donagan uses the same passage from Kant to make the same point (see "Alternative Historical Explanations and Their Verification," p. 76).

3. When normal conditions prevail at the time of acting we have the so-called normal case. (See *Explanation and Understanding*, p. 119; and also "Practical Inference," pp. 50–51.) For von Wright these conditions would include that (a) the agent is not prevented from acting, (b) he has not forgotten about the time, (c) his intention is still in effect (he has not forgotten it), (d) he has not otherwise changed his mind, etc.

Now the implications of this for a theory of explanation are striking. For, as should be clear, in the case of attempting to explain an action A we already have the fact that A has happened; hence, we can dispense with what Dray called "efficacy premisses" and normal conditions (for *ex hypothesi:* these have held good in the case at hand; otherwise there would be no action to explain). Accordingly, we do not really need to mention them explicitly in the explanations we give. This leaves the basic explanatory axis itself: E (intention or end in view) as mediated by B (means/end belief) to A (action). And since the action is "already there," in von Wright's phrase (*Explanation and Understanding*, p. 117), we need determine only the remaining two elements. At this point von Wright introduces the contention, or thesis, that I am principally concerned to dispute. He says:

It is . . . taken for granted that the agent considers the behavior [A] which we are trying to explain causally relevant to the bringing about of [E] *and* that the bringing about of [E] is what he is aiming at or intending with his behavior. Maybe the agent is mistaken in thinking the action causally related to the end in view. His being mistaken, however, does not invalidate the suggested explanation. What the agent *thinks* is the only relevant question here. [*Explanation and Understanding*, p. 97]

Now, in a way, what von Wright is claiming makes perfect sense. For if we do understand the notion of a means/end relationship, then we can understand how someone who intends E (to achieve socialism, for example) would do A (throw a bomb at a bank), if in fact he *believed*, all things considered, that A was the means to E. The issue, though, is not whether von Wright has correctly described this important relationship or even whether this relationship figures in our understanding of actions (for, clearly, it often does). Rather, the question is whether the citing of that relationship, in any given case, has the explanatory power claimed for it, as, for example, in von Wright's remark that "what the agent *thinks* is the only [note this *only*] relevant question here."

It seems to me that part of the force of von Wright's point resides in the particular examples he has used. Many of them are wholly unproblematic, commonplace examples—like pushing buttons to ring bells or turning handles to open doors or crying for help when drowning. And in these cases we already see an intelligible connection between intending E and doing A. We can say that the doing of A is the sort of thing done when someone intends E. One wonders, accordingly, whether asserting that the agent believes A to be a means to E really adds all that much in such cases. And, more to the point, one wonders whether merely showing that the agent believes A to be a means to E is sufficient, for explanatory purposes, in those cases where we cannot see the connection as an intelligible one in the first place.

If it is not enough in these latter cases, then it will not do simply to say that Brutus believed—even if in fact he did—that joining Cassius' conspiracy was the way of achieving his resolve to save the republican constitution of Rome from the threat of Caesarism. For unless we can understand how someone with this particular purpose could believe that doing this exact thing would be a way of achieving his goal, then we lack the essential standpoint from which we could explain his action. And to attain this we would have to be able to show that such an action does "make sense" in the light of the intention attributed to the agent.

In support of this point let us consider some examples where a perspicuous connection does not appear to hold between the agent's intention and the deed he performs and yet we do credit as fact that the agent believed a means/end relationship to hold between these things.

For instance, Augustine tells us that he supported a policy of coercion toward dissenters and of inquisition into religious beliefs and had done so to serve "love." Initially this explanation (or justification) appears to be a puzzling juxtaposition of deed and intent. Moreover, the puzzle is not resolved by our knowledge that Augustine did believe coercing Donatist schismatics to return to the catholic Church was a means to the end of Christian charity. And we do have reason to think he believed this; after all, he said that he did.

In short, we do not get a clear explanation of Augustine's support of coercion by citing his operative intention, to serve "love," and his belief that there was a means/end relationship. The problem is not in the evidence for the facts we cite but in the nature of the facts themselves. The deed and the intent do not cohere; their connection, even though mediated by a means/end belief, is still not clear. We need some additional information.

Principally, we would need to be told that Augustinian "love" had the well-being of others as its object. A bishop's love for his flock, like parents' for their children, sometimes requires actions harsh and punitive. Coercing dissenters has the effect of restoring them to fellowship with the Church and to the communion of the sacraments; forcing them to hear Christian admonition and reproof is to their benefit also. Hence, the policy of coercion does serve "love"; it is a means to the true well-being of those it coerces.[4] The troubling dissonance between deed and intention, which was perhaps deliberately played up by Augustine for rhetorical reasons, is removed by "filling in" the details of the picture. By *re-describing* deed and intent—which is what the "filling in" amounts to—the new information provides the looked-for coherent connection. I suppose following this same strategy would ultimately yield the kind of explanation we were seeking earlier in the case of the poor worker who threw a bomb to achieve socialism.

Consider now a somewhat different case. A primitive man, a "savage" or a "peasant," has inflicted a knife wound, accidentally, on his own leg. He attempts to "cure" the wound by cleaning the *knife* but he leaves the wound itself unattended. We are now offered as an explanation this (true) statement: the man wants his wound to heal and he *believes* that cleaning his knife is the means to this end. If the von Wright thesis is correct, then we ought at this point to understand why the man cleans his knife and lets his wound be. Yet the connection between the stated intention and the deed performed is not entirely clear; we do not understand the deed, then, despite the statement of the agent's means/end belief.

To remedy this defect in our understanding we seek additional information. In the case we are considering, the following bit of anthropological lore might render the connection perspicuous:

The savage and the peasant who cure by cleaning the knife and leaving the wound unattended, have observed certain indisputable facts. They know that cleanness aids, dirt on the whole impedes recovery. They know the knife as the cause, the wound as the effect; and they grasp, too, the correct principle that treatment of the cause is in general more likely to be effective than treatment of the symptom. . . . [T]hey fall back on agencies more familiar to themselves, and use, as best they may, the process of magic intertwined with that of medicine. They carefully scrape the knife; they oil it; they keep it bright.

4. Augustine's meditations on the ways of "love" can be found in *In Epist. Ioann.*, VII.8, X.10, and esp. X.7. In VII.8 he enunciates his oft-quoted precept "Love and do what you will" (*Delige, et quod vis fac*); it is ironic that many who cite this maxim approvingly do not know that it was being invoked in defense of coercion and inquisition. (See also Deane, *Political and Social Ideas of Augustine*, esp. ch. 6, pp. 172–220.)

Hence, the injured man "treats" the cause of his wound (the knife) to bring about the healing of the wound. (The example and quoted passage are from Kroeber, "The Superorganic," p. 175.)

This little story, added to the bare account with which we started, does seem to provide a more satisfactory explanation of the action performed. The new information "fills in" on our picture of the deed. This "filling in" exhibits the original elements more fully by in effect redescribing them; and, most important, it brings these elements into a kind of coherence. Their connection is made perspicuous.[5]

In the examples of the knife and of Augustine, the explanation offered on the von Wright principle, where merely citing the agent's *belief* in a means/end relationship is thought to suffice, was not satisfactory. If it had been, then there would have been no need to supply additional information. The proof is in the pudding: Can we say upon "filling in" that we understand the agent's *action* better than we did at the point where we knew only that he believed a means/end relationship to hold between what he did and what he intended? If so, I think we have in these examples a sort of counterinstance to the thesis of von Wright.

The warrant for using certain facts in an explanatory way is that their connection, where they are taken as standing in the deed-intention relationship, is an understandable or intelligible one. Two facts, one a deed and the other an intention, must be, under given descriptions, coherent one with the other; their conjunction, under those descriptions, is not in itself opaque or problematic. We have this warrant, then, insofar as the explicit material connection—as when we bring together Brutus' joining the conspiracy with his alleged intention to save the Roman constitution—is plausible. But if the investigator could not validate his reasoning respecting a particular material connection, then his bringing these details under the schema would lack force. For if the connection between a deed and its alleged intention is an opaque one, as it was in the knife wound example, then we cannot bring that deed and that intention, as described, under the formula to provide a fully satisfactory explanation.[6]

5. Cf. Davidson: "[W]hen we explain an action, by giving the reason, we do redescribe the action; redescribing the action gives the action a place in a pattern, and in this way the action is explained" ("Action, Reasons, Causes," p. 692).

6. The term "intelligible" is drawn from Gellner; in his case it refers to "a *conceivable* reaction of human beings to circumstances" ("Holism versus Individualism," p. 492 [italics added]; see also p. 494). The term is also used by Donagan ("Popper–Hempel

Historical Explanation

Or, to be more precise, if we use these facts in an explanation we are using facts we do not adequately understand. And here I think a distinction between explanation and understanding begins to emerge. The explanation so achieved is a minimal one; it is an explanation of sorts but it fails to satisfy the standard of *understanding*. This standard does not rule out the explanation as an explanation; it does, however, indicate a deficiency in an important respect. For an action-explanation should tell us something more than that the facts cited satisfy the basic schema. An explanation should yield understanding: it should provide a factual narrative that we can follow, an account of action that we can "re-enact."

There is even a sense in which von Wright's point about means/end beliefs concedes the logic of my argument. For, after all, if there were in every case a perspicuous connection between the two basic facts—the agent's intention and his action (considered here as a means to the end intended)—then there would be no need to insert yet a third fact: the content of the agent's means/end belief. Hence, the very fact that we sometimes do need to call in the agent's belief (and, presumably, it will be a somewhat odd or alien one) indicates that initially the desired connection does not hold between the agent's deed and his intention; and the very point of inserting what the agent believes in the matter is to effect this connection. By the same token, where the insertion of that fact does not render the initial connection intelligible, we do not consider the agent's action satisfactorily explained. The point of crucial difference between the inadequate attempt at an explanation and the adequate one, then, is not marked by the insertion of the agent's means/end belief (which we assume in any case) but, rather, by the es-

---

Reconsidered," p. 155), but without explication: "Considering what human history has been, an historian would be in a pretty pass if he were obliged to assume that the only actions he may succeed in understanding were rational. They must, indeed, be intelligible; but that is another thing." Along these same lines, the translators of Wittgenstein's "Remarks on Frazer's 'Golden Bough' " use the term "perspicuous"; Wittgenstein's own word is *übersichtlich* (see p. 35 and 35n). Wittgenstein's term has the sense of lucid or distinct, i.e., in that things are clearly arranged; his word suggests a synoptic or connective vision: hence, literally, a seeing of connections. In a similar vein Louch uses the term "transparent" (*Explanation and Human Action*, p. 163; and on pp. 120–121 he uses "intelligible," with the same meaning).

In each case the point is the same: we are concerned with the intelligible (perspicuous, coherent, transparent) connection of elements in a designated relationship. Here it is useful to note Scriven's notion of "parts whose relation we understand" (review, pp. 502–503); this is the crux of what I mean by "intelligible connection."

Explanation and Understanding

tablishment of an intelligible connection between the elements of the agent's action (his deed, his intention, and his means/end belief).

Not just this one relationship, that of deed performed to intention, must be satisfied by a set of facts. Indeed, two other designated relationships are equally basic: the relationship of situational motivation to deed and the relationship of situational motivation to purpose. The kind of argument that served to show that the facts must, in order to fulfill the intention to deed relationship, exhibit an intelligible connection would also show that they must exhibit the same connection for these other two relationships as well.

Consider the relationship of the agent's situational motivation to his formed intention. It could be alleged that we need only take account of his *belief* that a certain end in view or purpose, if achieved, would satisfactorily take care of whatever it was (i.e., his situational motivation) that moved him to act in the first place. This belief, in fine, is all we need in order to complete the required connection between the agent's situational motivation and his operative purpose. Again, it could be replied that merely being in possession of this belief is not enough.

The point here is the same one we met with earlier. Unless we can understand how someone having a particular situational motivation could believe that achieving his intention would resolve the situation he thought himself to be in, then we lack the essential standpoint from which we could understand his action and, hence, offer a full-fledged explanation of it.

Obviously, I am not suggesting that the investigator should discount the beliefs of agents and look only for "intelligible connections." Rather my claim is that if the connection of an agent's situational motivation and his purpose is not in and of itself clear and plausible, then the mere citation of the fact that the agent sincerely *believes* his purpose to be "responsive" to his perceived situation is not sufficient to make it so. What is necessary is that the material connection provided, as when we bring together Brutus' perception of the threat posed by Caesar (i.e., Brutus' "motivation background") with his alleged intention to save the republican constitution of Rome, be an intelligible one. If it is not, then we "fill in" our picture of the deed so as to exhibit these elements, the situational motivation and the agent's purpose as originally described, more fully. And, if we were to turn to the third leg of the triangle of explanation, the relationship of situational motivation to alternative ways of acting, we would find the same sort of objection, follow out the same dialectical moves, and reach the same conclusion.

In sum, the investigator is working with several rather precise relationships, which we are familiar with from our earlier discussion of the basic schema itself; and in giving an explanation, the historian is in effect asserting that the facts cited *can* stand to one another in the required relationships. This means that to fulfill each of the designated relationships the facts must exhibit an intelligible connection. There must be a "coherence," a line of perspicuous connection, between each pair of facts in order for the facts to serve as end points on a leg of the triangle and, thus, when all the points are covered, to provide the explanations we are seeking.

If my argument up to now has been sound, then simply "going to the evidence" to "value the variables" of the schema will not do, contrary to what von Wright suggests (see esp. *Explanation and Understanding*, p. 97; and also pp. 120, 142). The triangle metaphor at least has the virtue of indicating that the facts are always linked and cannot simply be "plugged in" as discrete units.

Moreover, it also follows that we must add a criterion to those von Wright has been prepared to acknowledge: it is not just that the facts be evidentially well supported or that the substitution of these facts be a consistent one throughout but also that the facts cited do, as we go round the triangle, exhibit coherence. For, on the principle that an explanation in which the facts are plausibly related to one another is a better explanation than one in which they are not, intelligibility of connection is *one* of the criteria that must be met by the facts. The logical role of understanding is simply that it is a criterion for *applying* the schema for action-explanations.[7]

Perhaps my point can be made clearer if it is put in the rather more familiar terms that von Wright himself has employed. Let us, in our general account of action-explanations, distinguish between "formal" and "material" validity (see *Explanation and Understanding*, pp. 120–121). A given explanation is *formally* valid if it provides us with facts that satisfy, at least in effect, the conditions or "premises," as von Wright calls them, of the basic schema. Now, of course, if any one of

7. We might describe the three criteria—evidential support, univocal substitution, intelligible or plausible connection—as "application principles" (the term is Braithwaite's) for the basic schema.

Explanation and Understanding

the facts provided is incorrect, that is, *not so*, then the explanation is said to be *materially* invalid. As von Wright comments of one of his own examples, "this explanation can be 'materially invalid' (false, incorrect) in the sense that the reason why A pressed the button was in fact different. But it is 'formally valid' (correct) as an *ex post actu* construction of premises to match a given conclusion" (*Explanation and Understanding*, p. 120).

I want to extend this distinction. I am proposing that an explanation in which the relationship of facts in any of the three principal dimensions, motivation to deed or motivation to intention or intention to deed, is not intelligible be regarded as *materially* invalid—as the explanations were initially, for instance, in the Augustine and knife wound examples. In other words, when we cannot understand *facts* said to be standing in a certain relation to one another, even though we can comprehend the relationship itself, as given in the basic schema, then we have a case of *material* invalidity; and this is so whether the facts are judged on other grounds to be true or false. Hence, beside invalidity due to falseness I would set invalidity due to implausibility. What we want in an explanation, otherwise formally valid, is both plausibility and truth. Materially valid explanations are both, and only those should count as full-fledged or wholly adequate explanations of action.

Indeed, now that I have made this second kind of material invalidity explicit—the kind we call *implausibility*—it is possible to find mention of it, here and there, in von Wright's own text. For instance, he tells us that "we cannot understand or teleologically explain behavior which is completely alien to us" (*Explanation and Understanding*, pp. 114–115) and the context indicates that this failure is at the *material* level, in our sheer inability to penetrate an alien form of life and thereby to understand its characteristic modes of behavior. (See also p. 29, on this point.) And, again, in terms that have a strong resonance with the argument I have been developing, von Wright asserts, "In order to qualify as *fact*, one could say, the material at hand must already have passed a test of explicability" (p. 166). Now, admittedly, von Wright's test can be read narrowly as requiring merely that we must *tell what some group or person is doing* (and in that sense "interpret" their behavior, putting it under some specific action-description); but his remark is suceptible of a wider reading, as it has in his own gloss on the passage, where he says, "it [the behavioral datum] must have been shown to be intelligible as action" (p. 206, n. 27).

So, my criticism of von Wright should not be taken as suggesting that he has totally ignored the *material* invalidity induced into "formally valid" explanations by unintelligible or implausible (material) relationships between the facts cited. Rather, I am principally concerned to show that he did not accord this factor *explicit* status and thereby failed to incorporate it into his account of teleological explanation. I am concerned, as I have already said, to show the inadequacy of von Wright's contention that all we need in order to "mediate" an explanatory connection between the agent's end in view and the action he performs is his *belief* that this action is a means to that end. (Recall: "What the agent *thinks* is the only relevant question here" [*Explanation and Understanding*, p. 97].) This belief may be all that is needed under normal conditions in order for the action to be done, but it is not all that is needed in order for the action to be understood.

Von Wright has provided no real role for understanding in his account of the logic of action-explanations. Although he has found a place for evidence and for true statements within the conceptual space occupied by his schema for teleological explanation, he has found no corresponding place for understanding and for plausible statements. Von Wright has failed to integrate understanding into his account of the teleological explanations of actions. And this, I think, is the foremost shortcoming of his book.

I think the concept of *understanding* that I have been discussing here fits the case of history particularly well. For I have contended that understanding consists in the ability, given a particular set of facts, to construct an unforced narrative. The essence of understanding does not reside in some datum of *experience*, say, an "aha!" or "hat doffing" experience (the latter phrase is F. Waismann's) or "seeing the light" or a "perception" of any sort. Rather, it resides simply in the telling and in the following of a plausible story, the factual details of which can be displayed as instantiations of the elements of the basic schema for action-explanations.

I think this may well represent what von Wright had in mind when he explicitly contrasted a "psychological" construal of understanding (as *Einfühlung*) to what he called the "intentionalistic" construal or "semantic dimension of understanding" (see *Explanation and Understanding*, p. 6) and contended that understanding "is a semantic rather than a psychological category" (p. 30). And this idea of understanding,

Explanation and Understanding

as the capacity to tell or follow a particular story, certainly fits in nicely with his perception that "behavior's intentionality is its *place* in a story about the agent" (p. 115).

If my reading of von Wright is sound, or even suggestive of a tendency in his thought, then he is much closer to the *verstehen* tradition, or at least to Collingwood, than he thought. (See *Explanation and Understanding*, p. 33.) For Collingwood put great emphasis on the category of action with its attendant features of motivation background and purpose (cf. von Wright's schema of practical inference) and his idea of re-enactment can be taken simply as a peculiar way of saying that we understand a deed when we can put it in place in a plausible story about the agent's motivation background and his purpose.

Indeed, the accounts offered by each man are curiously complementary. Each has chosen to emphasize a single major feature in the logic of historical explanation. Von Wright has emphasized the basic schema—the logical framework—for action-explanations and tried to make that explicit; whereas Collingwood has concentrated on the factual filler side of things and on making clear the principle that understanding provides the connective or "narrative dimension" in an action-explanation.

It may well be that Collingwood distorted the role of understanding by emphasizing it as he did. For he made it appear that an explanation can go through on understanding alone, just from putting together the agent's thought with his deed in a perspicuous way. But, as we have seen, an action-explanation derives its force not just from facts in perspicuous connection but from these facts *when placed within their proper framework*, the framework provided by the basic schema.

Even so, there is a point to Collingwood's emphasis which needs to be brought out and which von Wright, in his very lucid account of the schema for action-explanations, has failed to notice. It should be evident that no matter how much we elaborated or added to the basic conditions of the schema, there would always have to be some rules (semantic rules) for *applying* the schema to data. The so-called semantic dimension is indispensable. The only question is whether a certain criterion belongs there or, alternatively, in the schema, as one of its conditions. And, unless we wholly *identify* understanding with explanation, there will always be some elements of understanding that belong in the semantic dimension. My own position is that they ought to be distinguished—and here I agree with von Wright—but that they should be integrated, not separated, in an account of the logic of explanations in history and social science—and here we disagree.

I have been contending that an *integrated* model of explanation, where von Wright's schema is applied in accordance with Collingwood's criterion of narrative understanding, is peculiarly well adapted to serve as the model for explanations in history. My point is that the idea or form of an action-explanation is given in the schema; at this level we perceive the basic outline of any such explanation. For it is in terms of the schema that we exhibit our conception that action is being considered as a means to an intended end, or as part of accomplishing it, and so on. But for *facts* to count as satisfying that schema in a given explanation we must not only see them as instances of the elements in the schema but also see them as exhibiting, materially, an intelligible connection.

We can view re-enactment, then, as the *way* of establishing facts that will satisfy the conditions of the schema for action-explanations; re-enacting shows that these particular facts do "fit together," and do so consistent with the evidence. It shows this because to re-enact an action under investigation *is* to get to the deed performed by "going through" the thought-factors cited, and one could not do *that* unless the material connections between these facts were intelligible ones. Re-enacting, then, is tantamount to saying that these connections are intelligible; if they were not, the investigator could not re-enact the deed and neither could anyone else. Hence the historian's main task *is* "to think himself into this action," as we have been told (*IH*, 213), for this is how he satisfies the criterion of intelligible or "coherent" connection. The indispensable factor allowing us to mesh a particular set of facts with the empirically vacuous schema R is the operation of re-enactment. Or to put the matter somewhat differently, intelligibility of connection is a criterion for *applying* a principle of inference for actions to a set of facts—a criterion for *using* these facts within the framework provided by the basic formula or schema—and this criterion is satisfied by re-enactment.

Now it might be well to add at this juncture what no one would deny, that the facts in question can only be "established" by going to the evidence. For, after all, it is by reference to our body of evidence that we would decide that E_1 (Brutus' attempting to save the constitution) *is* a fact (a true statement of the agent's intention) and that E_2 (his getting rid of an envied political rival) is not. But the point is that there are *two* distinct relations involved and not just one: the relation of facts to evidence as true or false and the relation of facts to one another as perspicuous or opaque. Hence, it is one thing to say that the relationship of facts in a given historical account is a plausible one and another to say that the facts cited are evidentially well supported and, hence, in that sense, true.

There is, however, some confusion posed for my account of re-enactment by the claim that two distinct relations are involved here. It is always open to someone to claim, as von Wright and Cebik have done, that re-enactment should really be taken as operating in the *evidential* domain, as concerned with establishing whether factual statements are true or false.[8] Moreover, the potential for confusion is compounded when it is noted that re-enactment could provide a way to verify, in the sense of confirm, what the evidence tells us. Indeed, I have already suggested (in Chapter Three) that re-enactment could be taken as confirming that the thought attributed to the agent on the basis of evidence was indeed the thought that lay behind his action. But it should be equally clear that this confirmation could come in other ways too (as, for example, a diary account might confirm an eyewitness report). And, more important, I think it would occur to someone to treat re-enactment as a mode of verifying facts only if he already believed that it had an explanatory character as well. Hence, I think there would be little point in attempting to collapse re-enactment into a *mere* method of verification—even though it could, and sometimes does, play the role of establishing facts from evidence.

I think it necessary, in light of my argument about the indispensable role of understanding in action-explanations, to treat re-enactment as playing the somewhat different role of *validating* facts for explanatory use. By this I mean simply that, however the investigator works his evidence, the facts he puts into "place" in accordance with the schema for explanations must have passed the test of understanding, of re-enactment.

Of course, one could make understanding into a criterion for fac-

8. Von Wright in his "Replies," esp. pp. 411–412: to an earlier version of this chapter, which was read as a paper at a conference on explanation and understanding in the human sciences (held in Helsinki, January 1974); Cebik in his essay "Collingwood: Action, Re-enactment, and Evidence," esp. pp. 68, 82–89. It is unclear whether Cebik wants to drop re-enactment altogether or to reinterpret it, limiting it to the working up of evidence.

tuality—so that nothing could be counted as *true* that was not also, in its particular context, understandable. I cannot see, though, that this would in any way dispute my claim that the criterion of understanding must be satisfied in an explanation and that the point of re-enactment is to validate, to establish each fact by showing that these particular facts do plausibly line up.

In any case it follows from my account that if certain facts are intelligibly connected and if this particular reconstruction is also evidentially sound, then these facts can be put in place under the basic sketch to provide the explanation we are seeking. But if the historian cannot re-enact, he goes to the body of available evidence or he finds new evidence. He observes more minutely: facts are discerned that were not previously stated or the facts already discerned are described more judiciously. He tries to "fill in" the picture so that the crucial facts do "cohere." If one cannot do this, if one cannot re-enact, then one cannot understand the action under scrutiny no matter how large the body of evidence.

Six

General Laws and
Principles of Action

In the previous chapter, I argued that any full-fledged explanation of an action involves assertions of intelligible connection, although it may not state them explicitly. Indeed, the argument I have conducted would require specific assertions that (1) the agent's doing A in the light of his situational motivation M is intelligible, (2) his purpose E is an understandable reason for his doing A, and (3) this purpose is "responsive" to his situation as he conceived it and, hence, that the connection of this particular purpose with this particular situational motivation is a perspicuous one.

Although the historian brings these elements of understanding together in a sort of triangulation to "think himself into this action," each one could stand on its own. In this chapter I will consider these elements as individuals, as molecular components of the reasoning involved in re-enactive explanation, and inquire into the logic of the use and justification of any one of them. I will not be concerned, I should add, with the logical nature of the fundamental principle of inference—the basic schema—that underlies this reasoning but, rather, just with the assertions of intelligible connection that have been assigned the role of validating facts for use under the schema.

Specifically, I want to show that these particularized judgments of intelligibility, in order to perform their job, must be susceptible to a certain generalizing move. And then I want to delineate the character of these *generalized* assertions of intelligible connection more fully, principally by distinguishing them from empirical general laws and from what Dray has called principles of action.

Collingwood's re-enactive explanation of Caesar's invasion of Britain, to cite one example, depends on several general judgments of intelligible connection; at least two of these appear crucial to his explanatory account. In its supposal of alternative courses of action, Collingwood's account presupposes the general assertion: when a military leader is faced with hostile interventions by x and when he proposes to curb these interventions, then an invasion is an intelligible way of acting. And in its establishment of a purpose relevant to the agent's situational motivation, Collingwood's explanation presupposes the following general assertion: when a military leader thinks that the pacification of x can be accomplished by an application of force, then his trying a punitive action against x or attempting to conquer x is understandable. Moreover, although it seems a mere truism to say that if the leader intends a conquest of x then his invading their land is a plausible thing to do, nonetheless, Collingwood must have regarded this judgment as holding for his explanation to have gone through. These judgments justify alleging that intelligible material connections hold between the specific facts cited in his explanation.

My point is that the connecting of facts on each of the lines of the triangle of explanation is founded logically in a *general* assertion of intelligible connection. My argument is designed to show, not that an assertion of this sort is textually part of an explanation or explicitly part of the historian's reasoning, but rather that it is included among its logical grounds.

Now, in our explanation of Caesar's invasion, we could summarize the agent's intention as "Caesar was attempting to conquer the British tribes." This, as it stands, is not general, but we can easily make it so by replacing the terms designating particular objects (Caesar, British tribes) with "general designatory terms which include the originally designated objects amongst their extensions." (See Danto, *Analytical Philosophy of History*, p. 221, for the passage quoted.) By taking this step we would get "a military leader was attempting to conquer certain tribes."

The rationale for this generalizing move is that it serves to show that the assertion of a particular detail is connectible with another. For its effect is to subsume the particularized assertion, as a special case, under a general assertion of appropriateness: thus the judgment that Caesar invaded Britain with the intention of conquering the tribes there is warranted, as a special case, in that "intending *C*" (wanting to conquer certain tribes) is an intelligible reason for "doing *I*" (invading their lands).

Consider a somewhat similar case. We hear that "whenever John eats spinach, John breaks out in a rash." We want to say that there is a "connection" between "*his* eating and *his* developing a rash." We realize, of course, that this does not happpen to him "just because he's John" but because he has "a certain allergy." So we move to something general: whenever anyone who has this allergy eats spinach then he breaks out in a rash. If we were not persuaded that John has a relevant trait (the allergy) which leads by some "lawful connection" to his rash whenever he eats spinach, then we would not assert that he got the rash *because* he ate the spinach. Our particularized assertion about John and *his* rash requires, for the particular connection asserted really to be there, the generalizing move. And we, in effect, have subsumed our particularized assertion, as a special case, under a general assertion of some "lawful connection." Again, it is the general assertion that warrants the particular connection we have made. [1]

There is, I think, an interesting parallel between the generalizing move in the case of specific *reasons* and that move in the case of a *causal* regularity exhibited by a single individual. In each case we start with a particular occurrence (John breaks out in a rash, Caesar invades). And in each case we connect that occurrence with some distinct, but apparently relevant, fact which is supposed to account for it (John ate the spinach, Caesar wanted to conquer the British tribes). We ultimately allow for this connection of particular facts only where the connection is itself susceptible to the generalizing move we have been discussing.

Suppose, though, that we have a presumed "case" of the general formula that does not go according to rule: Morton had that certain allergy, ate spinach or something like it, but he did not break out in a

---

1. See Morton White, *Foundations of Historical Knowledge*, pp. 48–49 for the example and for the passages quoted (and, also, p. 83). The logic of the point is spelled out, more adequately in my opinion, by Donagan (see "Popper-Hempel Reconsidered," pp. 135, 137–142); the terminology of "a special case" I owe to Donagan.

rash; Arthur wanted to conquer the Picts and the Scots but this just was not an intelligible or plausible reason for invading their country. In other words, the cases of John and Morton, or of Caesar and Arthur, are alike in all the relevant respects except that where "he breaks out in a rash," or, alternatively, "his invading is a plausible thing to do," holds in the one case it does not in the other. Well, if we do suppose this, either the cases are not really alike in the relevant respects (e.g., not alike between Morton and John or between Arthur and Caesar) or the supposed connection between the occurrence and the fact that accounts for it does not hold. That is to say, unless, for every person, the connection of those facts holds upon being generalized—the various persons being alike in all the *other* relevant respects—then the fact as cited in a particular case (Caesar wanted to conquer the British tribes) cannot account for what allegedly followed from it (Caesar invaded). Plainly, then, the explanation of the rash, by referring it to an allergy and the eating of some spinach, really requires a general conditional statement on the order of (x) $(Fx \supset Ox)$. And, equally plainly, the explanation of an action really requires, logically, these *general* assertions of intelligible connection.[2]

If we restrict the relevant assertion of connection, by introducing historically or individually particular terms or by likewise restricting the subject variable (e.g., to Caesar alone), then we simply fail to indicate the generic connection of C as such (e.g., attempting to conquer) with I as such (e.g., invading). Indeed, by bringing in these restrictions we leave unspecified exactly what it is about the agent or his behavioral conditions that is going to constitute the explanatory connection in his case. Only by specifying what the elements of this connection actually are and by indicating that the connection does hold as plausible, for *people* generally with that sort of purpose in mind and not just for Caesar, can we establish the connection in the individual case.

My argument so far has been designed to show that the explanatory operations of re-enactment do require connection-justifying grounds and that this role is played by general assertions of appropriateness. The *generic* relationship that holds at this general designatory level un-

---

2. I have adapted this argument from Danto (see his *Analytical Philosophy of History*, pp. 207–208); a similar argument is developed by Donagan ("Alternative Historical Explanations and Their Verification," pp. 60–62).

derwrites the particularized assertions of appropriateness with which we started. ("Attempting to conquer is an intelligible reason for invading" supports our judgment that Caesar's invading Britain is plausible in the light of his purpose to conquer the tribes there.) Presumably, if this generic relationship did not hold, then neither the investigator, nor anyone else for that matter, could justifiably "perceive" a connection of appropriateness in the particular case of Caesar and, hence, could not "think himself" into Caesar's action from this stated purpose as his starting point.

Since the notion of a *generic* relationship is more complex than might be evident, we might pause here to note its crucial features. (a) The obvious feature is the difference in levels: in a particularized relationship the elements are particular objects; in a generic relationship the elements are named by "general designatory" terms. (b) There is, however, a second and equally important distinction. When we say, "Caesar invaded Britain in order to conquer the tribes there," we are referring to a deed performed and to an instance of intending C. But when we talk simply of "invading" in relation to an intention such as "wanting to conquer certain tribes," we are talking of *categories* of action and intention. We might describe each such category as an *action-universal*. (c) This distinction of action-universals from performances would hold even at the level of particularized descriptions. Thus, "Caesar's invading Britain in 54 B.C." could be taken as naming a performance exemplifying an action-universal. But what is the action-universal that this performance exemplifies? It could be "invading" but it could also be "invading Britain"—or even "Caesar's invading Britain," since he did it more than once. It is important, then, to keep clear as to the distinction drawn in (a), between levels of descriptive discourse, and that drawn in (b) and (c), between action-universals and action-exemplifying performances.[3]

The notion of a *generic* assertion is meant to mark both of these crucial distinctions. For, first, such an assertion is not descriptive of particular performances at all. Generic assertions do not refer to action-exemplifying *performances* but, rather, to the *action-universals* themselves. Such assertions hold between the categories—the descrip-

---

3. I have been influenced in my thinking about generic assertions of appropriateness by Landesman's article, "Actions as Universals," esp. sec. III, pp. 250–251, and by Danto's paper, "Causation and Basic Actions," esp. pp. 110–112.

tive contents themselves—in terms of which particular performances, exemplifications, are described. And, second, the terms of a generic assertion are "general designatory." In sum, then, a *generic* assertion of appropriateness is one which asserts that the relationship is intelligible between, say, *I* and *C*, where *I* and *C* are action-universals under general designatory descriptions and where they are conceived as the end points on any line of the triangle of explanation. Such an assertion would be conventionally read as saying something like "*I* [invading] is appropriate in the light of *C* [wanting to conquer]."

Moreover, it seems intuitively obvious that to say "*I* is appropriate in the light of *C*" is just to say "for all persons *x*: if *Cx* then *Ix* is appropriate or intelligible." In short, these connection-justifying warrants can all be translated into statements having the form "for all persons *x*: if *Cx* then *Ix*." Each such generic assertion can be rewritten as a lawlike general hypothetical which states what is appropriate.

It would appear, however, that any argument designed to show that explanations by re-enactment do require *general* hypothetical premises has a certain unwelcome drift to it—unwelcome, that is, to Collingwood or to those who share his philosophical predispositions.

First, there is a kind of formal identity between hypotheticals of appropriateness and what might be called regularity laws. They share a certain formal element; each can be brought under the uninterpreted formula "for all *x*: if *Fx* then *Gx*." Second, hypotheticals of appropriateness do warrant a connection, albeit one of plausibility, between particular facts. In saying generically for the facts "if *C* then *I* is plausible," these hypotheticals seem to connote some empirical or quasi-empirical connection between *C* and *I* as sorts of facts. Finally, hypotheticals of appropriateness can be said to function as the connection-justifying premises in a piece of explanatory reasoning, where we do connect a particular *I* with a particular *C* as being "plausible in the light of *C*."

However, given all this—lawlike form, suggestion of matter-of-fact connection, premise role—a question naturally arises. Why cannot we just replace these general hypotheticals of appropriateness with regularity laws? For a regularity law, in the interpretation we are considering, asserts that whenever *C* happens then *I* happens, specifying the matter in two ways: as a general law (*I always* happens) or as a probability law (*I usually* happens). Any such generalization tells us what, given the satisfaction of certain antecedent conditions (C), does happen; it states what we can count on to happen always or usually. It might be said that hypotheticals of appropriateness seem to be mere grammatical variants, less precise perhaps, of regularity laws and that they are therefore replaceable by regularity laws.

Now, the issue here is not whether individual re-enactment explanations presuppose, as premises or grounds, general connection-justifying statements or even whether they presuppose them in the form "for all persons x: if Fx then Gx"—for all this has been granted. I would argue further that regularity laws and general hypotheticals of appropriateness are distinguishable as two different types of statement possible under the formula $(x)\ (Fx \supset Gx)$. Each is equally an "interpretation," in some loose sense, of that formula. If this is so, it follows that we cannot argue for the necessary role of regularity generalizations in historical explanations simply by pointing out that any connective inference must logically presuppose a statement of that particular form. Nor can we foreclose the matter by asserting that "the empirical interpretation" of $(x)\ (Fx \supset Gx)$ is a "general law" (as Danto does, *Analytical Philosophy of History*, p. 208).

For the whole point in dispute is whether we must use the "empirical" or "general law" interpretation of the formula. The issue is simply how we should interpret this formula once its logically necessary role has been admitted. The question is whether general hypotheticals of appropriateness should be dispensed with in favor of regularity laws or whether the two have a logical difference which would underwrite their remaining distinct.

The issue, as I see it, comes down to whether we could formulate acceptable regularity laws to supplant general hypotheticals of appropriateness in the role of connection-justifying premises for historical explanations—at least for those explanations which connect details of the agent's deed and thought under the category of plausibility. To do this would require, if we take Hempel's classic account of the function of general laws in history as our touchstone, that we be able in any explanation to derive the explanandum from a regularity law together with certain statements of fact, called "statements of initial condition," which satisfy the antecedent clause of the generalization. It would be admitted, I think, even by the proponents of this position that it is quite difficult to frame an acceptable law, one which meets the criteria

Historical Explanation

for a law *and* which would allow an explanation to go through; this is especially true when we try to formulate a *general* law.[4]

For example, let us restate, as a general law, one of the hypotheticals presupposed in Collingwood's explanation of Caesar's invasion: "Whenever a military leader is faced with hostile interventions by x and if he proposes to curb these interventions and if he thinks that this can be done only by an application of force, then *he always invades.*" The main objection to this candidate "law" is that we would not entitle it a general law because it is defective in regularity. We can think of several important counterinstances to this putative "law." We know that sometimes, as in Vietnam, air raids are employed rather than invasions; or an inhibiting sanction can be leveled by economic embargoes or by blockades as well as by invasion. So even if we insisted that our rule of appropriateness be interpreted as a regularity law, the particular candidate we have advanced would not be a *general law* because it is defective in regularity. We can always supply what Morton White has called "superficial generalizations," as in our cited example, but the problem is that these are almost never true. (See White, *Foundations of Historical Knowledge*, pp. 63, 65.) It is unlikely that we could find any such general law.

We could, of course, maintain our claim in favor of regularity laws if we are willing to let probability laws count as well as general laws and if we are willing to allow a nondeductive type of support for explanations covered by laws. Hempel, in speaking precisely to this point, suggested a distinction between a " 'deductive-nomological' kind" of explanation and an inductive-probabilistic kind. In the latter sort the regularity law is in "probabilistic-statistical form" and it covers the event to be explained, not deductively, but by conferring a "high inductive probability" on it. In developing his point, Hempel assimilated the probabilistic law to a statistical model in which the probability is "close to 1" and claimed that a "law of this type may be invoked to

4. My use of the terms "law" and "general law" is the conventional one, as spelled out, for example, in C. G. Hempel's article "The Function of General Laws in History" and in his article with P. Oppenheim, "The Logic of Explanation." In these articles the following law traits are stated: (1) A statement is a law if and only if it is (a) "lawlike" and (b) "true" or, at least, unexceptionably confirmed. (2) A statement is "lawlike" only if (a) its "domain" is non-finite (universal scope, e.g., all physical objects in all spatio-temporal locations); (b) it is in the form "$F \supset G$" or a logical equivalent; (c) it is universally quantified and contains no individual constants; (d) it is (dis-) confirmable by reference to matters of fact; (e) it can sustain counterfactual or subjunctive conditional statements. (This final criterion [e] was added by Hempel in his essay "Aspects"; see esp. p. 339.)

General Laws and Principles of Action

explain the occurrence" of the event described in the explanandum.[5]

If we follow Hempel on this point, we could, it is true, qualify our regularity generalization with some such term as "usually"—so long, that is, as the indicated frequency was quite high ("close to 1"). In so doing we convert the generalization from a general law to a probability law. But the move to replace "always" with "usually" is of dubious value in the face of a large number of counterinstances. For unless generalization can, given the satisfaction of its antecedent conditions, provide for the deduction of the explanandum or, failing that, afford a high inductive support for it, then that generalization is not a regularity law in the sense required by Hempel.

I might add that Nagel actually proposed a probabilistic account of Cassius' plotting against Caesar. In so doing he referred to the following generalization, "In ancient Rome the relative frequency (or probability) was high (e.g., greater than one-half) that an individual belonging to the upper strata of society and possessed by great hatred of tyranny would plot the death of men who were in a position to secure tyrannical power" (*Structure of Science*, pp. 22–23; see also pp. 18–19). But the probability value he selected was not "close to 1," as Hempel would have it; hence there is good reason to doubt that such a generalization could afford more than *low* inductive support for the occurrence of the event it was called upon to explain.

So, whether we treat the covering relationship as deductive or inductive, the fact remains that the putative regularity laws run up against a sufficient number of counterinstances to be either untrue general laws or loose probability laws conferring only low inductive support. I do not believe, in short, that we could successfully restate the hypothetical presupposed in Collingwood's explanation in the form of a law—either general or probabilistic.

The line of argument I have taken is susceptible to certain circumventing moves. One such move, and a reasonable one, is to claim that the general law used in my example was the wrong one. Accordingly, it might be suggested that the law should be cut back so as to assert simply "whenever a military leader wants to curb hostile interventions by x then he always (or usually) levels some inhibiting sanction of

5. See Hempel, "Reasons and Covering Laws in Historical Explanation," pp. 144–145; and also "Explanation in Science and in History," esp. pp. 96–103, and "Deductive-Nomological vs. Statistical Explanation." Hempel first introduces this distinction explicitly in his "Logic of Functional Analysis"; see esp. pp. 301–302.

force against *x*." This amended law is achieved by replacing the relatively determinate happening "invading to conquer" with the less determinate "leveling *some* inhibiting sanction of force." Such a law might be used to connect the agent's situational motivation with his intention, although the statement of intention is, admittedly, vaguer than a historian is normally satisfied with. And since the revised law absorbs the alleged counterinstances (air raid, embargo, etc.), it can now be said that we have a regularity law which is not infirmed by the counterinstances I previously adduced.

Even if we grant that the counterinstances alleged against the first candidate-law do not count against the second, it seems that the shift to the second candidate-law still carries with it unwanted consequences for the regularity law analysis. The first candidate-law would have allowed us to derive, given certain statements of fact which satisfy its antecedent clause, a deed under an invasion description. But this possibility no longer obtains with the second candidate, for here we can only derive some sort of punitive sanctions description. The problem is that the second law-candidate, and others like it, I would suggest, is too loose, too fuzzy, too unrefined to allow for the subtle discriminations we need in the explanation of behavior. Thus, although the second regularity law may be better in one respect (i.e., is less open to counterinstances), it is worse in another respect, that of deriving the event under an invasion description. And since Hempel has specified that we must be able to derive—deductively or inductively—the explanandum itself from the law together with certain statements of initial condition, this weakness would appear to be a serious one.

Nor is the law as it stands immune from counterinstances. For example, diplomatic initiatives or a mere "showing of the flag" might occur as well as punitive sanctions. This raises the question whether the second candidate-law is a regularity law in the sense required by Hempel.

The important point, though, is that the second candidate-law does not satisfy the criteria put forward by Hempel. Insofar as we try to satisfy both of Hempel's criteria, the having of an acceptable regularity law and the ability to derive the explanandum—the deed to be explained—from the generalization, neither candidate-law is satisfactory.

This leads us to a consideration of the analysis advanced by Danto. Although Danto claims that his account of the role of regularity laws

General Laws and Principles of Action

is "essentially a variant of the Hempelian model," he departs significantly from Hempel on one important point. (See Danto, *Analytical Philosophy of History*, p. 228, for the passage quoted; a similar remark occurs on p. 222.) In Hempel's account we try to derive the deed under the description given in the explanandum, but Danto seems to think that it is highly unlikely that we can find acceptable laws which would allow us to do this. He suggests, accordingly, that we try to derive the deed under a *redescription* of it; before the derivation can go through we must, Danto says, replace the given description of it "with one of greater generality" (see *Analytical Philosophy of History*, p. 227; also p. 223). What we try to derive is not the description, as given in the explanandum, but the relevant classificatory heading under which the deed as described is to be subsumed. Danto's analysis depends on distinguishing two levels, the explanandum level—in which the descriptions are particular—and the classificatory heading level—in which they are general. Hempel's account is modified in that we shift the derivation focus from one level to the other.

I do not think, however, that Danto's analysis represents a basic alteration in the regularity law model or that his analysis succeeds in saving that model. For Danto's account still requires that we be able to derive the relevant (and explanatory) *redescription* of the deed from a regularity law. And, in the example we have been considering, we could not derive even this from the second candidate-law. We could not, supposing provisionally that the law were acceptable as a regularity law, derive the relevant heading "attempting to conquer" under which the explanandum should be subsumed; rather, we could, as I have shown, derive only the rather vague heading (or redescription) "leveling inhibiting sanctions." My argument against the second candidate-law holds whether we are using Hempel's criterion or Danto's: it is not merely that we cannot derive the explanandum from it; we cannot derive even the relevant classificatory heading under which the explanandum should be put. It is just as true to say that we could not derive the crucial *redescription* of the event (an attempt to conquer) as it is to say that we could not derive the initial *explanandum description* (an invasion).

I should add that Danto is not particularly concerned to derive *precisely* that redescription of the agent's deed which would be most useful to the working historian. He would tend to see what I have called a vague redescription as simply a statement "of greater generality" than the more precise one "attempting to conquer." The essence of Danto's case seems to be that some things—in the case I am citing it is something rather vague—can be deductively derived; the other things have to be "subsumed" under what can be derived. Hence, the more specific redescription "attempting to conquer" can be subsumed under the rather vague umbrella "leveling inhibiting sanctions" and the deed (an invasion) can be subsumed under that same umbrella also. So, in a way, it all comes out well in the end. For even though we can derive only a vague redescription of the deed from the law, we can on Danto's model subsume the things we really want (the other descriptions) under it. Moreover, since one of these subsumed descriptions ("attempting to conquer") is a redescription or way of classifying the other ("invading"), we do have the explanation we sought after all.

There is, I think, a problem with Danto's analysis. Let us allow for the moment that we do have a true regularity law "whenever a military leader wants to curb hostile interventions by x then he always (or usually) attempts to level some inhibiting sanction of force against x," which would allow us to move deductively (or inductively) from what amounts to the agent's situational motivation ("wanting to curb hostile interventions") to something else, however indeterminately it is described ("leveling inhibiting sanctions"). The fact remains that to get beyond *this* point certain additional explanatory moves are required. For instance, we need at a minimum to get from "inhibiting sanctions" to "invading." Or, if we wanted something more specific (say, "attempting to conquer") to serve as our explanatory redescription of "invading," we would need to get to *that* from "inhibiting sanctions." How do we justifiably make these additional moves?

Danto's answer is that we *subsume* one description under another, where the second is "one of greater generality." Even so, this does not really allow us to dispense with what I have called generic assertions of appropriateness. For these nondeductive explanatory moves in Danto's analysis would themselves have to be covered by such assertions, or by *something* that can take the role of licensing the connection of the descriptions in question. Otherwise, we have no basis for saying that "invading" can be subsumed under "leveling inhibiting sanctions" or that "attempting to conquer" is a redescription of the deed to be explained.

There is something altogether too casual about what Danto is claiming. It seems that his argument comes down to saying that we deductively derive what we can with the help of regularity laws; for the rest, we get by as best we can: we just "subsume." But I would suggest that unless we can deductively *derive* the crucial explanatory redescription, the one that the historian is going to use in his narrative, by means of our regularity law, then there is very little left of the sort of analysis Hempel was trying to advance. A gap exists which must be closed for Danto's analysis to be able to save Hempel's.

Moreover, even if we were to give full credit to Danto's analysis, it still does not allow us to replace all generic assertions of appropriateness with true regularity laws. Indeed, Danto's analysis would tend to underwrite the claim that laws and hypotheticals of appropriateness are logically different and that they play distinct roles, one functioning in explanatory *derivation* and the other in explanatory *subsumption*.

I am, of course, leaving it open that some connection at some level of generality could be mediated by true regularity laws. But I am also suggesting that where certain crucial connections cannot be deductively established, in particular those that otherwise would require generic assertions of appropriateness, it is because there are no true regularity laws to do the job. If this is not the case, it is difficult to see the point of Danto's argument.

Now, Danto does provide us, in his chapter, "The Problem of General Laws," with one "law" that would allow us to deduce the relevant classificatory heading under which the explanandum cited could be put. Danto's law goes as follows: "Whenever a nation has a sovereign of a different national origin than its own citizens, these citizens will, on the appropriate occasions, honour that sovereign in some acceptable fashion." Danto argues that from this law we could deduce the classificatory heading ("honouring a sovereign") under which the explanandum ("putting out American flags side by side with Monagasque flags") is to be subsumed. (See *Analytical Philosophy of History*, p. 221.)

Let us first consider here simply the question whether the explanation provided seems suitable: whether, in short, saying something like "The Monagasques are putting out American flags side by side with their own in order to honour their sovereign, an American by birth" has explanatory force. I think that it does. But why? It has it, I would suggest, not because the "honouring the sovereign" part can be deductively derived from a law or because that part is a redescription of the explanandum ("putting out American flags," etc.) but because that part gives us the purpose or intention of the deed that is being explained.

The really interesting thing about Danto's argument, and about this example which bears so much of the weight of his argument, is that it avoids all mention of intentions, or even of situational motivations. The whole analysis is denatured, as it were. We are given simply deeds under a description, redescriptions of these, and the deductive derivation—perhaps at a very high level of generality—of *one* of the redescriptions. But the cost of avoiding reference to "thoughts" (purpose, situational motivation) in favor of mere redescriptions of deeds is, I think, a heavy one.

For it seems to me that much of Danto's argument rests on a very dubious claim, that *explaining is simply redescribing*, at least in the case where the redescription is one "of greater generality." (See Danto, *Analytical Philosophy of History*, esp. p. 220; and also pp. 219, 223–224, 227, 230, 242–243.) But this will not do: some redescriptions are just redescriptions; they redescribe but they do not explain, even when they are "of greater generality." Caesar's invasion of Britain could be redescribed as an increase of pressure on a landmass or as the kicking about of stones and the relocation of sand and soil. It was that; these redescriptions are true and they are of "greater generality." But they do not explain; and they would not have an iota more explanatory force even if they were to be deductively derived from a law. What gives a redescription, if we want to call it that, explanatory force is not simply that it is a redescription "of greater generality" but, rather, that it states some relevant thought-factor of the agent. In short, the move to description "of greater generality," as I described it in my account of generic assertions of appropriateness, must be firmly anchored to the points of the triangle of explanation.

Danto treats the application of a classificatory heading to an explanandum simply as a redescription of the deed without even telling us in terms of *what* it is a redescription. Now it is quite clear that Danto wants to leave redescription open on this point. But it is also clear that, in his extended sample explanation of the Monagasques putting out American flags, the explanandum was put under a general heading which tells us what the Monagasques *intended* by their act; that particular redescription, at least, was a redescription in terms of the

General Laws and Principles of Action

agents' thought. (See Danto, *Analytical Philosophy of History*, pp. 220, 228, 232.) [6]

One point, I think, must be admitted: insofar as we do regard an action as done for a reason, we must classify (redescribe) that deed in terms of thought (purpose, etc.). And this point is simply a restatement of a contention which Collingwood argued for throughout *The Idea of History*.

There is another point, though, which Danto's analysis serves to alert us to, however obliquely. We cannot rely on the "surface" of our descriptive language to chart our way through to an explanation. The essence of the difficulty, as I see it, is that our *descriptive* terms in satisfying action concepts (deed, purpose, motivation) do not wear a clear label identifying their role. We cannot tell, just by inspecting the terms used in a sentence or two of ordinary historical narrative, whether, say, "attempting to conquer" is going to be part of describing a deed performed, or part of stating a situational motivation, or part of what is going to be said in giving the agent's purpose.

The descriptive terms for action concepts have a way of slipping around the barn, so that they turn up here in this guise and there in that one. This fact underlies, I think, the strong feature in Danto's analysis: it allows us to explain actions by redescribing them (e.g., we effectively explain an invasion by redescribing it as an attempt at conquest). But the basic reason for this explanatory power of redescription is not so much that we can redescribe a deed in other terms, although it is clear that we can, as it is that we do redescribe it, in *explaining* it, with terms that designate an agent's purpose or his situational motivation.

The whole point of redescribing is found not in what we say but in the logical role each element has in a given explanation as determined by its place on the triangle of explanation. Insofar as the issue in an explanation is one of justifying or licensing redescriptions, this is done not by deductive derivations and subsumptions, but by referring one of these elements to another (e.g., a deed to a purpose). Thus, when the agent does A in order to achieve E then "attempting E" is a licensed redescription of doing A and this recasting of A in these terms does have explanatory force.

6. For another criticism of Danto along these same lines, see Olafson, "Narrative History and the Concept of Action," esp. pp. 267–273, 289.

I would argue, in short, that Danto's example of the Monagasques, and ultimately his entire analysis of explanatory redescriptions, is acceptable just to the extent that it presupposes the basic analysis of action we are already familiar with from our study of Collingwood. Wherever these redescriptions depart from the lines of the triangle of explanation, as they ineluctably must, given the loose rein Danto has put on them, Danto's account is unconvincing.

With this point made, let us return to the question of the *truth* of Danto's law, "Whenever a nation has a sovereign of a different national origin than its own citizens, these citizens will, on the appropriate occasions, honour that sovereign in some acceptable fashion." Unfortunately, this "law" cannot be regarded as acceptable, for there are many counterinstances to it, as just the history of the British monarchy since the Reformation would show. (See Scriven, review, p. 502, for an example.) I will grant, however, that Danto's "law," if it had been unexceptionable, would allow us to deduce the relevant purpose under which the explanandum cited could be subsumed. So it might be well to modify my contention about regularity laws somewhat: I would want to admit that there might be some such laws which could afford the selective derivation of a relevant purpose and, hence, provide *one* of the premises of connection in an explanation. But Danto's example fails, as I have pointed out, in that his law is defective in regularity.

I would not want to argue that an acceptable regularity law could never be formulated. I think, if we accept Danto's amendment to the Hempelian model, that some parts of some historical explanations could conceivably be supported by regularity laws, whether of the general or of the "usually" sort. My contention is that any such case would be a *rara avis*; and pointing out isolated instances does not support the *general* reconstructive account of the logic of historical explanation advanced by the proponents of the regularity law model. We could not reconstruct every or even most historical explanations along the lines advocated in the model. The point that I made at the beginning of this discussion still stands: it is quite difficult to frame an acceptable (clear, complete, and true) law-form regularity generalization, one from which we could derive—deductively or inductively—the explanandum (Hempel) or, alternatively, the relevant purpose under which the explanandum is to be subsumed (Danto).

Essentially, then, it would not be profitable to restate generic asser-

General Laws and Principles of Action

tions of appropriateness as regularity laws. What we need to show, in order to allow a given action-explanation to go through, is the *plausibility* of a certain purpose of the agent in the light of his situation-conception and of the deed that he performed in the light of these elements of his thought. And the warrant for such claims to plausibility is provided by a set of hypotheticals each of the form "for all persons x: if Fx then Gx is intelligible or appropriate." My contention is that these hypotheticals, these assertions of appropriateness in generic form, typically take the place in the logic of historical explanation that Hempel and others have assigned to laws. It follows, moreover, since re-enactment explanations are supported, logically, by generic assertions of appropriateness and since these are not replaceable by regularity laws, that such assertions are not reducible to laws. These two kinds of statements are logically different.

It happens, though, that just as we have finished drawing a sharp distinction at this point, the question arises in yet another quarter. For what I have called a generic assertion of appropriateness bears a family resemblance to what Dray calls a "principle of action." (See Dray, *Laws and Explanation*, pp. 131–137, esp. 132.) The resemblance consists largely in three particulars. First, each type of statement is distinguishable in concept, in what it asserts, from a regularity law (see Dray, *Laws and Explanation*, p. 128). And, second, the role assigned to these two types of statement is the same in each case: they function as connection-justifying grounds in the explanation of actions determined by thought. Finally, there is the rather minor similarity that such terms as "appropriate," "intelligible," or "plausible" occur in statements of each of the two sorts. There are, however, significant points of difference and I think it would be helpful, in clarifying my own account of the matter, to bring these out.

The most important difference is that Dray's "principle of action" is evaluative; it belongs to the same general type as the logic of game theory, to the grading of actions as *sensible* or *rational*. The characteristic locution for giving an explanation, according to Dray, is that x was "the reasonable thing to have done" (*Laws and Explanation*, p. 135). The general hypothetical which supports such explanations takes the form: " 'When in a situation of type C_1 . . . C_n the thing to do is x' " (*Laws and Explanation*, p. 132). Dray's claim, as I see it, is that a "principle of action" is normative in what it asserts: it states that one thing which the agent *should* do *if he acts rationally*; such a principle tells us what is *"appropriate* in a rational sense" (*Laws and Explanation*, p. 136). [7]

In my analysis, on the other hand, a generic assertion of appropriateness does not make reference, oblique or otherwise, to some abstract norm of rational conduct, presumably applicable in a given case; rather it tells us only such things as what action(s) would be appropriate, in the sense of "fitting" or understandable or intelligible, if the agent did act for certain reasons. What we have, between Dray's case and my own, are two distinct types of statement: the one, insofar as it functions as a premise in an explanation, presents something as the rational thing to do; the other, functioning in exactly the same role, presents something as what plausibly could happen.

It seems to me, moreover, that there are some serious internal problems with Dray's claim that we explain a given action by bringing it under a particular normative principle of rational conduct. One of these problems has been effectively stated by Hempel: "Dray seems to assume (i) that, given a specification of the circumstances in which an agent finds himself (including, I take it, in particular his objectives and beliefs), there is a clear and unequivocal sense in which an action can be said to be . . . rational under the circumstances; and (ii) that, at least in many cases, there is exactly one course of action that is [rational] in this sense" ("Reasons and Covering Laws in Historical Explanation," p. 153; see also "Aspects," p. 468).

Each of these assumptions, if made, would clearly be problematic. Dray's account, since it does call for selecting out just *one and only one* course of action as *the* rational thing to do, suggests that there is not only a single clear "sense" of the term "rational" but also that there is only one correct standard, indeed a single universal standard, of rationality. I think it evident, though, that there is not a *single* standard of rationality.

---

7. Endorsing a phrase of Walsh's, Dray says that "principles of behaviour" give us "knowledge of how [men] *should* behave" (*Laws and Explanation*, p. 136). This particular point is further clarified in a later essay; there Dray says that "a statement like 'Rulers do not normally invade neighboring territories if they are satisfied with what they have' [an example cited by Scriven] may quite intelligibly be interpreted as stating a 'norm' in the sense of reminding us of what it is reasonable to do—and thus, of course, of what people in fact do, except when they act foolishly, ignorantly, arbitrarily, and so on. . . . And this would assimilate explanation in terms of normic generalizations [i.e., in the terms Scriven has proposed] to what I have called the 'rational' kind" ("Historical Explanation of Actions Reconsidered," p. 122). For additional discussion, see Dray, *Laws and Explanation*, pp. 124, 126, 135.

General Laws and Principles of Action

Even if we were to choose a restricted and well-defined sense of "rational," that of game theory, there are still different standards for rational conduct which one could follow in a given case: one could play a winner-maximize game or a loser-minimize one, and so on. If we move to vaguer senses of "rational," ones closer to the interests of historians and to ordinary life, we will find an even greater number of substantive standards, and correspondingly "imperfect" ones as well.[8] This variety is exhibited not only in the history of thought, what with its "natural law" and "light of reason," but also today, where we confront as *standards of rationality* everything from Marxist "revolutionary praxis" or existentialist "absurdism" to "scientific method" and its derivatives, "rational egoism" and the many varieties of "utilitarianism."

Without this assumption of a single, coherent standard of rationality that covers the agent's action, however, Dray's argument loses its grip on the individual case. For we are no longer in a position to select out just one action as the rational thing to do. Hence, even if we allowed the claim that we do explain by reference to normative principles of rational action, we would not, in a great many cases, be able to derive that one single action which was the rational thing to do.

One might seek to remedy Dray's position by bringing in the idea of a network of principles of rational conduct, some of which are deployed to eliminate certain possibilities and others to "cover," as rational, what remains. Even so, it would be difficult to achieve this in Dray's case since there is nothing in his account that answers to what I have called a basic schema or sketch for the explanation of action. There is no conceptual framework, in contrast to the case with generic assertions of appropriateness, that could organize this network of principles and give it focus. For it is, ultimately, not the assertions of appropriateness that select out one deed as the done thing but, rather, the principle of inference—the schema itself—which they subserve.

Mention of a schema for action-explanations, or lack of one in Dray's case, does serve, I think, to point out yet another deficiency in Dray's account. Dray seems to think that, in an explanation of a deed, it is sufficient to say what the rational thing to do is. But, as has been pointed out many times, first by Strawson and most cogently by Hem-

8. Watkins, in a very helpful essay, distinguished three levels of rationality, in descending order: (a) optimal rationality, (b) game theory rationality, and (c) "imperfect" rationality. (See "Imperfect Rationality," esp. pp. 199ff, 205–206, 209.)

pel, we cannot explain "he did *x*" *simply* by showing, even if we could, that "*x* was the rational thing to do." For as Hempel aptly put it: "[T]he information that agent A was in a situation of kind C and that in such a situation the rational thing to do is *x*, affords grounds for believing that *it would have been rational for A to do x*, but no grounds for believing that A did in fact do *x*" ("Aspects," p. 471).[9]

On the other hand, it seems needlessly concessionary to Dray's view to suggest, as Hempel does,[10] that we would need to supplement a principle of rational conduct with some statement of initial condition to the effect that the agent was "rational" at the time, meaning thereby that he would actually *do* the rational thing. My contention here is, not that the suggested insertion of this condition is tautologous, but simply that it is pointless. It still leaves explanations of actions on the spurious foundation of principles of rational conduct.

What we do need is a principle of inference that allows us to go from the specified "reasons" of an agent (principally, from his situational motivation and relevant purpose) to the action he performed without requiring, at the same time, that the needed connecting of these facts be mediated by principles of rational conduct. I think the schema for action-explanations, working in tandem with general hypotheticals of appropriateness, does allow us to bypass explanatorily empty talk about what is normatively rational and does provide a ground for explaining deeds by reference to the thoughts of an agent.

I would suggest, finally, that the reason Dray adopted his notion of "principles of action" in the first place and why it has continued to exercise a fascination ever since is that these "principles" really are logically distinct from regularity generalizations and really are immune from empirical disconfirmation. Now some people have concluded that Dray's "principles" are *moral* ones because they are general norms or prescriptions for action and because they are not disconfirmable by reference to matters of fact.[11] But this, I think, is a mistaken conclusion; rather, they are *like* moral principles in these two respects. Perhaps, though, it would be useful to consider the second of these two similarities more closely.

9. At this point Hempel cites Passmore, review, p. 275, against Dray. See also Strawson, review, p. 268, and Leach, "Dray on Rational Explanation," pp. 65–67.

10. See "Reasons and Covering Laws in Historical Explanation," p. 155, and "Aspects," p. 471.

11. White has interpreted Dray's position, with its talk of *ought* and *should*, as a form of moralism (see *Foundations of Historical Knowledge*, pp. 182–184).

General Laws and Principles of Action

There is, I think, at least a *prima facie* difference in logical type between saying that men always *do* seek their own pleasure and saying that they always *ought* to. The difference is clear in what would tend to "disconfirm" each statement: providing counterinstances of what men *actually* do would serve in the first case; providing countervailing "moral" arguments or reasons would in the second. By the same token, when Dray asserts that all agents, when in a situation of kind C, *must* do x, he is not giving us a regularity generalization; this assertion is of a different logical type, drawing ultimately on some substantive standard of *rationality*, and it cannot be disconfirmed by citing contrary instances of what agents, in such a situation, actually do.

Dray says, "It is true that finding a large number of negative instances—finding that people often do not act in accordance with it— would create a presumption against the claim of a given principle [of action] to universal validity. But it would not *compel* its withdrawal . . . ." (*Laws and Explanation*, p. 132). Indeed, we would not even, in the face of negative instances, have to give up the statement that a certain person held to a certain principle of action: "that statement would not *necessarily* be falsified; and if it were retained, we could still explain in the rational way those of his actions which *were* in accordance with it" (pp. 132–133). Dray concludes, "The connexion between a principle of action and the 'cases' falling under it is thus intentionally and peculiarly loose" (p. 133). This makes it clear, I think, that Dray's principal distinction is between what he calls "rational necessity" (see *Laws and Explanation*, p. 154; also pp. 55, 158, 161) and empirical regularity. The point is that we must know, and can know, "that a particular action [rationally] *had to be done*" ("Historical Explanation of Actions Reconsidered," p. 105); but the principle of action that tells us this is, logically, immune from disconfirmation by reference to what actually does or does not happen.

In a rather straightforward way Dray's point about contrary instances here actually tends to strengthen the criticism I made earlier that we cannot move from a statement, even presumably a true one, of what an agent ought rationally to do to the fact that he actually does it. Indeed, so long as the logical connection between a principle of action and its contrary instances is so "peculiarly loose" as to rule out empirical disconfirmation altogether, it is difficult to see how one could ever derive an actual performance of a deed from a rational norm. If this is so, then appealing to such norms (or principles of action, as Dray calls them) can never in and of itself have explanatory force for an action performed.

Ultimately it is immaterial to Dray's argument whether there really *are* or could be adequate and true general laws. For, if his notion of the logical-type difference between two kinds of explanation is granted in the first place (as the difference between explanations that tell us what "always or usually happens" and those that tell us "the rational thing to do"), then general laws, or their lack, and so-called disconfirming instances, or their lack, are simply *irrelevant* to the latter kind.

Dray clearly sees the principle of action as *the* basic alternative to regularity laws and "rational explanation" as the *only* real alternative to the "covering law" model (see "Historical Explanation of Actions Reconsidered," esp. pp. 121, 131). Indeed, I think the strategy of this essay of Dray's is to argue for precisely this point. That one dissents on points of detail here is less important than how much has already been accepted, in letting Dray draw up the agenda for the "other type" on the model of "rational explanation." I have tried to show that the range of types is wider than the two Dray has cited and that my own account, especially on the point of generic assertions of intelligible connection, is, despite superficial resemblances, radically distinct from what Dray has called "rational explanation."

The essential nub of the difference is, I would suggest, whether empirical regularity and the notion of disconfirming instances have any place, really, in the logic of the explanation of actions. Dray denies that regularity generalizations have any logical role to play at all in the explanation of actions done for a reason; he rules them out not only from the role of "covering law" but from "rational explanation" altogether. However, as will become clear in the next chapter, there is a role for regularity generalizations, and for possible disconfirming instances, in my reconstructive account of the logic of re-enactment explanation.

Seven

The Role of Regularity Generalizations

In the previous chapter I argued that what is involved in a re-enactment explanation, at the point where a premise for particular material connection does function, is not a regularity generalization; rather, it is a statement of intelligible connection in generic form. Regularity generalizations—in particular regularity *laws*—are not required as connection-justifying grounds in an explanation.

But this is not to imply that regularity generalizations play no role at all. I would suggest, rather, that they function as inductive supports for generic assertions of appropriateness. Where these assertions perform the first-order job of licensing a particular connection of specific facts in re-enactment explanations, regularity generalizations perform the second-order job of confirming the assertibility of these generic hypotheticals of appropriateness.

The point of bringing regularity generalizations into the picture is that they provide a necessary condition of asserting as true any generic hypothetical of appropriateness. For example, we would be justified in asserting "if a military leader proposes to curb interventions by x, then invasion is a plausible course of action to take" only if invasions *do sometimes occur* for the reason given. Of course, this regularity generalization would be a "loose" one, not an "always" or a "usually" one.

Historical Explanation

It might prove useful to back up a bit and fill in behind this point. For there is, I think, a tighter logical connection between assertions of appropriateness and regularity generalizations than I have yet indicated. This connection underwrites the inductive support role that I have assigned to regularity generalizations, albeit "loose" ones.

In any explanation, where we attempt to explain an event by referring it to the agent's situational motivation (leaving aside for the moment any reference to the agent's intention), that situational motivation as described should provide an understandable reason for the agent's action. Conversely, his deed as described should be plausible in the light of the situational motivation we have ascribed to him on the basis of evidence. We want a relation of plausibility to hold between the agent's deed (as described) and his situational motivation (as described). For this relationship to hold we need at a minimum to be able to show that the deed performed is relevant to the situational motivation, and vice versa. And we would, of course, want this relationship of plausibility (and hence of mutual relevance) to be reproduced as well for the other basic relationships (that of intention to deed and that of situational motivation to intention).

This relationship of *relevance* is established, in these sorts of cases, by probabilistic reasoning and the probability values required are given by regularity generalizations—which are themselves, for the most part, loose or low-level ones. It follows, accordingly, that regularity analysis does provide an indispensable support for the generic assertions of appropriateness which re-enactment logically presupposes.

To see the character of this thesis more clearly, let us consider an example: that of the Scandinavian incursions into Western Europe during the early feudal age and, in particular, the settlement of Northmen along the lower Seine (later Normandy) and its incorporation as a seigneury under the king of West Francia.

Without entirely neglecting the mouths of the Rhine and the Scheldt, the Vikings' activities from about 885 were directed more and more to the valleys of the Loire and the Seine. In the region of the Lower Seine, for instance, one of their bands was permanently installed in 896, and thence sallied forth in all directions in search of booty. But these long-distance raids were not always successful. The marauders were defeated in Burgundy on several occasions, and under the walls of Chartres in 911. In the Roumois and the neighbouring region, on the other hand, they were masters, and there is no doubt that in order to feed themselves during the winter seasons they were already obliged to cultivate the land or have it cultivated for them; the more so since this settlement was a centre of attraction and the first arrivals, few in number, had been joined by other waves of adventurers.

If experience had shown that it was not impossible to curb their ravages, it yet seemed that to dislodge them from their lairs was beyond the powers of the sole authority whose business it was to do so, i.e., the king. For regional government no longer existed: in this horribly devastated area, whose centre was now the mere ruin of a town, the machinery of local command had totally disappeared. Apart from that, the new king of West Francia, Charles the Simple (crowned in 893 and universally acknowledged after the death of Odo, his rival), appears from the time of his accession to have planned to come to an agreement with the invader. This plan he tried to put into effect during the year 897, by summoning to his court the chief who at that time commanded the Northmen of the Lower Seine, and making him his godson, but this first attempt was unsuccessful. But after this it is not surprising that, fourteen years later, he should have taken up the idea again, addressing himself this time to Rollo, who had succeeded Charles' godson in the command of the same 'army'. Rollo, for his part, had just been defeated before Chartres and this reverse had not failed to open his eyes to the difficulties with which the pursuit of plunder was beset. He considered it wise to accept the king's offer. This meant that both sides recognized the *fait accompli*—with the additional advantages, so far as the king and his counsellors were concerned, of reuniting to their dominions, by the ties of vassal homage and the accompanying obligations of military aid, an already full-blown principality which thenceforward would have the best reasons in the world for guarding the coast against any further depredations by pirates. In a charter of the 14th March 918, the king mentions the concessions granted 'to the Northmen of the Seine, that is to say Rollo and his companions . . . for the defence of the realm'. [Bloch, *Feudal Society*, pp. 28–29] [1]

This example is an interesting one for several reasons. For one thing, the considerations involved in the explanation can be put in such a way as to make the outcome appear implausible if not paradoxical: Charles regains a territory by giving it to the people who took it from him and Rollo, in order to acquire a territory he already controls, becomes the subordinate of a king who cannot oust him militarily. Accordingly, the explanation requires some care to avoid this element of implausibility. For another thing, the action in question is a mutual or reciprocal one and requires the cooperation of the two

1. I am indebted to Phillip R. Craft for calling this example to my attention and for suggesting some of its amplification.

principal agents: Rollo receives from Charles a kind of title or tenure with respect to a certain "holding" (a "tenement," in this case of territory) and gives Charles in turn his "homage": his loyalty and service (in this case, military support). Finally, Charles's action is sufficiently like the earlier example of Caesar's invasion of Britain to make useful comparison possible.

Charles was in a situation of hostile confrontation between himself and his political-military associates, on the one hand, and the Northmen, on the other. The situation could easily degenerate into armed conflict and indeed had done so on numerous occasions. (Let us designate a situation of this sort with an *H*—for hostile confrontation.) Charles's situational motivation was complex and included a number of elements: he wanted to curb these incursions of the Northmen (the raids, maraudings, and ravages as Bloch calls them); he had had some success in doing so by force of arms but was not able to stop them entirely; the Northmen had gained control of some territory and were beginning to settle there in numbers, and they could not be dislodged militarily from this stronghold; at the same time Charles had reason to believe that his opposite number among the Northmen, Rollo, would welcome a termination of this uneasy situation. The crucial fact that emerges from all this, and that serves to differentiate this situation from the one Caesar was faced with by the Britons, is that Charles and the Northmen were in a kind of stalemate, where force could curb the ravages of the Northmen but not dislodge them from their settlement. This was the uncomfortable *fait accompli* which Bloch described and hence I will designate this complex motivational background, put in general terms, as *F*).

So, Charles enlisted Rollo in a reciprocal accommodation. Since the accommodation involved certain salient features of feudal vassalage, I will designate action of this sort with a V. However, it should be borne in mind that reciprocal accommodations on this order are not peculiar to the feudal period. (Indeed, the main details of the *action* taken in the famous Mayflower Compact would be described in roughly the same way, that is, designated with a V, even though the situational background in that case was vastly different from the one we are here considering.)

Now, our problem is to make good the claim that the situational motivation alluded to (in general terms, as *F*) is relevant to the deed performed (described, in general terms, as V) and, hence, support the

Role of Regularity Generalizations

assertion that the relationship of the one to the other is a plausible one. It does not appear that the connection between *F* (finding the stalemate or *fait accompli* uneasy) and *V* (reaching the reciprocal accommodation indicated) is an analytic one. For, clearly, we can regard *F* as holding without its being absurd or in any way self-contradictory that *V* does *not* hold. In fact, an outcome of roughly this sort had actually occurred in 897, when Charles made the leader of the Northmen his godson, that is, when he did a *G* rather than a *V* (which involves, we should recall, a tie more like feudal vassalage than like adoptive kinship). Hence, since the relationship of *F* to not-*V* is a logically eligible one, we must ground the relevance relationship of *F* (finding the stalemate uneasy) and *V* (reaching a reciprocal accommodation on the model of vassalage) in something other than a logical entailment.[2] Indeed, it is difficult to conceive any a priori way of determining a relevance connection here, for the matter is both too complex and too specific to be amenable to treatment by such notions as logical entailment or the a priori calculus of chances.

It is possible, nonetheless, to support the claim to plausibility in the case at hand. We can do so by showing, in *probabilistic* fashion, that *F* (finding the stalemate uncomfortable) is relevant to *V* (reaching a reciprocal accommodation of the sort we have been discussing).

The establishment of relevance by probabilistic reasoning actually would require several steps. Initially, at step one, it would involve two points. First, we would have to be able (at least in principle) to generate a probability value for *V* (occurrences of the action attribute sought here) in relation to a very inclusive, very basic but very neutral reference class (in the case under consideration, it is occasions of hostile confrontation: designated by *H*). Thus we would get, schematically, a regularity generalization "if *H* then sometimes *V*," which has, we can assume, a rather low relative-frequency probability value (let us call it *n*: where *n* is some number—in this case it is most likely well below

2. The claim that I am concerned to dispute here was actually put forward at one time by Alan Donagan (see his "Explanation in History," pp. 436–437 and 439 in particular). But Scriven pinpoints well what is at issue here: "[T]he relation between a psychological concept, for example, and the behaviors (even rather generally described) that instantiate it . . . is simply consonance. It is not analytic that a man who is very upset will speak sharply to his children when they ask for money to go to a movie or for any favor, nor even probable, but it is perfectly understandable." (Review, p. 503.) There is not high probability in such matters, I would agree. What I want to argue, though, is that *consonance*, which is at issue, can be established by probabilistic reasoning.

125

½—or, if not a number, then a loose phrase like "sometimes but not terribly often"). Alternatively but still schematically, we could write down the regularity generalization in question as $p(V, H) = n$. Now, second, it seems evident that we could exhibit the positive relevance of the sort of situational motivation Charles had—that is, F (finding the stalemate uneasy)—to action described as V (reaching an accommodation through vassalage) only if, when we "partitioned" the basic reference class by inserting the details of F, we got a resultant probability value greater than the one with which we had started. (Likewise, we could exhibit a negative relevance if the resultant probability value were less than the one with which we had started; but, of course, the relevance force we are after here requires that the difference represent an increase in probability value: for we want the relevance of F to V— within the reference class H—to be such as would improve the probabilistic weight attached to V's occurring.)

Putting this point more formally now, we can say that F (finding the stalemate uneasy) is relevant to V (reaching reciprocal accommodation) within the basic reference class H (of hostile confrontations) where $p(V, H)$ is *not* equal to $p(V, H.F)$—meaning that the probability value of the one is not equal to that of the other. (We are assuming throughout that the indicated relevance of F to V is a positive one, one where the difference in value represents an increase.) On the other hand, if the partition were to make no difference, then we would say that the inserted detail is not relevant. Put more formally, we would have shown the apparent irrelevance of F to V within H where $p(V, H)$ is equal to $p(V, H.F)$.[3] We have in this notion of probabilistic relevance or irrelevance a device for dealing with the problem of exhibiting relevance so as to provide grounding for the generic assertions of plausibility we make.

In order to test whether this analysis is in accord with our intuitions, let us consider possible partitions of the basic reference class which are clearly irrelevant. For instance, one would not suppose that the dating (D) of the event in a year designated by an odd number would be a relevant consideration. Most likely then, though $p(V, H.D)$ will have

3. It should be borne in mind that the probability values I am referring to are not those of classical, relative-frequency probability theory: for in that theory a probability value represents the *limit* toward which the relative frequency of an attribute tends in an *infinite* sequence of events. The values I am suggesting are *partial* probability values; they represent the relative frequency of attributes within a historically available, finite sequence of events. They are, in short, the values provided by regularity generalizations.

some probability value, the insertion of D will not mark any change in value from the original "untreated" case $p(V, H)$; hence, these values are identical and D is judged irrelevant. It would be implausible to account for V by reference to D. And it was, no doubt, an implausibility of this sort, that is, one based ultimately on the notion of probabilistic irrelevance, which figured in our original judgment of implausibility as regards the knife wound example (in Chapter Five).

My example of the odd-year factor is deliberately improbable, especially in the historical context we are considering. For as Bloch points out, though chronicles were kept at the time (see pp. 27–28), the people of the period had a rather poorly developed date sense by our standards (see pp. 65, 74–75, and esp. 84). Even so, I want to use this example again to take us to the second step in my account of the probabilistic establishment of relevance, the step at which we are concerned with comparative partitionings of a basic reference class (here H: hostile confrontations).

Let us begin by considering the relevance relationship involved, were we to match up the strange property D (dates of odd-numbered years) against F (finding the stalemate uneasy—which serves to describe the situational motivation Charles presumably had). In such a case we would most likely find that (i) $p(V, H.F)$ is equal to $p(V, H.F.D)$, which suggests that the insertion of D (the odd-year factor) would make no difference to V (the type of action in question) in a reference class already partitioned by F; but that (ii) $p(V, H.D)$ is *not* equal to $p(V, H.D.F)$, which suggests that F (finding the stalemate uneasy: here a particular sort of situational motivation) does make a difference to action of that type even though the reference class has already been partitioned by the date factor. We could say then that, while D (the odd-date factor) is irrelevant to V (reaching accommodations on the model of vassalage) in the reference class H (of hostile confrontations), F (finding the stalemate uneasy) is relevant.

However, I think the relationship just examined is susceptible of a more exacting characterization. For (ii) $p(V, H.D) \neq p(V, H.D.F)$ does not indicate the simple irrelevance of D; rather it indicates, more precisely, that whatever difference the partitioning of H by D had made to V (and we determined earlier that it had really made no difference at all) that difference was outweighed, or overruled, by the insertion of F. Hence, it would be more accurate to say that the difference made to V by the insertion of D into the reference class, whatever that difference is, was "channeled" or "filtered" by the insertion of F.

This relationship of "outweighing" is important because sometimes the partition of the reference class by some element E actually does make a difference (unlike the case with the odd-year date factor) and yet that difference could still be "channeled" in the way I have indicated. For example, if we were to take a mere subset of F (which is a complex situational motivation and includes such elements as E: "curbing hostile incursions") and then were to partition the reference class with that element (E), we would very likely get the first-step result that $p(V, H) \neq p(V, H.E)$, which suggests the relevance of E (the element) to V (the type of action) in that reference class. However, we would also get the result, when we moved to the second stage, that (i) $p(V, H.F) = p(V, H.F.E)$ but that (ii) $p(V, H.E) \neq p(V, H.E.F)$.[4] These two results would be in accord with our expectations. For the first-step result says, as to simple relevance, that E (the element: "curbing hostile incursions") is relevant, within the basic reference class, to V (the type of action: "reaching accommodations on the model of vassalage"). But the second stage says that that relevance is overruled ("channeled" or "filtered") by the insertion of F. And, presumably, a similar set of results would be reached if we took any other element, for example, the fact of settlement and the beginnings of a rudimentary agriculture (a fact that Bloch himself put considerable emphasis on—see pp. 27, 30, and esp. 38), and matched that against F.

It would seem, however, that introducing this second relevance relationship—that of outweighing or overruling—opens my account to an interesting rejoinder. For one could say that all the analysis has shown is that the sort of thing designated by F is statistically relevant to the event-type V *only* in relation to things that are statistically irrelevant or to things that are statistically less relevant. I have failed to show, however, that F is anything more than merely "relatively relevant" to V; in particular, I have failed to show that it is *intrinsically* relevant. This then becomes the point at issue.

I do think, though, that a further elaboration of the relevance rela-

---

4. For technical reasons, we would need to read E here as "occasions of curbing hostile incursions" (and that *only*) and scan F as designating occurrences of the *other* traits as well as, or instead of, that one. This will allow us to have exhaustive and mutually exclusive partitionings in these formulas.

tionships already deployed could meet this objection. It should be noted that the first relevance relationship, the relationship of simple relevance, is in fact satisfied; for we can show that F is relevant to V (in the very broad reference class H) and is relevant on its own, so to speak, and not in relation to some other, presumably irrelevant or less relevant factor. (Here we would rely on the formula $p[V, H] \neq p[V, H.F]$.) Nonetheless the request for an establishment of intrinsic relevance does seem in order. For it is still open to question whether it is F *per se* that is relevant to V or whether it is some factor internal to F, a factor that would need to be brought out explicitly, or some descriptive detail that would need to be explicitly added to F that is in fact the principal bearer of the relevance relationship.

To deal with this issue, we would need to specify a third and final relevance relationship of F (finding the stalemate uneasy) to V (reaching a reciprocal accommodation on the model of vassalage): that no partition of F makes a difference to the probability value already available in $p(V, F)$. In other words, this third relevance relationship is satisfied where F becomes the focus of attention and itself serves as the basic reference class and where the probability value of $p(V, F)$ is *unaffected* by the insertion into F of any of a variety of details.

The value in question would presumably be unchanged after the insertion of such apparently irrelevant details as an odd-year date factor (D) or a difference in the length of names (N) between, for example, Charles and Rollo. It would be unchanged were we to add the fact of a standing necessary condition—like the presence of oxygen in the atmosphere: (O)—which is relevant to all situations and all events but has no peculiar relevance to the particular action-explanation details presently under discussion. And it would be unaffected if we were to take any element (E) of F, for example "curbing hostile incursions," and bring that out as an explicit partitioning factor. (In short, we would be relying on the formula $p[V, F] = p[V, F.D] = p[V, F.N] = p[V, F.O] = [V, F.E]$, etc.) On the other hand, where this equivalence did *not* obtain, as in $p(V, E) \neq p(V, E.F)$, then this third relevance relationship would *not* hold.

We can call the relationship here of F to V a relationship of intrinsic relevance because that relevance is not "channeled" or "filtered out," in a series of partitionings, by any inserted factor. There is nothing outside the explicit description we have given of F which, if added to F, would make any difference. And there is no feature inter-

Historical Explanation

nal to F which, if F were partitioned by that feature, would screen out a part of F and thereby change the picture with respect to V. The relevance relationship so established between V and F is stabilized: here the reference class F as described is intrinsically relevant to V.

The emphasis I have put on the description of F (which includes such things as finding the stalemate uneasy, and so on) is crucial here. Where does this description come from? How does one decide that something is to count as a part of that description? And how do we determine what kinds of things are extrinsic to F (as described)? We need some sort of rule of closure, some principle for determining a range of objects such that some are to count in and some out in a description of F. We need, to put the matter somewhat differently, a way to limit, to localize the partitionings of F.

There is a sense in which what I have called intrinsic relevance is a "relative" notion: it is relative to the epistemic situation of the historian in two crucial respects.

For first and most important, when the historian asserts that V (reaching a mutual accommodation) is plausible in the light of F (finding the situation of stalemant awkward), as Bloch must surely have thought when he offered his explanation of Rollo's envassalage to Charles, V is here being regarded as descriptive of the agent's deed and F of his situational motivation. The historian is already within the framework of action; there is already available a set of fundamental categories (deed, intention, etc.) into which the data are to be sorted. And the basic arrangement of these categories, as we have it in the triangle of explanation, would simply be presupposed in any attempt to establish the mutual relevance, at the material or descriptive level, of V and F. Hence, the very fact that F and V are regarded as descriptive of objects that hold places in a specific relationship—in the case at hand, that of situational motivation to deed—controls and delimits the range of things that can be considered for insertion into these places.

Moreover, the sorts of things that could figure in any partition of F (which designates in general terms the motivational background Charles had, under the description we have given it) are themselves circumscribed on the basis of evidence available to the historian. For, ultimately, his narrative account and the thinking that lies behind it will come to reflect a certain "picture of life," for the deed and the agents and the period under study. This picture, which is itself supported by available evidence, will allow him to interpolate some things into his narrative, but not everything.

The history of Charles the Simple and Rollo, or of the Scandinavian incursions or of feudal Europe, would be drastically disordered if, for example, the facts and attendant attitudes of twentieth-century transportation or mass-media communications or military technology were to be superimposed. Or if we were to try to take into account twentieth-century standards regarding such things as property holding and political legitimacy. Interpolations of this sort would be out of place; the partitioning of Charles's situational motivation (F) by these things would be incompatible with the historian's "picture of life" for that period and, hence, would not be allowed.

There are definite epistemic restrictions on our capacity to partition, or to fiddle with partitioning, a historical reference class. The most important of these are the constraints provided by our model of action-explanation itself and then those provided by evidence available to the historian and by his "picture of life" formed thereby for the period under study. The second class of restrictions is, admittedly, a rather vague one; but its function is clear enough. It is simply a way of indicating that there is nothing known to the historian or includable in his narrative account of two things, say an F and a V, each under a fairly definite description, which would disrupt the bearing of relevance between things of the one sort (or class F) and those of the other (class V). And, though both these provisos restrict considerably the range of application of what earlier was called "channeling" or "filtering out," neither of them presents any particular difficulty in itself. So, I think it quite allowable to say that a relationship of intrinsic relevance could be established using the rather simple mechanisms of probability value and probabilistic (or statistical) relevance with which we are already familiar.

In sum, now, I have argued that a relationship of relevance can be established between factors in an action-explanation—factors which stand to one another as situational motivation to deed, or as intention to deed, or as situational motivation to intention. And we are, of course, considering these factors under the *material* descriptions they have when standing in any of these basic relationships. For example, we might be considering the two factors already cited above, where the one is described as belonging to class F (finding stalemates uneasy) and the other to class V (reaching reciprocal accommodations on the model of vassalage). Specifically, then, the relevance of F to V would be established insofar as the indicated relevance relationships are satisfied:

(a) *simple* relevance, the relevance of F to V within a basic reference class (H: of hostile confrontations)—and here we would rely on the formulas $p(V, H) > 0$ and $p(V, H) \neq p(V, H.F)$

(b) *outweighing* or *overruling*, where F "channels" the relevance of other factors as being either irrelevant (I) or less relevant (L)—and here we would rely in particular on the formulas $p(V, H.I) \neq p(V, H.I.F)$, $p(V, H.L) \neq p(V, H.L.F)$

(c) *intrinsic* relevance, where the relevance of F, already established in (a) and (b), is *unaffected* by other factors in a series of partitions, subject to a sharp demarcation of these factors by specific epistemic considerations—and here we would rely on the formula $p(V, F) = p(V, F.I) = p(V, F.L)$, etc. [5]

Or, alternatively, we could say that the relevance of F to V, already established in (a) and (b), is preserved (that is, not screened out by other known factors) under (c) conditions of epistemic constraint of the sort which characteristically operate on the working historian.

It might prove illuminating at this point to look again, briefly, at an important difference between the explanation of Caesar's invasion of Britain and that of Charles's mutual accommodation with Rollo (or "reconciliation" as Bloch called it, p. 29). The situational motivation, when described in general terms, is in each case strikingly similar. What differentiates them, principally, is that in Caesar's case there was the prospect that military pressure would make a difference but in Charles's case there was not. Hence, we get a well-constructed description of Caesar's motivational background without including the fact of stalemate (and indeed we would have no reason to include it, given the evidence at hand); and a situational motivation of this sort can be shown to be relevant to a deed described as invading. By the same token, we get an apt characterization of the motivation of Charles the Simple only by including the fact of stalemate. And

5. My account of establishing relevance through probabilistic reasoning is much indebted to Wesley Salmon's essay "Statistical Explanation." See, in particular, his discussion of statistical relevance (p. 186 esp. and also pp. 205, 215–216), screening-off (pp. 198–199), and homogeneity of the reference class (pp. 187, 190, 200, 207, 209). What I have called *intrinsic* relevance is roughly equivalent to Salmon's notion of *epistemic* homogeneity (see esp. pp. 188, 194, 224).

Role of Regularity Generalizations

Charles's situational motivation, when described in general terms as F (finding the stalemate uneasy, etc.), can be shown to be relevant to a deed described as reaching reciprocal accommodation. Change the description of situational motivation in either case, by adding the stalemate factor to Caesar's sort of motivational background or subtracting it from Charles's and the relationship of relevance between situational motivation and deed would be disrupted. Indeed, the disruption might be so great as to make Caesar's invasion appear implausible, on the one hand, and Charles's accommodation with Rollo implausible, on the other.

The point in each case is to provide a characterization of the agent's situational motivation which is relevant to the sort of deed under consideration. But we should take care not to overdo this point. For the relationship of relevance I have been discussing in this chapter is a rather weak one and its holding between, say, a particular kind of deed and a particular kind of situational motivation is by no means an exclusive matter. Thus, even where we had an apt characterization of the sort of motivational background Caesar had, there would no doubt be an indefinitely large number of courses of action to which it was relevant (not just invading but also blockading and showing the flag and even taking diplomatic initiatives, to name but a few). And, likewise, there are no doubt, given the sort of situational motivation Charles had, an indefinitely large number of types of action to which *it* could be regarded as relevant: cases of envassalage, adoptions to kinship, exchanges of hostages, linkages through marriage or treaty, and so on. It would be no different with the actions we have been considering. Take just the single instance of invading: there must surely be an indefinite but large number of differing situational motivations (for Caesar one, for Cortes another) that could stand as relevant to a deed so described. And if we were to vary our pattern, by turning to the other main action-explanation elements (intention to deed or situational motivation to intention), we would find that this "indefinitely large number" business holds there as well.

Nonetheless, the important relationship I have tried to capture in my analysis, that of relevance, would be present in all these illustrations. Now, on the assumption that plausibility or appropriateness of connection would normally be taken for granted in these cases but would not even be allowed where the relationship of relevance was disrupted (recall the point made about Caesar and Charles), an impor-

133

tant conclusion becomes available. One could not legitimately assert a connection of plausibility or appropriateness unless there was a relationship of relevance between the factors said to be so connected.

Here relevance is established by probabilistic reasoning: by exhibiting on the basis of the probability values involved, for two factors (say, F and V), that certain probabilistic relevance relationships are fulfilled —those of simple relevance, of outweighing, and of the preservation of relevance under conditions of epistemic constraint. Since the probability values required are the values provided by regularity generalizations—for the most part loose ones—it follows that regularity generalizations, in virtue of their role in probabilistic reasoning, are logically ingredient to the establishment of relevance.

We can say that every (generic) assertion of appropriateness is inductively supported, if true, by a corresponding regularity generalization. But this tells only half the story. We can put the matter more precisely, and more formally, by saying that a truth condition of any generic assertion of appropriateness is that its elements, say, F and V, are so related that a regularity generalization could be formulated (as $p[V, F] = n > 0$) and that such a generalization would satisfy the matrix of probabilistic relevance relationships. This truth-condition claim does provide for a logical connection between generic assertions of appropriateness and regularity generalizations and it does so by indicating clearly that the connection is mediated by the role such generalizations play in probabilistic reasoning.

I am not saying that the assertion of appropriateness is true only where we actually have the regularity generalization in hand, or know it to exist. Or true only where the probabilistic reasoning has actually been done, with the desired result. An assertion of this sort can be called a true statement only if someone is able, given the facts of the world, to produce such a generalization and to conduct the probabilistic reasoning required so as to establish relevance. Where we cannot thus establish relevance, our assertion of appropriateness is unsupported and thereby doubtful. Such an assertion would then be out of place: appropriateness could not legitimately be asserted there.

Whoever wants to deny this condition (as a necessary one) must be prepared to say that a hypothetical of appropriateness can be true or can be asserted regardless of whether such a regularity exists. I do not see, though, that one could maintain this view. To do so would be tantamount to saying that there is an affinity between two elements, say, I and C, such that the descriptive content of C (curbing interventions) does comport with that of I (invading), despite the fact that there is no case at all where instances of either have ever actually gone together. The man who disagrees with my point would have to say that *any* degree of regularity in the connection of instances is immaterial to his claim. He would be committed to believing that the affinity existed even though there was *no* degree of regularity in the instances, and could be none.

More important, he would be committed to believing that the affinity existed irrespective of whether it could be established that the one descriptive content was even relevant to the other. Indeed, he would have to believe that the establishment of probabilistic relevance is itself immaterial, that it is of no significance at all, one way or the other, to his claim.

What is at issue is the kind of support required by an assertion of appropriateness, or plausibility, and the kind of reasoning that would be involved in providing this support. We must be able to support the *assertion* of such judgments with at least "loose" regularity generalizations, specifically those that could satisfy a set of probabilistic relevance relationships. It follows that one could not say, justifiably, that two action-concepts, C (curbing interventions) and I (invading), are plausibly connected or that they have an affinity, at the material or descriptive level, when instances of each have never gone together or when, though there might be some degree of regularity between instances of the two kinds, it could not be established that the one sort of thing was probabilistically relevant to the other.

It is not just that a person would have no rational basis for saying, in the total absence of any relevant concurrence of their instances, that the connection of C (curbing interventions) and I (invading) is an intelligible one, it is not clear even that it would make sense to say it. For how could it be a meaningful claim—how could it ever be *true*— that an intelligible material connection exists between C and I unless instances of each *could* go together relevantly, in some practicable state of affairs? Clearly, then, the fact of relevant connection *to some degree* is not immaterial. If this is not granted, then it would have to be allowed that an assertion of plausibility is capable of surviving demonstration that two factors said to be plausibly or intelligibly related were actually totally irrelevant to each other. Allowing this takes us to the verge of self-contradiction. For it seems that it would make more sense to deny such an assertion.[6]

There is considerable bite to my truth-condition claim. It precludes contending that regularity analysis and the establishment of relevance by probabilistic reasoning are immaterial to an assertion of plausibility of connection. (Cf. White, *Foundations of Historical Knowledge*, pp. 81, 83.)

And, paradoxically, precluding this contention is precisely what is required if the theme of re-enactment is to be preserved in an analysis of historical explanation. For just insofar as it is claimed that regularity analysis and probabilistic reasoning are themselves irrelevant to judgments of plausibility, the distinction between the intelligible and the unintelligible—on which these judgments depend—is dissolved. There is no foundation for such distinctions. And this result goes against the principle from which we started: that in re-enactment the discriminations made are real ones and that in the successful re-enactment the factors selected are plausibly connected.

It is important to avoid a possible misinterpretation of the argument I am making. My claim is not that assertions of appropriateness are sanctioned by reference to degrees of regularity, so that the higher the degree the more intelligible the connection. Indeed, my argument supports a very different claim: that it is not the level of the probability value involved but, rather, the probabilistic establishment of relevance that sanctions such an assertion. My point has been that where relevance cannot be established we cannot justifiably make these assertions.

Regularity generalizations and hence the level or degree of regularity (read off in the form of a relative-frequency probability value) are only obliquely related to assertions of appropriateness—the connection being mediated by the notion of establishing relevance. Thus, with an eye to Brutus' joining the conspiracy of Cassius, we would consider the relevance of J (joining a conspiracy of assassination) to D (countering despotism) to be established, regardless of what particular value $p(J,D)$ has in fact, only if the indicated value would afford satisfaction of the matrix of basic relevance relationships: that is, the relationships

6. Cf. Wittgenstein's remark: "From its *seeming* to me—or to everyone—to be so, it doesn't follow that it *is* so. What we ask is whether it can make sense to doubt it" (*On Certainty*, p. 2e, sec. 2).

of simple relevance, where D is relevant to J within some very inclusive reference class, of "channeling" or "filtering out," and of the preservation of relevance under conditions of epistemic constraint.

Regularity generalizations are invoked in my analysis in virtue of the contribution they make to probabilistic reasoning in establishing relevance. But no particular degree of regularity, no particular level or cut-off point ("close to 1" or "at least ½") is mandated; the levels required are indefinitely variable, for what particular value will do the trick in a given matrix depends on what *other* values happen to be involved.[7]

In short, a generic statement of appropriateness does not assert or imply or entail any particular degree of regularity. Even regularity generalizations contributing low-level probability values would suffice, in a given matrix, to yield probabilistic relevance. And such generalizations are enough to support an assertion of plausible connection inductively; they are the only support required here. There should be nothing surprising in this: for example, all three of the illustrations I have used in this chapter—the accommodation between Charles and Rollo, Caesar's invasion, the adherence of Brutus to the conspiracy of Cassius—involved characteristically low-level generalizations. Indeed, I tend to regard these as representing the typical case in history.

Accordingly, I have thought it sufficient to say that evidence for the truth of any generic assertion of appropriateness could be found within the entire range of regularity generalizations. But it seems that the required degree of regularity, in most cases, is going to lie somewhere between "never" or "just this once," on the one side, and "always" or "close to 1," on the other. And, since the specification of something more exact within this range does not seem called for, and since the general tendency appears to be towards the lower end, we need go no further than "loose" regularity generalizations.

A generic statement of appropriateness such as "J is appropriate in the light of D" *means* that there is an intelligible material connection between J (joining a conspiracy) and D (countering despotism). It says

7. I have said that a *zero* probability value could not support an assertion of plausibility. But this can be regarded as a special case—a limiting case—of the analysis I have offered. For a zero probability value could never afford satisfaction of the matrix of relevance relationships and, hence, could never figure in the establishment of a truth condition for an assertion of intelligible connection. Accordingly, I have stipulated that the contributed probability values must be greater than zero: that is, there must exist some degree of regularity where we assert appropriateness ($p[J, D] = n > 0$).

that D as a reason for doing J is intelligible or that doing J for such a reason is understandable. Now something, I have argued, is entailed by such an assertion *when it is a true one*: it implies that J (joining a conspiracy) and D (countering despotism) actually do go or "fit" together sometimes.

Surely then, it could be countered, talk of appropriateness, as holding between D and J, can be construed as pointing to the fact that the things named by D and J are implicated in a *nomic* regularity network. For to say that they "belong" together or "go" together indicates that there are some conditions which, together with an instance of D (curbing despotism), would bring about one of J (joining a conspiracy). Hence, such talk obliquely refers to a complex scheme of conditions and consequences which, if it were filled in more than just sketchily, would take the form of a regularity *law*. In other words, it might well be contended that a generic assertion of appropriateness implies, when true, that a regularity law *could* (*empirically* could) exist, insofar as it implies that there are some conditions which, together with an instance of D, would bring about one of J. This brings us to an important argument of Morton White's.

It might well be contended, along lines White has suggested, that there exists, or would exist, if we could state all these conditions fully and clearly, an empirical law "for all persons x: if x is D and if x satisfies certain other conditions, say R, S, and T, then J happens." Accordingly, one could reasonably claim that a general statement of appropriateness ("J—joining a conspiracy—is appropriate in the light of D—curbing despotism") is equivalent to the statement that there *exists* such a law. (Whether the law is conceived as an "always" one or as a "usually" one is a matter of indifference to the argument as I am advancing it.) [8]

Of course, the alleged equivalence could be said to hold without anyone being in a position, in a given case, to state all of these conditions; indeed, some of them may not even be known, or ever known at all. Moreover, a reason for this difficulty in stating conditions could

8. It is important to note that the equivalence is to the statement that there exists a law; hence White has called his position "existential regularism" (see *Foundations of Historical Knowledge*, esp. p. 60; and also pp. 56–57, 61). The basic idea of "existential regularism" was anticipated by Donald Davidson; see his "Actions, Reasons, Causes," esp. pp. 698–699; and also his "Causal Relations," pp. 91–92. I should add that my own position, in the first part of this chapter, is much indebted to White's book, especially to ch. 3 ("Explanatory Statements"), pp. 56–104 (in particular pp. 60, 75).

readily be given: it is due to the inherent complexity of human affairs. (See White, *Foundations of Historical Knowledge*, p. 97.) Even so, anyone who was prepared to assert the equivalence would believe— and this strikes me as the very heart of White's analysis—that a generic assertion of appropriateness (of the form "for all persons x: if Dx then Jx is appropriate") is true if and only if a certain empirical law could exist. (See White, *Foundations of Historical Knowledge*, pp. 60, 80, 84, 94, 103.) In short, a reasonable argument could be made that the postulated existence of a regularity law is a truth-condition for a generic hypothetical of appropriateness.

Now suppose we were inclined to buy White's argument. It would be readily agreed at the outset, I imagine, that the consequence of this argument is something quite remote and abstract, particularly in light of the admitted fact that we can expect to satisfy this truth-condition only rarely, not having the laws themselves stated or any real prospect of ever having many of them stated. Hence, we are really asserting merely that the fact of existence of such a law, and not the fact of the law itself, is the truth-condition. This is just a logical point meant to show how hypotheticals of appropriateness and regularity laws are related conceptually. We are making no claims on facts that we do not have, nor are we claiming to produce laws that we cannot.

Even so, admitting White's argument has the effect of reintroducing regularity laws into the logical structure of re-enactment explanation. For if the *existence* of a law is the truth-condition of a generic assertion of appropriateness, then we supplant my earlier truth-condition claim, which in effect is satisfied by producing even a "loose" regularity generalization (so long as relevance can be established), with a much stronger one: that the existence of a law is the truth-condition in question.

At the same time, White's analysis is rather accommodating to a general strategy of retaining assertions of appropriateness. What he has said affects the *logic* of their use but not the fact of their continued usefulness. For the very complexity of the law that the investigator would have to produce, but cannot produce, to fill in the merest "sketch" of the nomic regularity network in a given case provides the reason for his use, or presumption, of a hypothetical of appropriateness. Moreover, since the conditions requiring fulfillment are so numerous, it should be clear why D (countering despotism) and J (joining a conspiracy of assassination) do happen together only sometimes, rather than always or usually, and why we actually do have only "loose" regularity generalizations rather than laws.

Indeed, White's analysis provides a rationale for saying that we have in hypotheticals of appropriateness something that will never collapse into empirical laws; for we "have" the hypotheticals and we do not and probably will not have the laws. The laws are like far distant heavenly bodies; they exert very, very little gravitational pull on the hypotheticals of appropriateness. There is no prospect of the one being drawn into the other. There is only the slight pull of loose regularity generalizations already noted: assertions of appropriateness are not absolutely free-floating in explanatory space.

White's analysis seems so concessionary on points I want to make that it sets one to wondering why I do not just accept it. There seems to be so little real ground of difference: I make the capacity to formulate regularity generalizations, albeit "loose" ones, that would satisfy relevance relationships eligible for truth-condition status but allow that D and J (where one is appropriate in light of the other) are actually in some sort of regularity matrix; White starts from this point and says that the *existence* of the law that would state nomic regularity, if it could be formulated, is the eligible truth-condition.

Exactly what is at stake in deciding between White's criterion and my own? It seems that something like the following is at issue: it is clear that the truth-condition I favor can be satisfied, even by "low level" regularity generalizations; it is not clear that White's truth-condition can be satisfied at all. How can we say that such-and-so law *exists?* That is, how can we say it short of actually producing the law?

There is, White argues, a fairly ready way of supporting the claim that a general law *exists*, and hence of allowing for the satisfaction of his stipulated truth-condition, without being able to state the law fully and clearly or even to know *all* of its conditions. We can, he says, provide *inductive* support for the claim that such-and-so law exists.

We can start by producing loose regularity generalizations; for raw regularity data, even of a low probability value, offer an order of evidence for these existence claims. We can begin with a quite loose generalization like "if P then sometimes T," which has a fairly low relative-frequency probability value (say below ½, i.e., $p[T, P] < ½$). Now, where we have this value and it can be raised by adding Q to P, so that "if P and Q then often T" has a higher probability value (say ½), then we can say that this provides inductive support for the claim that there exists an empirical law which has P and Q among its antecedent conditions and T, either always or usually, for its consequence. (See White, *Foundations of Historical Knowledge*, pp. 86–87.)

It seems to me that the crucial consideration lies at this point. In my analysis, loose regularity generalizations can function as the needed inductive support for asserting appropriateness or intelligible material connection between, say, D (countering despotism) and J (joining a conspiracy). The truth-condition for the general statement "J is appropriate in the light of D" is the *fact* of a corresponding relevance-satisfying generalization or, to put the matter precisely, of the state of affairs that this regularity generalization formulates. But in White's analysis, loose regularity generalizations function to support the claim that there *exists* a regularity *law*. The law itself is the truth-condition and the support that loose regularity generalizations offer to, say, a causal attribution or one of appropriateness is indirect, mediated by way of the law. Hence, laws *per se*, as distinct from mere regularity generalizations, play a logically necessary role in White's account of action explanations; whereas in my account the logically necessary role in question is taken by regularity generalizations *per se*, insofar as these are required by a piece of probabilistic reasoning, rather than by laws.

Now, if it can be shown that these loose regularity generalizations *cannot* inductively support the claim that a law exists, this would constitute a decisive inhibition on White's analysis; for *laws* would be removed as the crucial linchpins that hold assertions of appropriateness in a linkage with regularity generalizations. On the other hand, in extricating hypotheticals of appropriateness from this conceptual entanglement with regularity laws, we would be removing laws from the logical structure of re-enactment explanation altogether, at least to the extent that it was claimed they have a *necessary* role there.

Let us return to White's inductive support argument, to see if it can be sustained. The logic of White's argument is that *increasing* probability value, as we add conditions to P, constitutes the needed evidence that a law exists. To say this, though, it seems we would need to know not only the probability value of "if P and Q then often T" (say ½) but also the value of that formula when some third condition is added, say R, and know that the probability value of "if P and Q and R then quite often T" is higher than ½.

Historical Explanation

Suppose we did know all this. Would that provide evidence for saying that there *exists* a law, the antecedent clause of which is *partially* formulated as "if P and Q and R"? It would do so only if it provides adequate evidence for saying that a law exists that has antecedent conditions *other than* "P and Q and R." Now it is not clear in my mind that it does.

In any event, White has provided no criterion for what is to count as *good* or *adequate* inductive evidence for the statement that a law exists. We are left, then, with the rather crude claim that increasing relative-frequency probability value, of the sort I have been describing (i.e., a probability less than ½ increases to ½ and then to something greater than ½), constitutes such a criterion.

The matter is obviously complex. But I would suggest that the concept of "inductive evidence for a statement" is *formally* like the notion of statistical or relative-frequency probability. On this suggestion, the logical relation of *confirmation* between statements h (hypothesis) and e (evidence) would be represented as c (h, e) = v (where v is the inductive evidence value). I do not want to argue for this suggestion; I do want to point out that we have reason to believe that White would accept it.[9]

Of course the argument comes on the question what value v should have in order for us to say that h (here the statement that a law *exists*) is confirmed by e (here the statement that relative-frequency probability value is increasing). I suspect, on the basis of one of his passages, that White would opt for *at least* "close to 1" (see *Foundations of Historical Knowledge*, pp. 92–93; also p. 102).

In any case, though, I do not see how we could intelligibly talk this way unless we actually had some regularity laws to provide the data necessary to establish a value for v in the matter we are discussing. Since White admits that in history and the other social sciences we have no such laws, or very few, we would have to rely on our experience with natural laws. I have no reason to believe, however, that in

9. For a brief discussion of adequate inductive evidence, see Hempel, "Aspects," p. 381–393, esp. p. 385. Hempel distinguishes between what he calls "inductive" probability and "statistical" probability by saying that the former is " a quantitative logical relation between statements" and the latter "a quantitative empirical relation between kinds or classes of events." Although he says these two "must be sharply distinguished," he goes on to say that they "have a common formal structure . . . in virtue of which both of them qualify as probabilities" (p. 385). The passage of White's I have in mind is the one about "constant conjunction" on p. 80 of his *Foundations of Historical Knowledge*.

natural science one would take mere increasing relative-frequency probability value as providing the required confirmation. What would also be required, at the very minimum, I suspect, is the actual achievement of a fairly high relative-frequency value with "if P and Q and R and S then very frequently T." Hence, that regularity generalization would itself have to be close to "close to 1" to meet this criterion and to give the desired value to v. From this it follows that there would have to be regularity generalizations in history and in social science which actually have the fairly high relative-frequency value in question. Since White does not produce much in the way of examples of these, and appears to think there are not many, and since we already have reason to think that there are very few "strong" regularity generalizations in history, the setting of this standard would prove quite destructive to White's analysis.

All of this is somewhat speculative; for, as I have already said, White does not provide us with a criterion for adequate evidence in the first place. It may well be that this is ultimately an unimportant issue in White's eyes and that he does not deal with this problem because he is already committed to determinism. For it seems this is the only way White's analysis could go through in the absence of such a criterion. I will not press this point, though, since White never actually argues for, even though he does affirm, a determinist view. (See *Foundations of Historical Knowledge*, pp. 5, 96–97.)

White could claim that increasing relative-frequency value constitutes adequate evidence, not for saying that a *law* exists, but, rather, for saying that some (nomically) regular *state of affairs* exists. But this move is open to the same objections that have just been lodged above. Moreover, it would actually be very damaging to White's analysis because it breaks down the alleged equivalence of saying "we have reason for believing that an existential regularity exists" and saying "we have reason for believing that a *law* exists." For it implies that what is a good reason for saying the former is not a good one for saying the latter. Since White's positing of laws in the first place was based on this alleged equivalence, the bridge whereby he would pass from belief in the existence of a state of affairs to belief in the existence of a law would be forever down.

Nonetheless, let us allow (just for the moment) that mere increasing relative-frequency probability value *is* sufficient to the matter at hand. I do not think even this concession would save White's analysis.

Historical Explanation

White's central claim, as I read it, is that, starting from "if P then sometimes T" and given the fact of increasing probability value, we can provide adequate inductive evidence for saying that there exists a law that has P as a *part* of its antecedent clause and T as its consequence. The problem is that we may have evidence for saying that *a* law exists; but we do not seem to have evidence for saying that it will contain either P or T. It might be, rather, that the law will contain some as yet unknown (but true) *redescriptions* of P and T—or, indeed, not even contain entities such as P and T at all.

The point is that the satisfaction of White's criterion of increasing probability value establishes the existence of no *specific* law. Hence, even if we allow that criterion, we could not claim to have evidence that a law *exists* such that P and T are included in its relevant clauses. And, if existential regularism requires that we be able at a minimum to specify a *part* of the law that is said to exist—and I think it does—then this point about redescriptions is surely fatal to White's basic analysis. [10]

Unfortunately, only one thing could ever really satisfy White's postulated truth-condition—that a given regularity law with certain specific antecedent conditions exists—and that is the production, with all of its detail, of the law in question. It seems that White is actually locked into the Hempelian position, insofar as his account of existential regularism ultimately does, on its law side, require the production of a law or, failing that, of a nearly lawlike regularity generalization. With this point established, we can move back from the strong but inaccessible criterion favored by White to the weaker one that I have been advocating.

In my account, asserting appropriateness between two factors, say D (countering despotism) and J (joining an assassination plot), requires simply their mutual relevance, but not their implication in a nomic network. Relevance is established by probabilistic reasoning, in which regularity generalizations—for the most part merely "loose ones"—play a necessary role. The necessary condition, in my argument, requires merely that there *exist* a relationship between the two factors

10. My argument is an adaptation of one by Davidson ("Actions, Reasons, Causes," pp. 697–699, esp. p. 698). Davidson alleges that it is an error to think "that singular causal statements necessarily indicate, by the concepts they employ, the concepts that will occur in the entailed law" (p. 698). Davidson cites the example of ordinary language predictions about the weather, and the kinds of low level regularity statements we might generate here, over against truly scientific meteorological laws.

(e.g., D and J) such that a regularity generalization, though not necessarily a law, could be formulated and such that this generalization would satisfy a matrix of probabilistic relevance relationships. And *this* condition can be satisfied whether or not the generalization (in the form $p[J, D] = n > 0$) could be amplified in the direction of ever-increasing probability values.

It is clear then, if my argument for what might be called "existential probabilism" has been acceptable, that regularity generalizations are required and can function to provide inductive support for generic assertions of appropriateness. The argument I advanced against regularity laws does not apply in this case. For we can get loose regularity generalizations, even though we cannot get the general laws or the probability laws that Hempel has described—and even though we cannot attain the very high probability values that White's position appears, upon analysis, to require.

In saying this, moreover, I have provided a significant qualification to Dray's (and Collingwood's) contention that there is a logical-type difference between explanations that use or presuppose assertions of appropriateness and those that subsume deeds under "covering" regularity generalizations. For it must be granted, I have argued, that re-enactment explanation does depend, insofar as the probabilistic establishment of relevance is concerned, on at least loose regularity generalizations—though not necessarily on regularity generalizations in law form.

I believe, finally, that I have disposed of the troublesome claim that, since hypotheticals of appropriateness do not assert the same thing as regularity generalizations and since they cannot be reduced to or replaced by them, we have gotten rid of any need to confirm the truth of these connective principles by using regularity analysis. Insofar as our question has to do with the warranted assertibility of appropriateness, our answer is to be found in the probabilistic establishment of relevance. To this extent our justifying grounds for particular connection at the material or descriptive level, our generic assertions of appropriateness, are for their truth logically parasitical on the regularity generalizations that probabilistic reasoning requires.

Eight

On the Logic of Explanation by Re-enactment

What we have done, if my argument in the previous chapter is sound, is to assign a role to regularity generalizations different from that found in Hempel and in the "science of human nature" of Hume and Mill. I have argued that the role they assigned to regularity generalizations is actually played by generic assertions of appropriateness. Rather than "cover" explanations, as premises from which we derive the explanandum or, alternatively, the agent's purpose, regularity generalizations warrant the assertibility of general hypotheticals of appropriateness. They are one step removed from connection-justifying grounds; their job is to support the statements, these generic assertions of appropriateness, which do fill that role.

It also follows in this analysis, however, that *any* assertion of appropriateness—whether generic or individualized—does indicate, albeit obliquely, an actual empirical connection. In this respect it is different from an aesthetic judgment or a moral one, from a prescription of normative rationality or a conceptual truth.

Now, if I were arguing merely that a historian must use, or tacitly presuppose, assertions of appropriateness and if I had otherwise indicated my acceptance of the basic Hempelian analysis, in either its inductive or its deductive form, then I would be open to a devastating

146

The Logic of Explanation

critique. For it could be claimed that these assertions of appropriateness amount, in actual *empirical* content, to nothing more than weak regularity generalizations and that such generalizations are not sufficient to support explanations of the sort Hempel had specified in his two models. This charge would clearly be just: if all I had done was simply to replace regularity laws with weaker regularity generalizations, then I would be convicted by the very standards that I had originally acknowledged. Or if all I had done was tie in judgments of appropriateness with probabilistic relevance, then I would be open to the telling charge that explanation by re-enactment, despite the great hullabaloo raised about laws and the other initial disclaimers, really is governed by regularity analysis and by essentially statistical considerations.

However, these charges are not effective against the general position I have been trying to construct. This is the point at which appeals to the logical framework of my discussion of assertions of appropriateness would become important.

In my analysis, the explanatory force of a nondefective re-enactment, in the case of any given action, is not provided by generic assertions of appropriateness. These were not conceived as freestanding hypotheticals, on the order of Hempelian laws, which "covered" instances of J (joining a conspiracy) and D (countering despotism) thereby allowing for a "deduction" of the particular deed to be explained—in the example at hand, Brutus' deed. Rather, the re-enactment was regarded as explanatory only insofar as it could be conceived as an instantiation of a basic schema for action-explanations. Generic assertions of appropriateness operate in the individual case within a conceptual framework that organizes the network of hypotheticals employed, or presupposed, and gives it focus. It is not these hypothetical assertions that govern the placement of the various facts and select out a deed as the done thing in that particular behavioral circumstance but, rather, the principle of explanatory adequacy—the schema—which they subserve.

Here assertions of appropriateness serve to *validate* the particular set of facts as the instantiation of the schema R in the case at hand. But it is the schema itself that allows us to go from these particular facts, from these thought-factors and this deed of the agent, to the explanation "he did x because he thought y."

At this juncture it would be well to recall that the flow of particular facts into the explanatory system is from the investigator's body of available evidence. Without evidence, without data, the apparatus I have been describing would yield no explanations. So, when I talk about validating facts, I am distinguishing this from producing them or verifying (confirming) them evidentially. Validating has to do, not with whether facts are evidentially founded or with whether a given piece of evidence "leads" to a certain conclusion, but with whether facts (presumably supported by evidence) are plausibly or intelligibly related to one another.

The crucial idea involved in validating is not evidential truth but understanding. And my point has been that an explanation which yields understanding, an explanation in which the various thought-factors and the deed performed are intelligibly connected, is a better explanation of an action than the one which does not. The model that integrates the basic schema with the standard of understanding is the preferred one for the explanation of actions in history.

Thus, for facts well grounded in the available evidence to count as satisfying the basic schema in a given explanation we must not only see them as instances of the elements or "places" in the schema but also see them as exhibiting materially, under the description we have given them, an intelligible connection. For example, the explanation of Brutus' deed involves the assertion that his joining the conspiracy of Cassius is plausible in light of his desire to counter the threat posed by Caesar to the republican constitution of Rome. This assertion would validate these facts for use under the schema, where one of them would take the place marked *deed* and the other the place marked *situational motivation*. But ultimately it is the generic form of the assertion which actively discriminates what is intelligibly related in a relationship of plausibility, thereby providing the apt characterization that "*J* (joining a conspiracy of assassination) is plausible in view of *D* (wanting to counter despotism)." And since our singular assertion about Brutus is but a special case of this generic assertion and can be said to hold in virtue of it, I have emphasized that intelligibility of connection at the generic level underwrites or warrants the insertion of a set of facts as fulfilling of conditions under the schema.[1]

1. Scriven has distinguished evidentiary (or "truth-justifying grounds") from what he calls "role-justifying grounds" in an explanation (see "Truisms," esp. pp. 446–448). Generic assertions of appropriateness have been discussed in my book principally as "role-justifiers"; they perform this function when they validate, in a given case, treating *that*

The Logic of Explanation

Assertions of appropriateness, then, can be seen as operating in the logical space intermediate between a very high-order but empirically vacuous explanatory schema and a determinate body of available evidence. The schema specifies the sorts of connections that must hold if an explanation is to go through. Here it would be useful to have in mind the lines of what was called earlier the triangle of explanation.

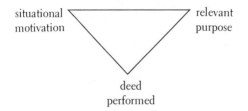

The body of evidence provides the detail of content that, subject to the test of understanding, of re-enactment, can satisfy the terms of the schema. Assertions of appropriateness validate a particular instantiation of the schema, consistent with the available evidence, by warranting as intelligible or plausible the holding of these specified connections betwen particular data provided by the evidence.

I think we are now in position to see, despite superficial resemblances, the main differences between Hempel's account of the logic of action-explanations and the one I have been offering. They are two radically different basic models for explanation. The model Hempel was explicating presents explanation as the logical operation of *deriving* from premises, either with deductive certainty or with inductive high probability, the deed that wants explaining. The other is the *instantiation* model I have been discussing.

When we explain re-enactively we simply exhibit certain specified connections as holding between particular thought-factors and between these and the particular deed we are explaining. Ultimately these specified connections are spelled out in what I have called a schema for action-explanations (i.e., the formula R). An explanation,

---

specific deed (Brutus' joining the conspiracy) and *that* specific situational motivation (his wanting to counter the despotism of Caesar) as fulfilling conditions, i.e., as taking the roles specified therein, of the schema for action-explanation. In providing "role-justifying grounds" these assertions are very like what Scriven calls "truisms"; however, truisms differ from generic assertions of appropriateness in that the former are, as Scriven puts it, "guarded generalizations" ("Truisms," pp. 463–468, esp. p. 465).

in the individual case, is given simply in virtue of presenting this particular action and these particular thought-factors as an application of
the schema R. Hence, all explanatory re-enactments are governed by
and their conclusions derive explanatory force from it. Accordingly,
we could say, "schema for action-explanations intelligibly instantiated = a full-fledged explanation of a particular action." Or we could
say, alternatively, that where one can re-enact the deed by "going
through" a particular instantiation of the schema we have an explanation that passes the test of understanding.

This instantiation model provides the logical context of my entire
discussion of general hypotheticals of appropriateness. Now I have admitted to a certain similarity between these and Hempelian regularity
laws. Specifically, I have indicated that hypotheticals of appropriateness are like laws in that the use of each is concerned with the explanatory *connection*—at the material or descriptive level—of, say, a
particular instance of J (joining a conspiracy) with a particular instance
of D (countering despotism). But I would want to add that the actual
use in the case of each is quite different.

The Hempelian use of a general hypothetical is to show, where possible, that *types* of J and D are connected in a regularity law. Hence,
we are able to *infer* from an instance of D (a so-called initial condition) to an instance of J (the deed to be explained). General assertions
of appropriateness, however, are not really used to infer from a D to a
J. Rather, they affirm the claim that D and J are intelligibly connected
so that, for example, an instance of D could be the situational motivation to which an instance of J stands as an action to be taken.

So, we do have two quite distinct *uses* of general statements, the
Hempelian and the re-enactive. In one case, the Hempelian, they are
used for purposes of inference: to connect one sort of instance with
another inferentially. In the other case, the re-enactive, they are used
for purposes of *justification:* to warrant a connection of particular facts
as plausible or intelligible, thereby validating the subsumption of these
facts under the schema in a given explanation.

Interestingly, this difference between inferential and justificatory use
is mirrored even at the point where regularity generalizations are
themselves introduced into my account of the logic of explanation by
re-enactment. For I argued that a necessary condition of asserting appropriateness between two factors, say, J (joining a conspiracy) and D
(countering despotism), is their mutual relevance and that relevance is

to be established by probabilistic reasoning, in which regularity generalizations (typically sublawful ones) play a necessary role. The logical relationship between the existence of a piece of probabilistic reasoning and a judgment of appropriateness is that of truth-condition for an assertion. Hence the "covering" regularity generalization (e.g., $p[J, D] > 0$)—insofar as it could satisfy a matrix of relevance relationships—would be said to support inductively, or confirm, an assertion of appropriateness (e.g., one that says "D is an intelligible reason for joing J").

Even at this level in my analysis, moreover, there is no inference to the conclusion that Brutus *joined* the conspiracy of Cassius, no logical detachment of the deed (J_b), afforded by Brutus' desire to counter the despotic threat posed by Caesar (D_b) together with the fact that J_b and D_b are mutually relevant. There is no freestanding, detachable conclusion because the probabilistic establishment of relevance between the one sort of thing, J (joining a conspiracy), and the other, D (wanting to counter despotism), does not allow for such a conclusion. Rather, the conclusion would always take the form, ". . . then (by probabilistic reasoning) J_b is *relevant* to D_b." Thus, were we to make explicit the actual functioning of a regularity generalization in an explanation, we would find no ground for an inferential argument from instance to instance (e.g., from a D to a J). There is in this point, too, an interesting logical symmetry between a judgment of appropriateness and the piece of probabilistic reasoning that would be invoked to support it.[2]

It is, of course, no accident that two different patterns for explanation have developed: the one characteristic of explanation by re-enactment (the instantiation-justification pattern, which we have just been

---

2. I am indebted to Ilkka Niiniluoto for the criticisms of my position to be found in his interesting paper "Inductive Explanation, Propensity, and Action." The development of my views in this and the previous chapter indicate two points about probabilistic reasoning, in the case of action-explanation, which run counter to the general drift of his thinking. First, probability statements (in a matrix of relevance relationships) have a justificatory, rather than an inferential, role. And, second, such probabilistic reasoning does *not* take the form of an argument, in which an instantial or event-happening conclusion is inferred (inductively) from premises. This latter point is directly opposed to Niiniluoto's own constructive account (in which he develops the idea of a *propensity* argument). I would want to add as well that the low value (i.e., the low relative-frequency probability value) of the propensity statements typically invoked in action-explanations would also militate against—strongly, in my view—any notion of inductive *inference* here.

noting) and the other characteristic of "covering law" theory. Each pattern belongs to a different basic model of explanation. Ultimately, what is presupposed is that there are two irreducible kinds of activity in the world: action and causality. The one model is clearly suitable to actions, what with its apparatus of purposes and motives, and the other to physical causation.

I realize that, in saying this, I am putting things the way Collingwood did. Hempel, no doubt, would want to deny this basic dualism or, at least, to say that it makes no difference to the explanations we give. His position is that the model of explanation is invariant between cases of explaining actions and cases of causally explaining physical events. Accordingly, he wants to endorse the deployment of the causal model as the only, or the basic, one.

To argue as Hempel does seems to me perfectly reasonable, since he does not make the elementary mistake of confusing the two explanatory models. His claim is that the action model reduces to, or requires, the causal one. Indeed, one could not argue this case intelligently without seeing the alleged difference in the first place. The point of Hempel's argument is to show that the distinction is not a deep one, that it cannot be sustained under analysis.

On the other hand, one could argue that the distinction is really there, that the models have a deep difference and that analysis reinforces our initial perception of the difference. It is this point that I have been trying to bring out.[3] I think the arguments we have considered up to now tend to support my noncausalist point, as *prima facie* sound.

It seems, however, that in the analysis I have given there is still some ground left for maneuver by those who advocate a necessary role for general laws in the explanation of actions. I have been arguing that generic assertions of appropriateness perform their job of connection-justifying grounds individually and piecemeal but that they do it in tandem, so to speak, within the conceptual framework provided by the schema for action-explanations R. Now it could be suggested that the entire set of hypotheticals in the case of any given explanation be regarded as a single, amalgamated assertion of appropriateness. Would not there be in such an event, the advocate of the general law argu-

3. I recommend a reading of the first two chapters of von Wright's book, *Explanation and Understanding*, in connection with the argument of the last few paragraphs. (See also his later book, *Causality and Determinism*, esp. pp. 48–53, 57–58, 128.)

The Logic of Explanation

ment asks, a regularity generalization that corresponds to this consolidated hypothetical of appropriateness?

We might, following this suggestion, take the piecemeal assertions of appropriateness which functioned in Collingwood's explanation of Caesar's invasion of Britain and formulate these as a single composite hypothetical. Thus, we would take the three crucial ones that served to fill in the lines of the triangle of explanation, thereby getting: "(a) If a military leader wants to curb hostile incursions and (b) if he proposes to accomplish this pacification through conquest and (c) if invading could be judged as a means to, or as a part of, accomplishing this pacification, then his invading is an intelligible or plausible course of action."

The claim is that this hypothetical could be restated in regularity form: "if (a) and (b) and (c) then the military leader invades (with degree of regularity)." This hypothetical in regularity form is not, as it stands, a regularity *generalization*. However, it would become one if we were actually to check out the regularity involved—looking at cases drawn from past and present in Europe and India and South America and so on—and to assign a relative-frequency probability value to it. The claim, then, is that corresponding to the *composite* assertion of appropriateness is a hypothetical formula which can take a high probability value. Thus we might say "if (a) and (b) and (c) then the military leader invades quite often (i.e., with a considerable degree of regularity)."

I do not see, however, that there is any difficulty posed for my analysis in acceding to this claim. For I could argue that the relationship of my amalgamated general hypothetical of appropriateness to a corresponding regularity generalization, if indeed there is one, is exactly the same as the relationship of the component piecemeal assertions of appropriateness to their corresponding regularity generalizations. In either case, the regularity generalization would merely take its role within a matrix of relevance relationships, thereby satisfying a truth-condition for the hypothetical of appropriateness; in so doing it would provide an inductive ground for *asserting* appropriateness in that case. This is all that my analysis commits me to saying and saying this does accommodate the claim currently being urged.

Of course, our putative regularity generalization would likely have, as it appears to have in the example cited from the explanation of Caesar's invasion, a higher probability value than any of its constituent regularity generalizations. This is merely to say that the drift of that explanation as a whole has a sounder empirical weight than does any single one of the assertions of appropriateness which go to make it up. But this is surely to be expected, given the analysis already offered of the nature of the empirical commitment of any general hypothetical of appropriateness.

This point, by the way, adds another reason why the fact of relatively low-grade inductive support was not troubling in the case of any given constituent assertion of appropriateness. However, the reason here is not that the probability value of the whole ensemble is "close to 1" or even that the value increases incrementally toward that point each time we add in another relevant condition; rather, it is principally that the addition of relevant information always serves to *raise* an initially low value for any one of the constituents. (This point is developed in an interesting way by Newman; see his *Explanation by Description*, esp. pp. 44–45, 63–64.)

Even so, it is worth noting that where there was a regularity generalization corresponding to an amalgamated hypothetical of appropriateness that generalization would not, in all likelihood, be a regularity *law*. Certainly the regularity generalization just cited, allowing that it is one, is not a law. If we were actually to do the regularity analysis what we would get, I am suggesting, in almost all cases is not something that happens "always" or "usually" (close to 1) but, rather, something that at most happens "with a high degree of regularity." And this would not satisfy the advocate of the general law position, since what he requires is not just that there be a regularity generalization but that it be a law.

Presumably, though, this defect could be remedied. We could do so by expanding the antecedent clause of any of these regularity generalizations, by taking in more of the facts which were said to have fulfilled other of the necessary conditions of the basic schema in any given explanation. We could, for example, simply take the whole set of facts cited as fulfilling these conditions in the case of the explanation of Caesar's invasion, suitably generalize our description of each of them, put the whole thing in hypothetical form, and get a regularity law. Or, at least, this is what is being claimed.

Here we could say:

IF (a) a military leader is bothered by hostile incursions by x and wants to curb these incursions, and

(b) invading is one of the courses of action along with D, S, and E, that he might take, and

(c) he proposes to pacify x through conquest, and

(d) this proposal is not overridden by any other purpose that he has, and

(e) he does not prefer any of the alternative courses of action—D, S, or E—to invading, and

(f) invading can be judged a means to, or part of accomplishing, what he proposes, and

(g) he is able, personally and situationally, to invade,

THEN he invades always or usually ("close to 1").

If we were to take this step and to lay all of it out in hypothetical form, doing as a general practice what we have just done in this one case, the plausibility of the general law argument would be altogether dissipated. For clearly this hypothetical as it stands is *not* a regularity generalization and, hence, not a law: it is simply a generalized version of the facts whereby we had explained Caesar's invasion in the first place.

Indeed, the conviction that the whole "if . . . then . . ." statement just cited is a regularity law actually precedes, in the case at hand, any assignment of probability value to it by regularity analysis. So much, then, for the claim that it is really a regularity law. In fact, the formula just cited might conceivably, in its complete form, have no probability value at all. It would, for example, not have one if the particular set of facts mentioned in the formula had occurred only once, i.e., only once as a set.

I should add that there is a problem posed for White's analysis in that these one-instance, lawlike assertions count as evidence *against* the claim that there exists a law. The reason for this is clear enough. We have increasing relative-frequency probability values as we move from "if P then sometimes T" to "if P and Q and R then very frequently T." But when we come to the stipulated one-instance "If . . . then . . ." formula in question, it has no probability value at all (for there cannot be regularity in just one instance). Hence, we no longer have increasing relative-frequency probability value at this point. And since having these incremental increases constitutes, in White's account, our sole evidence for saying that a law *exists*, we must conclude on our evidence that a law does *not* exist. So, the one-instance "law" is a serious problem for White's "existential regularism," more serious than he allows (see *Foundations of Historical Knowledge*, esp. p. 26; also pp. 27, 37).

In any event, the "law" here was not used, nor could it have been presupposed, to cover Caesar's invasion, since *this* law can exist only after the facts are already put in their places, as fulfilling conditions of the schema for action-explanations. The "law" has no independent existence; as such, it cannot even be said to "confirm" or "justify" the explanation offered. Such laws are, Olafson says, "parasitic upon the rational [or re-enactment] explanations that have been given and thus really add nothing to our understanding of the events in question" ("Narrative History and the Concept of Action," p. 289).

All that we really have in any of these so-called laws is just the instantiation by singular facts of the basic schema itself. Putting these facts into a different form, by giving each a generalized description, is explanatorily empty and serves to disguise the essential character of the explanation we have given. For what governs each of these instantiations, and gives the singular facts cited therein explanatory force, is simply the schema for action-explanations.

The regularity "law" referred to in each case is itself nothing but a peculiar way of instantiating the self-same schema or principle, with those very facts this time under a generalized description rather than under a singular one. Or, to speak more precisely, it is merely a peculiar way of instantiating what I earlier called, following Ryle, the hypothetical *associated* with that principle.[4]

What my argument comes to, then, is that explanations in history, at least of the sort we have tried to capture with the notion of re-enactment, are not governed by regularity laws, or by the belief that some such laws exist.

Explanatory conclusions have the same standing whether we fluff them up into "law" form or not; for these conclusions are essentially independent of any "corresponding" laws, or even regularity generalizations. The facts cited in an explanation are instantiations, true enough; but they are instantiations of a principle of explanatory adequacy rather than of a general law.

There is another move available to the general law advocate. It is open to him to grant the point that the "law" developed by generalizing the facts of a given re-enactment explanation is not *as it stands* a

4. Ryle uses the term "corresponding" rather than "associated" in reference to these hypothetical statements (see " 'If,' 'So,' 'Because,' " pp. 326–328, 330–331).

regularity generalization. He could, however, still argue that it is susceptible of becoming one and that it would actually be a law if we were to establish by regularity analysis that what is said to happen does happen always or usually. He could then go on to argue that the conferring of law status on the facts, in the way I have just indicated, is a necessary feature of *confirming* the explanation offered.

The move is, however, of doubtful soundness. For it could be contended that any "law" established in this way would have precisely the same status as the principle of explanatory adequacy itself. The only way this particular deadlock could be broken, to the advantage of the general law position, is to show that the basic schema itself is some sort of empirical generalization. So, this would become the exact point at issue.

The dialectic of this argument has, I believe, served to bring out one point of interest. I suspect that the reason the general law advocates might have for wanting to graft regularity analysis onto explanations by re-enactment is that they actually do suppose the citing of the specific facts in question to be explanatory. This marks a common ground between the two positions I have been discussing and accords a measure of validity to the position I have been advancing. Accordingly, since it is accepted that the set of singular facts cited is truly explanatory, the argument for general laws goes on to conclude that a regularity law *must* be involved. The logic of this argument is that if we do have an explanation, then we must have it, somehow, in virtue of regularity laws.

That this is a phantom argument is something I will have to show. If it is true that what governs an explanatory re-enactment is the schema for action-explanations and that the singular facts cited are, in effect, an instantiation of that principle, it seems that advocacy of the general law position can take but one direction. The only recourse would be to claim that the basic schema is itself a general law. Or, what amounts to the same thing, to assert that the "if . . . then . . ." formula associated with the schema is a general law.

Nine

The Basic Schema:
A Question of Status

It is evident that we must devote some attention to the question of the *logical* status of the principle of explanatory adequacy itself. In particular, we must attend to the contention that the "if . . . then . . ." formula associated with the foundation principle could have the status of a general law. In short, we must consider whether that formula is an empirical statement. For if it is, that would reinstate the general law analysis, and on a far stronger basis than it has had up to now. Indeed for my purposes, the acceptance of the claim that the associated hypothetical R' is a general law would be decisive, since it would have the effect of grounding my entire analysis of the logic of re-enactment explanation in a single general law.

The formula for R' which follows would then be conceived as a law:

IF   (1) any person x is in a particular situation which he proposes to deal with in a certain way, and

     (2) one of the courses of action he might take is A, although alternatively he might take courses B, C, or D, and

     (3) his purpose is to handle the situation by accomplishing such-and-so thing, and

     (4) this purpose, or end in view, is not overridden by any other purpose that he has, and

158

The Basic Schema

(5) he does not prefer any of the alternative courses of action—B, C, or D—to doing A, and

(6) doing A is judged by him to be a means to, or part of accomplishing, his purpose, and

(7) he is able, personally and situationally, to do A,

THEN x does A.

It is, of course, obvious that the hypothetical formula R' is simply the general form of the conjectured "law" (in Chapter Eight) for military leaders invading, a law which was alleged to cover Caesar's invasion of Britain. The question now, and it is the crucial question, is whether the general formula R' itself is a law.

Arguments of two types could be developed in an attempt to show that the formula R' is a general law. We could describe them briefly as the indirect argument and the direct one.

The indirect argument proceeds by starting with some proposition about the meaning of the term "explanation" or about some feature believed to be essential to all explanations, and then arguing that the truth of this proposition requires that whatever plays the role of connecting the "he did w" part to the "because v" part in an explanation be a general law.

The other argument, the direct one, proceeds by examining the specific hypothetical formula associated with the schema and affirming, on the basis of this direct philosophical analysis, that the formula is an empirical statement. It would, of course, follow that if the formula was in all other respects like a general law and also was an empirical statement, it would be a general law.

In each case then, whether by the indirect or by the direct route, it would be concluded, given the analysis I have offered, that a general law *must* be involved at some point in explanation by re-enactment. Danto has provided an interesting account, of the indirect sort, in his book *Analytical Philosophy of Knowledge* (pp. 122–125; see also pp. 128–132).

This argument, which I have adapted to my own terminology and preoccupations without, I hope, distorting it, goes roughly as follows. Danto begins by saying, "In the typical case, we suppose ourselves to have explained . . . matters successfully when we show that something was . . . caused to happen, by the . . . other event[s] to which we have referred" (p. 123).

This simple account, Danto thinks, mandates a certain standard for

159

what an adequate explanation is. It is this: one event or set of events v cannot explain another event w "if, given that v occurred, w might not have, everything else being equal . . ." (p. 123). Danto's point is that "reference to v seems hardly explanatory if its occurrence is compatible with both the occurrence and the non-occurrence of w . . ." (p. 123). In short, where "the non-occurrence of w [the event to be explained] is compatible with the occurrence of v [the set of initial conditions]" (p. 123) there cannot be an *adequate* explanation of w by reference to v.

We can, of course, put Danto's point in a somewhat different idiom; we can put it in terms of true statements about v and w. Thus, we can say that w can be explained by v only where " 'w happens' cannot be false if 'v happens' is true . . ." (p. 123). Or, alternatively, we might say v can explain w only where the falsity of w is incompatible with the truth of v. Danto defends this second, true-false, way of putting his point: "[I]t seems to me a common feature of all possible explanations that they must fail if the explanans is true [e.g., v] and the explanandum [e.g., w] false: for what then has been explained?" (p. 125).

I take this criterion, which is intended to spell out an essential feature of all explanations, to be the initial proposition, the starting point, of Danto's argument. He goes on to say that "all this suggests that the *form* of an explanation should be deductive," that v and w "are related exactly as the premise and conclusion of a valid deductive argument" (p. 123). And this requires, of course, a "tight connection" (pp. 122, 128) between them, one that has the "odor of entailment" (p. 130). Thus, he generates out of his original truth-relationship criterion the notion of what he calls a "Deductivist criterion" (p. 125).

It is easy enough now to see his next step. Where v and w have the "tight connection" of a premise and conclusion in a valid deductive argument, they have it in virtue of the statement "if v then w." The Deductivist criterion can be satisfied, then, only by some such statement, of the form "if y then x," suitably generalized and functioning in *every* explanation. (For Danto's argument as to generalization, see *Analytical Philosophy of History*, p. 208, item [iii].)

Now it follows from this, if Danto's argument is correct, (a) that there must be a connective principle of this form operative in every explanation by re-enactment and (b) that the connective principle involved here must be a general law. Let us assume for the moment that

The Basic Schema

Danto's "Deductivist criterion" and the first step, point (a), present no problems. What are we committed to? Simply that there must be a generalized connective principle of the form "if y then x" wherever we explain "he did x" by saying "because y." And, of course, we are aware that this connective form might require us to say that the non-occurrence of the action designated by x is incompatible with the occurrence of the things that satisfy the conditions designated by y. If our proffered explanations cannot live up to this constraint, then we do not really have the requisite "tight connection" between x and y and we have thereby failed to conform to the original truth-value relationship which Danto has proposed for all explanations.

Now, one might say that since the v in "if v then w" is wholly unspecified—except as being the statement that "some event happens" or that "certain conditions obtain"—it could be satisfied by w. We would then have, as Danto himself recognized, a logical redundancy "if 'w happens' then 'w happens' " which nonetheless satisfies his deductivist criterion perfectly. But Danto specifically rules out all such explicit or syntactical redundancies. (See *Analytical Philosophy of Knowledge*, p. 123; also, *Analytical Philosophy of History*, p. 207.) And I think we can take Danto's stipulation that v and w here must be distinct events or things, not as an ad hoc device, but as a reasonable clarification of what the two criteria—the "semantical" (or truth-value relationship) and the "deductivist"—are asserting in his view.

Even so, it does not follow that whatever now satisfies the "if y then x" element required by these criteria must be a general law. For there are formulas which could satisfy it, without having explicitly (i.e., syntactically) any feature of logical redundancy, and still not be general laws. Indeed, as we think about it, analytic statements seem to be peculiarly fitted to satisfy Danto's criterion. For, after all, where we specify that w *cannot* be false where v is true or rule out that non-w might occur when v does, the relationship in those respects is the one that v and w would have if they were analytically connected—where the nonoccurrence of w is logically incompatible with the occurrence of v. And, were "if v then w" an analytic truth, it could not possibly be a general law.

Now it is certainly clear that Danto does not regard all analytic statements *per se* as logical redundancies. (Mathematical formulas, for example, are not in his view explicit or syntactical redundancies; see his *What Philosophy Is*, pp. 39–41.) So it is not clear exactly how

Danto would stand with respect to analytic statements, as to whether they should be included among or excluded from those that can take an explanatory role. In any event, Danto's argument is inconclusive so long as there are some statements that satisfy his criteria and that are logically necessary but not logically (that is, explicitly or syntactically) redundant.

Hence, it doesn't follow in any straightforward way that what satisfies Danto's semantical-cum-deductivist criterion must be a general law; for it could be an analytic statement. So, to make his point Danto must provide some argument to the effect that whatever takes the connection role, the "if *y* then *x*" role, *must* be a general law.

This is precisely the point at which Danto's argument breaks down. For he does not argue through to the conclusion he needs. Rather, he merely says that "the deductive model of explanation is most prominently identified as that of C. G. Hempel" and goes on to extol "it," presumably Hempel's version of the model, as "sound" (*Analytical Philosophy of Knowledge*, p. 124). In short, it would seem that he is merely assuming that only the general law analysis of Hempel can meet the "deductivist criterion."

That Danto explicitly makes this particular assumption is clear enough. He says, "[I]t is not easy to see how Donagan can, consistently with his assumption that historians explain, go on to affirm the deduction requirement, and at the same time reject the covering law requirement" (*Analytical Philosophy of History*, n. 1 to p. 229, on p. 310). But there is an easy rejoinder to Danto's remark: Donagan regarded the "covering law" to be an analytic statement and *not* a general law. It should be clear that I am not endorsing Donagan's claim but merely pointing out that in making it he is occupying the same logical ground as Danto. (See Donagan, "Popper-Hempel Reconsidered," pp. 132–133, 150.) Just because this is so, Danto must either show that the connective formula which takes the "if *y* then *x*" role *cannot* be analytic or that it *must* be a general law. Unfortunately, he does neither.

Let me add, now that I have made this point, that there is a deep dilemma for the regularity law position in Danto's argument. If the argument fails, as I believe it does, then we give up the sense of logical compulsion which has fueled the position all along, the notion that where we have an explanation we must have it, somehow, by virtue of a general law. On the other hand, if the argument succeeds we come up against the fact that we do not have the required regularity laws, ones sufficient to ground a deductive argument that yields the event to be explained, and hold little prospect of having them and, hence, have no explanations.

Indeed, the success of his argument is more cruel than its failure. For the maintenance of the criterion of deductivity from laws, as a necessary condition of explanation, rules out the alternative regularity law analyses, the inductive inference one offered by Hempel, White's "existential regularism," and Danto's own derivation and subsumption model. And, of course, it rules out all theories of statistical explanation (such as the one offered by Salmon).

Even so, Danto's argument does not seem to me a complete failure. It did, as I have pointed out, take one of its steps successfully. Danto was able to draw out the *form* "if y then x," suitably generalized, as a necessary consequence of his "semantical criterion" and he was able to require that y here be an event or thing distinct from x (and, hence, not a tautological reduplication of x). But it is also clear that for Danto's argument to have succeeded it would have required the insertion of a "lateral" argument, one conducted on grounds logically independent of the main argument itself, at the point of its concluding step. What would be required is a *direct* argument to the effect that the things which ultimately ground an explanation cannot be analytic statements and must be general laws.

So, the exact pressure exerted by Danto's argument on the hypothetical formula R' is not difficult to gauge. We need a direct argument that the formula is not analytic and that it is a general law. Such an argument does not, at first glance, seem particularly difficult to attain. For the view that the formula R' is a general law does appear initially plausible. It seems to represent, but in a highly schematic way, our experience of how an action happens. Presumably one could show that the formula is in some sense an inductive generalization based on vast experience. When the concept of action was first being formed, the various conditions in the "if . . ." part of the formula probably got put there because they had been observed to operate in a great number of cases. One's individual experience would, no doubt, lead to a similar result. In any case, the formula does seem actually to be confirmed by subsequent experience, no matter who has it.

Historical Explanation

Let us suppose all this to be so. Indeed, let us suppose, for the sake of emphasis, that the evidence of all experience of actions is totally favorable to the truth of this particular "regularity law." Even so, it still does not follow that the formula is a law. It could be a law, in the required sense of a regularity or general law, only if it is in principle possible to *falsify* what it asserts by reference to empirical observations and tests.

Since it could plausibly be maintained that the formula R′ is somehow immune to empirical falsification in what it asserts, there appears to be a decisive consideration against treating it as a regularity law. I take this to be one of the fundamental claims advanced by Donagan as an alternative to the view that the basic formula R′ has the status of a general law.

In Donagan's words: "No conceivable empirical evidence would count against the proposition that if you hold to your intention to bring about something, and believe that you must take certain steps to do so, then you will take those steps if you can." Why does Donagan say this? Because "any evidence which goes to show that you hold that belief but did not take those steps, although you could have, also goes to show that you did not stick to your intention." Donagan's proposition (that if you hold to your intention, etc.), then, is "an analytic truth which derives from the very concept of an intention." (See *Later Philosophy of Collingwood*, p. 185, for all three passages quoted.)

The peculiar emphasis of Donagan's account should not be misconstrued. He realizes that such things as time gaps or efficacy gaps would infirm the doing of an action X even where the agent could in some sense be said to have intended it. We can always account for these gaps, and in that way discount them, by building them into our understanding of the analytic truth.

Even so, Donagan notes, the question remains "whether there is a logical gap between intending to do something that is immediately within one's power and doing it." Donagan must, of course, deny this gap if his claim about the analytic status of his proposition is to be maintained. There is, he says, no *logical* gap between intending to act (intending to do X as a step to some desired end) and acting (i.e., doing X). This follows—once we have stated our proposition so as to absorb the other acknowledged gaps—from the claim that "what we mean by 'intending X' [is] that, in the absence of interfering factors, it

164

is followed by doing X. I could not be said to intend X if, even with no obstacles or other countervailing factors, I still didn't do it." [1]

Or, as the same claim has been put by another defender of the "teleological theory" of actions, "[I]t is *a priori* necessary that the [agent] realize the goal *if normal conditions obtain*, that is, if nothing interferes." This, he continues, is "analytic" of the "concept of goal" (Stoutland, "The Logical Connection Argument," p. 126; see also pp. 124–128). In short, the *doing* of X under normal conditions is part of what we mean by "intending X." Accordingly, it would be self-contradictory, or nonsensical, to say, given normal conditions, he intends X but he does not do X.

Something troubles me about this account and I will try to bring it out. For I am not convinced that the basic "if . . . then . . ." formula (R') expresses an analytic truth; and I say this because I am not convinced that the elements in the "if . . ." part actually *entail* that the agent does the specified action (designated here as X). In particular, I am inclined to deny that Donagan's claim about the meaning of intention-talk supports a thesis of logical entailment.

It may not be evident why I think this; so it might be well to review the argument with an eye to this particular point. We can begin with the fairly uncontroversial point that there must be something to "he intends X" other than the mere fact that "he does X"; for Donagan is not, after all, presenting these simply as synonyms. There must, in other words, be certain features over and beyond "he does X" which hold good when we say "he intends X." What are they?

From Donagan's own account it is clear what else might be involved in "he intends X": the agent would have a describable purpose, or end in view, and a belief that doing X is among the "steps" to that end. (Or the agent might believe simply that doing X *is* the accomplishment of his goal, or part of it.) Let us designate these two conditions as T. Now the question is, is it true that "if T then he does X"? No, clearly it is not, for we have left out "normal conditions" (N). So we

---

1. The two passages quoted in this paragraph are from Donagan, "Alternative Historical Explanations and Their Verification," pp. 78 and 80. In the latter of the two passages, Donagan is actually quoting with approval from Taylor, *Explanation of Behaviour*, p. 33. For Donagan's basic argument, see *Later Philosophy of Collingwood*, pp. 182–192, esp. pp. 185, 191; "Popper-Hempel Reconsidered," pp. 150–151; "Alternative Historical Explanations and Their Verification," pp. 77–81; and "Comment," pp. 225–226.

add them: is it now true that "if T and N then he does X"? For reasons that should be clear from our earlier discussion of the basic schema (in Chapter Four), we probably will not have a *true* formula until we get back to the hypothetical formula R'.

Now it can reasonably be believed of R' that it is true. Let us allow that this point is not in dispute here. We may still, however, entertain the possibility (or hypothesis) that the antecedent part is fulfilled while the consequent is not. The question then becomes whether given the instantiation of conditions (1)–(7) it would be *self-contradictory* to say "he does not do X." Presumably, the person who thought that the formula was analytic, that there was some intrinsic connection between its two parts, would say that it was self-contradictory. I believe that Donagan would say this, but I can see nothing in his account of intention that would require such a judgment.

In Donagan's account, "he intends X" breaks down roughly into three component elements: mentalistic factors, such as the agent's purpose and his means/end belief; normal conditions, such as his not being prevented from acting or his having the specified purpose at the time of acting; and the doing of X. Now, given Donagan's construal of "he intends X," we can readily see how he reasoned from that to the claim that the connection within the following hypothetical formula is one of entailment. For it is analytically true that "if he intends X (i.e., all the elements named above do hold good) then he does X." The truth-conditions of "he intends X" are such that it can never be true when "he does X" is false. Hence, it would be self-contradictory to assert both "he intends X" and "he does *not* do X." It was, surely, some such consideration as this that led Donagan to conclude that the formula R', or one very like it, is an analytic one.

But let us vary the picture here slightly. Rather than keep the three criteria of "he intends X" together in a single set, we could segregate out the "mentalistic" features (the purpose and means/end belief) and add in just the so-called normal conditions. We now have a truncated version of "he intends X," for we have only these two elements. From the argument of the previous paragraph it should be clear that where we provide *merely* these two elements then it does not follow—follow logically (deductively) or analytically—that the agent does X. And where we cannot say that "the agent does X" is deducible from these two elements, we cannot say that they *entail* it. Thus, where these two features of intention-talk are separated out, and treated as conditions for an action's occurring, it is not *self-contradictory* to say both that these features hold true and that the agent does not do a specified act. Hence the statement "if the agent has a purpose E and believes X to be a means to E and if so-called normal conditions prevail then he does X" is not an analytic one.

Indeed, for R' to be analytic (as also for Donagan's own hypothetical), "the agent does X" must appear both as a condition in the "if . . ." part and as the consequent "he does X." Thus, that (1) the agent has a purpose E and that (2) he believes X, all things considered, to be the means to E (or a part of accomplishing it) and that (3) normal conditions prevail and that (4) the agent does X would allow us to deduce the conclusion "he does X." Here the meaning of "intention," in Donagan's full-bodied sense—where (1)–(4) are its truth conditions—does generate a logical entailment between these four conditions and "he does X"; but the entailment is a trivial one and could not in any case be explanatory. For, by logical simplification, we could get from "(1)–(4)" *is true* that "(4)" *is true*; and (4) states that the agent does X; now (4) "the agent does X" logically entails "the agent does X"; but we could never explain p by p, as Danto earlier pointed out. Even if we were to leave out explicit mention of (4) we could, nonetheless, from the meaning *alone* (of "intention") supply it—and with the same result.

On the other hand were we to construe "intends X" as logically equivalent just to (1)–(3) alone, or to (1) and (2) with stipulation that (3) normal conditions prevail, then it would not follow deductively or analytically from *this* meaning of "intends X" that the agent does X. Now, it would follow here *if* the conjunction of (1)–(3) logically entailed "he does X," but this is something that would have to be determined independently of an analysis of the meaning of "intends X." And we have no evident grounds for a thesis of logical entailment in this case. My point, then, is that Donagan's argument from the alleged meaning of "intends X" leads either to a trivial (and nonexplanatory) entailment or to no entailment at all. Or, to put the point somewhat differently, where the *meaning* of "intends X" is the only ground offered, we would have to conclude that "if the agent has purpose E and believes X to be the means to E and if so-called normal conditions prevail then he does X" could not be an analytic statement.

The application of this argument to the formula R' is, I think, a fairly straightforward matter. For that formula can be regarded, quite plausibly, as an elaboration of the one just cited in the previous paragraph.

My argument is not, of course, intended as a verbal one. It is not an argument that depends on Donagan's choice of words. It would, unlike Donagan's own argument, work with *any* word in the "intention" family, as long, that is, as the logical distinction I have suggested, between "he does X" as a criterion and other criteria for using the word, is made.

My argument is simply that if we isolate those elements (the "reasons he did" and "normal conditions" part of action-talk) which belong on the "if . . ." side of the basic formula, then those elements are *conceptually* compatible with the nonoccurrence of X. This is going to be so whether we speak of the agent's intention or his purpose or his end in view or his aim or his goal or his wants or even his desire. This is the case because the point of the argument is a logical, not a verbal, one.

Of course, some of these words, like "intention" but unlike "desire," may well have the *doing* of X as a truth-condition of using that word properly. I have not chosen to deny this particular version of "intending X"; I have, however, disputed that it follows from this version that R', or any sufficiently similar formula, thereby has analytic status. For this is a matter to be determined solely on whether the agent's doing X (the action specified) is nontrivially entailed by the fact that the other truth-conditions have held good. And I have argued here that the so-called antecedent conditions in R', the conditions (1)–(7) on the "if . . ." side, do not *logically* entail "the agent does X."

I think the rub in Donagan's account comes from his reliance on a significant equivocation in the development of his argument. We might put this simply by saying that he has traded off between the global or full-blooded sense of terms like "intends" or "resolves" and the sense these have when we say, relying on the normal tests, that an agent has a certain purpose or aim. When we say that an agent has such-and-so purpose, we are saying that historians and journalists—or anyone, for that matter—can check records for what the agent said and did, make certain projections about characters and policies, and come up with a describable end in view which they attribute to the agent on the basis of this evidence.

Now this purpose is linked to doing the thing purposed in a quite evident way, no one would deny; indeed, it is linked as described in

R'. And in that formula we do register our belief that the agent who has that purpose, in the way specified there, does the action in question. In saying this, however, we are not committed also to saying that having the purpose, under the conditions specified in R', *logically entails* the doing of the action.

Clearly though, insofar as intention has come to include the doing of X as part of its very meaning, it will have a different sense from what it would have if it merely referred to purposes in the more restricted or "mentalistic" sense. However, it is an easy matter, where the same word ("intention") can be used to cover both the global and the restricted sense of the term, to trade back and forth between them. This is what has happened in Donagan's case. Hence, when he says that the agent has a certain intention, meaning thereby a purpose or end in view, he can move readily, relying now on the different, global sense of that term, to the claim that the agent must do, under certain conditions (the so-called normal ones already built into the global sense), the action specified. This is a transit by reference to meaning, but once the equivocation is spotted the argument loses its charm and the delusive conclusiveness of the claim that R' is analytic vanishes.

Actually, the claim that the formula R' is analytic by reference to the meaning of "intention" represents not only a significant equivocation, as I have tried to indicate, but also a complete about-face in the logical priorities involved. The claim ought to be the very reverse one: that the meaning of "intention" (in the so-called global sense) is mapped onto the formula. Hence, it is senseless to argue back from the meaning of "intention" to the relationship of elements involved in the formula R' in order to make *that* analytic. For the relationship itself, the structure of the act, as exhibited in the formula is logically primitive here and not the meaning of "intention."

Of course, it could be suggested that we are not really interested in a global sense of "intention" at all but, rather, in the restricted sense it has when congruent simply with "purpose." But, again, this suggested turn to meaning provides no support for the claim that the formula R' states an analytic truth. For the meaning of "purpose" in the restricted sense, whatever that meaning is, is not equivalent to the whole set of elements in the "if . . ." part of R'. The point is that whatever sense "purpose" has—and I have taken it to be roughly that of end in view— it cannot include *all* the antecedent-condition elements of R'. Therefore, the connection of purposes with the doing of the specified action must be mediated by certain other factors (i.e., by those indicated in the other conditions of the "if . . ." part of the formula) and these, by hypothesis, lie outside the meaning of "purpose." It follows, then, that the connection here is not by virtue of whatever meaning "purpose" has—and could not be so long as that term has a restricted as distinct from a global sense—and that the formula R' cannot be made analytic by reference to the meaning of *any* of its constituent terms.

Now some philosophers have concluded from this that the formula R', or any one reasonably like it, must be a general law (see, e.g., M. Martin, "Situational Logic and Covering Law Explanations," p. 395). But this does not follow. Indeed, for a formula like R' to have the status of a general law (and hence to be empirically falsifiable *in principle*) it is necessary that the antecedent part of the formula, the "if . . ." part, could be instantiated as true and the consequent part, *not* so instantiated. And this would require, in its turn, that these two parts be "logically independent" of one another.

Now I have argued that we cannot establish a relation of logical entailment, nontrivially, in virtue of the meaning of "intention" or of the meaning of any of the constituent terms of R'. Nonetheless it could still be maintained that the connection between the generalized explanatory considerations, given in the antecedent part of R', and the schematic consequence, "then the agent does A," is a conceptual, rather than a contingent, one. Though we cannot show this by reference to meaning, it might nevertheless be shown if we could establish that it is not possible to verify that the "if . . ." part is instantiated as true while the "then the agent does A" part is not so instantiated. And, of course, it would follow from this that the basic schema does not express a general law.

This brings us to an important argument by von Wright. For after indicating his own sympathy with the logical entailment thesis, von Wright suggests that "a good way of tackling" this problem of the logical status of the basic schema is by considering the verification procedures involved in any given case of action-explanation. (See *Explanation and Understanding*, pp. 93–94.) Clearly, von Wright seems to regard the issue of verifiability as a kind of argument respecting the nature of the "tie" that holds between the "if . . ." part and the part that says "then the agent does A" (the action specified) in a formula such as R'. The point, then, of considering verification is to prove (or dis-

The Basic Schema

prove) the logical entailment thesis (or, alternatively, the general law or causalist thesis) by means of it.

The argument itself comes in two parts. First, let us suppose we have a piece of behavior described as A. Now suppose we want to verify that the agent *did* A, as opposed to its just happening, that doing A was intentional on the part of the agent. To accomplish this, we would need to consider the motivational structure involved: that (1) the agent's intention was E and (2) his means/end belief was to do A (3) under normal conditions. In short, to say that A was an action *done* by the agent we would need to "shift" consideration from the action under its description A to such things as the agent's intention. (See *Explanation and Understanding*, pp. 109, 115.) We might say, then, that verifying (as true) the statement "the agent does A" necessarily involves a consideration of the agent's intention(s), his means/end belief(s), etc.

Let us suppose, second, that we started from the opposite end of the schema, with a purpose described as E. Now, suppose we want to verify that our agent has this intention. The traditional move here is to look for something "behind" or "outside" the agent's behavior. But this, von Wright thinks, is a mistake: an intention is not (and does not refer to) a neural event or an inner (mental) state or an identifiable experience of some sort. Rather, the intentionality is *in* the behavior (in that a particular sequence of behavior is "meant" by the agent or "understood" that way by others). In short, to say that an agent had a particular intention E we would need to "shift" consideration to the agent's behavior, to the aiming or intending "inherent" in what he does. (See *Explanation and Understanding*, pp. 114–115.) But even this formulation is not satisfactory, in von Wright's view, for it still suggests a particular location for the intention *vis-à-vis* the agent's behavior. Accordingly, he thinks it better simply to say that "the behavior's intentionality is its *place* in a story about the agent" (*Explanation and Understanding*, p. 115).

Intentions are "inherent" in behavior. Agents do not just "have" intentions; instead stories are devised in which "behavior gets its intentional character . . . from being *set* in a context of aims and cognitions. This is what happens when we construe a practical inference to match it [the action], as premises match a given conclusion" (*Explanation and Understanding*, p. 115). In the standard case, of course,

171

we do not tell the "story" of an action unless *some* behavior is there. Hence, the agent's intention and the other "premise" or antecedent condition elements enter the story because "we can single out some recorded item of behavior as being intentional under the description accorded to it . . . by these premises" (*Explanation and Understanding*, p. 116). But we want our story to be true; and this brings us back, again, to the question of verifying that a particular intention is present in the behavior of an agent.

We might establish its presence on the basis of his known character or temperament, or on the basis of his cultural and educational background (his tribal mores). But this is simply to fit a particular occasion of acting into a pattern of other occasions: how can we verify for any one of these that a particular intention is present? (See *Explanation and Understanding*, pp. 111–112.) Or we might try to establish his intention on the basis of what he explicitly avows. But what he says or writes on a given occasion is itself a piece of behavior and bears the same problematic relation to intention as any other kind or piece of behavior (see *Explanation and Understanding*, p. 113). And so it would be if we turned to what he *does*.

Von Wright's point here, I take it, is not to discredit these ways of establishing intention but, rather, to indicate that none of them takes us beyond the agent's behavior. In each case we look for the evidence of the agent's intention in something that he *does* (or has done).

Any establishment of intention supposes that the thing cited (be it a cultural pattern of behavior or a chance remark or a bit of conduct observed unawares) serves as a reliable indicator of the presence of a particular intention. The peculiarity with verifying intentions, then, is that all the things that count are themselves actions (in some sense) and, hence, are subject to construction by practical inference (that is, by reasoning in accordance with the basic schema).

In sum then, to verify that E was the intention which the agent had we would need to "shift" consideration from the intention under its description E to *some* "recorded item of behavior" (see *Explanation and Understanding*, p. 116). And this item of behavior either would itself have to be intentional in terms of E (and hence acceptable evidence that "the agent intends E" is true) or would have otherwise to be a reliable indicator.

The important result of this analysis becomes clearer now if we put our findings into the framework provided by the basic "if . . . then

The Basic Schema

. . ." formula: for it then is equally true that the conclusion "the agent does A" can be verified *only* by considering the agent's intention(s), his means/end belief(s), etc., and that the premises or antecedent conditions which elaborate this intention ("the agent intends E," "believes A to be a means to E," etc.) can be verified *only* by considering recorded items of his behavior as reliable indicators that he does so intend. In short, the facts that serve in the "if . . ." part of the inference schema and those that serve in the conclusion part are not logically independent of one another. Hence it is not logically possible both to affirm the premises and to deny the conclusion in any given case of action-explanation. And from this it follows that the facts in such an explanation are not in a contingent or Humean connection and that the basic inference schema is not empirically falsifiable, and hence that it could not possibly be a causal or general law.[2] Or, as von Wright has put it, "in this mutual dependence of the verification of premises and the verification of conclusions in practical syllogisms consists . . . the truth of the Logical Connection Argument [or Entailment Thesis]" (*Explanation and Understanding*, p. 116).

This argument, as it appears in von Wright's text (*Explanation and Understanding*, pp. 107–117), is a rather difficult one. Hence, I have in a few paragraphs above attempted a reconstruction and capsulization of it. In this simplified version—which I trust is faithful to the original—the argument is arresting and makes some very telling points, but on close inspection one finds that it lacks conclusiveness.

Its strongest feature, I think, is its treatment of the performance of the action A (where it is believed that A is a means to E) as evidence for the existence of an intention E. The particular virtue of this treatment is that it is neutral between the competing alternative theories, the general law and the noncausalist. For all that is being assumed in treating action A as a reliable mark of intending E (where the agent believes A is a means to E and where normal conditions prevail) is simply that the formula involved is *true*. (I mean true in the following way: when "(1)–(3)" is true then "the agent does A" is true.) But the specified truth-relationship here and the use of *does* A as evidence for *intends* E is consistent with either a general law (or causalist) "tie" between antecedent conditions and consequence or a noncausalist one.

However, as we think about it, we see that all von Wright's argu-

2. See von Wright, *Explanation and Understanding*, p. 93; also pp. 18, 139; and also *Causality and Determinism*, pp. 55–56.

ment requires is simply that for there to be a *true* statement about an agent's intention there must be some "recorded item of behavior" which stands as a reliable mark of that intention (or of its absence). To use some of his own examples: if von Wright really intends to visit Copenhagen he will reserve a place and buy a ticket before departure time; he will *not* fly to Peking two hours before his scheduled visit (see *Explanation and Understanding*, pp. 104, 111). Again, he might simply say that he has this plan or intention in explaining why he cannot make a conflicting appointment. Each of these is, or could be construed as, "a recorded item of behavior" and none of them is the action itself, under its specified description ("travels to Copenhagen"). Now, clearly, if we allow these other "recorded items of behavior" to be reliable marks of the agent's intention then we would have the possibility of verifying von Wright's intention without respect to whether he actually does or does not travel to Copenhagen. It follows, then, that we could have a suitably verified intention on von Wright's part to visit Copenhagen without his actually going there—so long, that is, as we based it on some "recorded item of behavior." Now, none of these items mentioned implies that von Wright actually *goes* to Copenhagen (even under normal conditions); hence, it is logically possible for there to be a verified intention ("to pursue *E*") together with the appropriate means/end belief (that "*A* is a means to *E*") and the prevailing of normal conditions—that is, "(1)-(3)" as instantiated is true—and it still *not* be the case that "the agent does *A*" is instantiated as true (e.g., it is not the case that von Wright goes to Copenhagen). If this is so, the verifiability argument does not support the logical entailment thesis.

There is, of course, an obvious move one could make here. One could say that, clearly, where some recorded items of behavior would tend to support *intends E* in a particular case but the agent does not *do A* (which is what he ought to do under normal conditions if he has the appropriate means/end belief) then we must conclude that, despite appearances, he did not really intend *E* at the time of acting. (Or did not really have the means/end belief then; or normal conditions did not really obtain at the time.) In short, the agent's doing *A* is the only conclusively reliable mark we can have of his intending *E* when it is true that he has the means/end belief which specifies that particular action and when conditions are normal. It would follow, then, from this that where "(1)-(3)" is instantiated as true then necessarily "the agent does A" is instantiated as true. And *that* conclusion could (logi-cally *could*) never be false where "(1)–(3)" is true.

Now, this would appear to reinstate von Wright's argument from verifiability as a conclusive argument for the logical entailment thesis. But the appearance here is misleading. For if we require the doing of the specified action as conclusive evidence of *intends E* (where "(2) and (3)" are presumed true), or if we take his *not* doing that action in the face of the presumed truth of "(2) and (3)" as conclusive evidence that the agent did *not* intend E, then the argument from verification already presupposes that the relationship of "(1)–(3)" to "the agent does A" is one of logical entailment. Hence, the argument from verifica-tion in this form could not *prove* the truth of the logical entailment thesis, since it is itself based on assuming that very thing. To think otherwise would be to beg the question. The most the argument in this form could do is to show, or exhibit, that this assumption was ac-tually being made; but the logic of verification here could never *prove* the assumption, since it already incorporates the standards of the logi-cal entailment thesis in what is to be counted as verified.

We reach the conclusion that the verifiability argument in the form von Wright has given it (as found in my reconstruction) does not es-tablish the logical entailment thesis. And where it does have the requi-site conclusiveness respecting the mutual dependence (for purposes of verification) of the action-conclusion and the intention-premise, it cannot be a proof but, rather, merely a rehearsing or exhibition of a prior commitment to the logical entailment thesis. Hence, the argu-ment from verifiability either proves too much or too little. [3]

I think my argument here has effectively undercut the claim that something like the formula R' can be *proven* to be analytic by refer-ence to the logic of verification. Even so, it is still open to philoso-phers to regard the entailment thesis as more or less embedded in that

3. In a recent paper, von Wright endorses the claim that "the omission of the action would . . . be a criterion or standard whereby we judge that the agent has changed his mind" ("Logic and Epistemology of the Causal Relation," p. 112). But in his book he says precisely of this view that to insist on it "would be dogmatism" (*Explanation and Understanding*, p. 117). The important point to note here is that only in the *book* is he concerned with the issue of verification and what follows from it. I have argued else-where that, although von Wright accepts the "mutual dependence" conclusion of the verifiability argument, he does *not* regard that argument as proving the logical entail-ment thesis. (See "The Problem of the 'Tie' in von Wright's Schema of Practical Infer-ence," esp. sec. 2.)

logic and for them to make this thesis a standard for the verification of the component elements in action-explanations. Indeed, I think we can take much of the advocacy of the logical entailment thesis as stemming from this particular view. I would like to examine the view, for on reflection I find that it too is highly problematic.

Characteristically, the philosophers who hold this view say that having a purpose E (i.e., having the goal or aim of accomplishing E) *entails* that, if the agent believes A to be the means to E—or part of accomplishing it—and if conditions are propitious, he does A. Hence an agent who has a purpose E will, under a *ceteris paribus* clause (in which all the other antecedent conditions of R' are presumed satisfied), necessarily do A.[4]

What the proponents of the purposes-entail view are suggesting, it seems to me, is that we can let the normal tests and standards suffice for all the other conditions in R' but that we require an extraordinary standard of testing for purposes. This suggestion lies behind the claim that where the agent does not do A, under the *ceteris paribus* clause (which includes that he believes A, all things considered, to be the means to E), then we cannot verify (as true) that he intends E. Indeed, we are in a position to *falsify* "he intends E."[5]

Now I will readily grant that there is an interesting rationale for the special treatment accorded to purposes here. For where a *ceteris paribus* approach is taken, everything covered by such a clause has to be satisfied before we can even get the tight "tie" of entailment: *intends X, does X*; therefore *does not do X, does not intend X*. Hence the conditions in the parenthetical clause have to be satisfied in a way that is different from the way in which "intends X" is satisfied. They can be satisfied by the normal tests (like the ones we used to "verify" von Wright's intention to go to Copenhagen) and in a sense must be, for otherwise we could never set up the mechanism of entailment. But "purposes" can then be conclusively satisfied by one thing only—

4. For example, see Donagan, "Popper-Hempel Reconsidered," p. 150. I also think my account will cover those philosophers who claim that "purposing to do X" represents a "dispositional bent" to do X and that when we tighten up our account by indicating the fulfillment of the other important conditions (as found in R') this "bent" amounts to a logical entailment. (See Taylor, "Explaining Action," pp. 60, 84, and esp. 82; and Stoutland, "Logical Connection Argument," p. 128.)

5. Recall Donagan's claim: "Any evidence which goes to show that you held that belief but did not take those steps, although you could have, also goes to show that you did not stick to your intention" (*Later Philosophy of Collingwood*, p. 185). See also his "Popper-Hempel Reconsidered," p. 150.

The Basic Schema

"does X"—and *no* amount of evidence, of the sort provided by normal tests, could count in its favor (unlike the case with the other antecedent conditions in R') *without* "does X."

At the same time, even to talk in the purposes-entail way suggests that we be able to identify purposes and confirm their existence independently of what the agent does. For, if this were not the case purposes could not entail deeds, except emptily (as in $F \supset T$), since there would be no such entity as a (verifiable) purpose. Nor could purposes entail deeds, except trivially, since *purposing* X would be nothing other than *doing* X—or would include that doing as part of its meaning. Of course, we no more want empty or trivial entailments in verification than we want them in explanation; for in each case they are fatal to the enterprise. So the point must be granted. But once it is granted all that is being said, really, is that it is the total set of conditions (the antecedent conditions of R'), suitably verified in the individual case, which conjunctively entail "does A" (the action specified).

If it is just the fact that (1)–(7) is *so* which logically entails that "does A" is *so*, then we are free to put this particular entailment in any of several ways. We could say, for example, that condition (7) the agent is (generically and situationally) able to do A entails, given the holding of (1)–(6), that (necessarily) he does A. And here it would be condition (7) that is singled out for the special treatment, for here it is only *does* A which could show conclusively that (7) held; it would take the action itself, over and beyond the evidence provided by normal tests, to verify that (7) was true. And the changes could be rung on this basic pattern *seven* times: thus condition (1) logically entails, *ceteris paribus* (that is, given (2)–(7)), that the agent does A, with the consequence that condition (1) is singled out for special verificational treatment. And condition (2) logically entails, given (1) and (3)–(7), that the agent does A, with the consequence that condition (2) is singled out verificationally; and so on.

But to talk of any one of the seven conditions entailing "does A," given the satisfaction of the other six, requires that we have normal tests and standards (over and beyond "does A") for identifying and verifying the holding of all these conditions. Clearly, we would have to require this for any six conditions in the *ceteris paribus* clause (otherwise we could not set up the vise of entailment between the remaining condition and "does A"). And, again, we would have to require it for the condition outside the clause, whichever one of the seven conditions it happened to be (for otherwise we would have the vice of empty or of trivial entailment).

Now, if this is so, if normal tests and standards have to be satisfied in every case for all seven conditions, then we see that (1)–(7) does *not* entail "does A." This follows, quite simply, from the fact that it is logically possible for us to identify and verify the satisfaction of the antecedent conditions of R'—that is, all the conditions (1)–(7)—irrespective of whether the agent actually does A. Hence, the holding of (1)–(7) is, within the context provided by verification, logically compatible with "does not do A."

Or, to put the point somewhat differently, the entailment thesis does not organize the logic of verification. Indeed, it is not even clear, now, that the argument in favor of such a view can be stated coherently. For the claim that we must presuppose a "tie" of logical entailment between the agent's purpose, means/end belief, etc. and his doing A (the action specified) *in order to verify* that the agent intends E requires that we have independent grounds, which could count verificationally, for saying *intends E*: if not we fail to make the case for entailment; but the logical entailment so generated seems to require that no such independent grounds can count in the case of verifying *intends E*. In order to be stated convincingly (as regards entailment), the argument requires an assumption which, when the argument is stated, is expressly said to be ruled out (as regards verification). This is objectionable: it verges on formal contradiction to say both that we must rely on normal verificational tests in the case of purposes and that we cannot. I see no way of avoiding self-contradiction here short of disentangling the two strands, verification and entailment, altogether.

With this point made, let me add that the actual *practice* of verification in the case of actions does not support a thesis of logical entailment. Historians and others who concern themselves with this matter do not regard purposes in particular as peculiarly difficult to verify. Intentions are intrinsically no more resistant to verification than are other so-called mentalistic factors—such as the agent's being situationally motivated in a particular way or his believing that A is a means to E or his preferring A to other such means. Hence, the historian does not require a triangulation between two verified factors—*does A*, as his first marker, and other instantiations of elements of R' (excepting *intends E*), as his second—to get at the peculiarly inaccessible purpose of the agent. Indeed, the practice of historians suggests that purposes are, for the most part, verificationally accessible over and beyond actions—otherwise historians could make no real use of such commonplace claims as that the agent changed his mind or that one purpose was overridden by another.

It is important to bear in mind, too, that the historian does treat the occurrence (or not) of the action specified as a piece of evidence. Now, sometimes this piece of evidence will outweigh a different piece in the historian's judging, say, of the agent's purpose. But this is no different from his believing Tacitus rather than Suetonius. And it should be sharply distinguished from the "falsification" of a statement of the agent's purpose of the sort recommended in the logical entailment thesis. For this enshrines a claim not about the weight of the evidence but, rather, about the impossibility of an agent's even having such a purpose (under certain conditions). And this impossibility can stand in the face of *all* evidence. We should take care to distinguish the issue of the evidential bearing of actions on purposes from the quite different issue of their being in a relationship of logical entailment.

Admittedly, there is a kind of coherence to the historian's reasonings; historians do work with the various "places" of the basic "if . . . then . . ." formula in mind. Accordingly, the historian can reason back from the agent's *not* having done A. He can take this as an indication that one (or more) of the places in the "if . . ." part will turn out, on this occasion, to be unfilled or to be filled with material that will prove, upon further investigation, to be evidentially unsound.

We should grant this: it correctly says that R' provides the groundplan of the historian's reasoning. Where the normal tests indicate that the agent intends E and believes A to be the means to E—and when all other conditions of R' are satisfied—the historian simply *expects* the agent to do A. In short, the historian takes R' (without regard to its ultimate logical status) as his principle of inference for the given case; his mode of reasoning indicates that he takes R' to be *true*. This is all we need say. It is not required additionally that the elements within the "if . . ." part and the specified action A exhibit a "tight" or "logical" connection.

It should, moreover, be quite evident that my argument has not been based on saying that where all the antecedent conditions of R'

are instantiated as true the specified action *sometimes* does not occur. What I am arguing would hold up even if the specified action *always* occurs, a point I am not inclined to dispute in any case. My contention is simply that the nonoccurrence of A in the situation specified, where the antecedent conditions of R' are all fulfilled, is not offensive to reason: it is not self-contradictory of the assertion that the conditions do obtain. The man who said "he does not do A," claiming that conditions (1) through (7) had been satisfied for the agent, would very likely be in error, I conjecture, but he would not be uttering anything absurd.

For we have examined the principal considerations—those of meaning and of verification—which have been advanced in support of the logical entailment thesis and have determined that neither of them provides a basis for saying that the basic formula R' is analytic. In fact, the arguments I have developed in order to canvass this issue have shown that there is not an entailment relationship between the elements in the "if . . ." part and the specified action (as "does A").

Once we have set aside the claim that the hypothetical formula R' is analytic, and hence have shown that an explanatory principle of this sort must be contingent or synthetic in character, it is open to us to advance further the argument that it is in fact a general law. This brings us to the argument of Churchland. For, after asserting that a formula very like R' is not analytic, he goes on to provide an interesting argument, of what I earlier called the direct sort, to establish its status as a general law.[6]

Or at least it appears that this is his intended strategy, for Churchland initially introduces his basic formula as being "prima facie a general law" (p. 215). And elsewhere in the article, quite consistently with that characterization, he calls it simply a "law" (pp. 215, 226, 229), a "law sketch" (pp. 216, 223, 229), or a "nomic principle" (pp. 215,

6. Churchland's own statement of his law, which he calls L_1, is as follows (from pp. 221–222 of his essay): (X)(Φ)(A) (If [1] X wants Φ, and [2] X believes that A-ing is a way for him to bring about Φ under those circumstances, and [3] there is no action believed by X to be a way for him to bring about Φ, under the circumstances, which X judges to be as preferable to him as, or more preferable to him than, A-ing and [4] X has no other want (or set of them) which, under the circumstances, overrides his want Φ, and [5] X knows how to A, and [6] X is able to A, then [7] X A-s.) Subsequent references in this chapter to Churchland's essay "Logical Character of Action-Explanations" will be given by page number only (in parentheses) in the text, e.g. (p. 215).

226; see also pp. 222n, 225, 226). Clearly, though, his preferred way of referring to it is as a "nomological" (pp. 216, 221, 226) or, more precisely, as a *"theoretical* nomological" (p. 225). But at other points, though, he refers to the basic formula with a different battery of terms. It is, he says, a "basic principle of the conceptual framework in terms of which we conceive ourselves" (p. 225; see also p. 215). In one place, he is even willing to refer to it as a "conceptual truth" (p. 226). In light of the difference in terms, and of the luxuriant variety of the terms themselves, one is not wholly clear as to what Churchland is prepared to argue for. I think that a coherent view of the logical status of his basic explanatory principle can, however, be teased out of the essay.

I should add that another of the curious, and perplexing, features of Churchland's argument is the rather casual way in which he introduces the claim that the basic formula is not "merely analytic" in character (p. 226). At no place does he *argue* against analytic status for the formula; he merely asserts his point. One reason Churchland is so casual and vague on this score is that his essay is written, not against Donagan, who does make a claim to analytic status for the basic formula, but against Dray, who does not. Dray seemed to think that the crucial formula was in some sense synthetic, although *not* empirically falsifiable (in that it was prescriptive or normative in character). Hence, the question of analytic status was never in dispute between Churchland and Dray; it was common ground between the two that it was not analytic. This is why Churchland merely asserted rather than argued the matter.

What was in dispute between them was whether the principle was empirically disconfirmable, and it is this point that Churchland is principally concerned to address. Accordingly, we should see Churchland's remark about not "merely analytic" in this context, as asserting the possible empirical falsifiability of the basic formula, and note carefully his claim that *epistemologically* the principle is "nomological" in character (p. 226; see also p. 223).

Churchland's argument is fairly simple. He indicates a number of traits that his formula obviously has, or reasonably could be said to have, and then suggests that these point to its being altogether like certain recognized laws of nature. We can call this an "asymptotic" argument, since it has the character of suggesting that the "curve" marked out by these similarities is such as to converge with an axis line marked out by "the standard D-N criteria," on which are to be found acknowledged general laws of natural science.[7]

Let me mark out the main stages of his argument briefly.

(a) Churchland allows that, since his hypothetical formula (called L_1) is not analytic, "the antecedent of L_1 could be true of some [person] without issuing in the relevant action" (p. 223; see also p. 225). It is, he goes on, possible to "conceive of circumstances which would falsify L_1"; although it is, he presses, really "difficult even to imagine [such] a case" (p. 224). Moreover, even if one could conceive of disconfirming circumstances, this "does not entail that such circumstances could (*empirically* could) obtain" (p. 224; see also p. 225).

(b) Of course, Churchland does believe that his law, L_1, though falsifiable in principle, is true "in the final empirical analysis" (p. 223). In any event, it should be clear that this candidate law is "immune from *casual* denial" (p. 215).[8]

(c) All this points, Churchland suggests, to the fact that L_1 is a "deeply entrenched theoretical nomological" (p. 225). It not only is a possibly falsifiable yet true general law but it also has the character of being central to our understanding of human behavior. It provides a "basic principle of the conceptual framework in terms of which we conceive ourselves" (p. 225). In other words, Churchland's argument approaches the general law axis at a point very high up the line. The law L_1 is more nearly on a par with "the principle of mass-energy conservation" (p. 225) than it is with "all copper expands when heated" (p. 225).

(d) The logical moral Churchland wants to underscore is that conferring "nomicity does not require that the universal in question be falsifiable independently of the entire framework of principles [laws?] of which it may be an integral part" (p. 225). He concludes, "the particular view of action-explanations being defended is but one aspect of the more general view that the common-sense conceptual framework in terms of which we conceive ourselves, *qua* persons, has all the rele-

7. Churchland is, throughout the essay, quite willing to locate his own candidate-law within the standard D-N (i.e., deductive-nomological) analysis we are familiar with from our earlier discussion of Hempel (see pp. 214–215, 229, 230, 234).
8. Especially is this so if we add yet another condition to the antecedent clause of L_1: the condition that unnamed "vitiating factors" are barred (see pp. 222, 224). The result may be to add "one more degree of sketchiness" to L_1, Churchland allows, but that does not change its status from law or law *sketch* (p. 222) to analytic truth.

vant structural and logical features of those lesser conceptual frameworks we call scientific theories (for example, molecular theory)" (p. 225).

(e) Churchland ends his argument, though, on a hesitant, almost apologetic, note. He states, rather defensively, that his claim of *"theoretical* nomological" status for L_1 may seem to some "a bizarre proposal" (pp. 225; the italics are his) and even that it might, damagingly, "smack of John Stuart Mill" (pp. 225–226). He feels, however, that he can demonstrate the essential "innocence" (p. 225) of his proposal: his point is that "whether a principle, such as L_1, enjoys nomic status is a function of the *kind* of role it plays in our judgments . . . concerning matters of fact" (p. 226).

Now, if I have Churchland's argument down correctly, we do have a strong case for treating the hypothetical formula R' (for it is in all essentials like Churchland's L_1) as a general law. In a nutshell his contention is that L_1 is empirically falsifiable in principle but well confirmed as true, that it is therefore a general law and, hence, analogous to a law of nature. But, unlike some laws of nature, it is deeply entrenched in a particular conceptual framework, in this case, the theory of persons and of intentional action, and, accordingly, is virtually immune from empirical disconfirmation. It is said to enjoy this peculiar status as a result of the role that it plays.

Without wanting to dispute the importance Churchland assigns to a hypothetical formula such as R' in the explanation of actions, I do think his account is open to challenge at several points but, crucially, at one point. The claim that R' is empirically falsifiable in principle is fundamental to Churchland's entire analysis. If that claim fails, then the general law claim fails and with it the whole asymptotic drift toward laws of nature. So, much does hinge on Churchland's claim that L_1, or what comes to the same thing, R', is empirically falsifiable in principle.

I do not think, however, if we examine the formula with any degree of care, that we could readily conceive its falsifiability. It is, after all, a highly schematic formula. The formula is not itself a factual statement, even a very general and high-order one; it is an unfilled specification, the satisfying of which does, admittedly, require facts. It would seem, then, that the formula as it stands, devoid of specific empirical content, is susceptible neither of confirmation nor of disconfirmation by reference to matters of fact. Hence, the *formula* is not the sort of statement that could be regarded, in practice or even in principle, as empirically falsifiable. But, clearly, what is being said when it is alleged that the formula could be falsified "in the final empirical analysis" is that it is disconfirmable through at least one of its instantiations.

This, then, is the very issue we want to address. And we will turn to it in the next chapter.

Ten

Practical Inference

Before taking up the thread of argument from the previous chapter, I would like to provide a brief terminological excursus and, in so doing, recall certain points made earlier on.

"Practical inference" (or "practical syllogism," as it is sometimes called) is a term with a long history, going back to Aristotle originally; and it has, in the course of time, acquired a variety of meanings. In my use of the term it refers to a specific mode of explanation wherein an action is accounted for by reference to the agent's situational motivation, purpose, means/end belief, and so on. We are, of course, familiar with this type of explanation, and with the set of conditions that figure in it, from my discussion (in Chapter Four) of the schema for action-explanations (designated R).

This schema, conveniently written down as "The agent does A because (1)–(7)," controls and is presupposed by individual explanations of particular actions. It would follow here that an adequate or nondefective explanation of an action is, in effect, an instantiation of this schema. We might, then describe it (the schema of practical inference) as an explanation sketch, or pattern, and particular explanations (that is, particular practical inferences) as detailed exemplifications of this pattern.

Our schema is susceptible of a philosophically interesting restate-

Historical Explanation

ment. Instead of saying "The agent does A because (1)–(7)" we could say "If (1)–(7) then the agent does A." This second or "if . . . then . . ." way of putting the formula (which I have designated R') represents the logical point that where we explain "q because p" we are equally committed to "if p then q." What we have said here, quite simply, is that the conditions which conjunctively warrant or license an explanation are the same as the conditions that warrant a connection, of the "if . . . then . . ." sort, between an action and the thought of the agent.

By the same token, what von Wright (and before him, Aristotle) calls the "practical syllogism" is itself simply another way of stating these same conditions, this time as premises to which "the agent does A" stands as a conclusion. It would be pointless to regard any one of these three forms (the action-explanation sketch, the "if . . . then . . ." formula, or the argument from premises to conclusion) as *the* basic form; rather, the use of any one of the three licenses the use of the two alternative versions.[1]

With this point in mind, let us return to the issue with which we were concerned in the previous chapter: that of determining the logical character of the "tie" which holds between the "agent does A" part and the "because . . ." part in the schema of practical inference. Now it is important to note that the substance of this issue is invariant whether the question of logical status is being asked about the schema in its form as schema of practical inference or about it in "if . . . then . . ." form or about it in its form as a syllogism. Let us resume our inquiry by again asking the question in its most convenient form: what is the logical status of R', of "If (1)–(7) then the agent does A"?

We could, given the fact that R' is not analytic, conceive the possibility that its antecedent is adequately instantiated as true but that the specified action does not occur. This is, of course, a logical possibility; it has already been granted in denying analytic status to the formula R'. Churchland claimed that, on the basis of this possibility, the conjectured nonoccurrence of the specified action would constitute the falsification of R'. But to say this assumes that the formula is of the

1. See von Wright, *Explanation and Understanding*, p. 27. Von Wright characteristically puts these conditions in argument form, with the conclusion (*does* A) introduced by a "therefore" (see, for example, *Explanation and Understanding*, p. 107; "So-called Practical Inference," p. 47). It should be noted, again, that my discussion of the three "associated" versions is based on the argument of Ryle's paper " 'If,' 'So,' 'Because.' "

right sort to be empirically disconfirmed in the way described. So this matter of empirical disconfirmability becomes the exact point at issue.

In order to resolve this crucial question, we might try a "thought experiment" in which the conditions specified obtain: the antecedent part of the formula, the "if . . ." part, is instantiated as true and the consequent part, the "then he does A" part, is not instantiated as true. Let us imagine, not our old friends Caesar and Brutus, but, rather, the assassin of President Lincoln.

The resolve and the opportunity are there; everything has gone according to plan. Booth stands in the President's theater box, aiming his loaded gun at the unwary Lincoln's head. But nothing happens. He just stands there with his revolver cocked, as if in a waxworks tableau.

The experts come in. The doctors can find, through medical examination, no evidence of paralysis or of any other disorder that would have physically incapacitated Booth at the crucial moment. Nor can the theologians or the psychoanalysts find appropriate evidence that the will of God or the Unconscious of this man stayed his hand at the very moment of execution. Psychologists and sociologists are no more helpful. Historians and journalists probe: did his intention change? did he forbear? was his situation-conception or its requirements altered? It appears not. Lawyers and judges are at a loss for words.

This is an odd story to tell or, at least, one with a very odd ending. Nonetheless, it is a possibility we can conceive: such a thing could (logically *could*) occur. It would appear to be the classic case for which we are seeking. Normal tests indicate that the conditions of the antecedent part of the formula were adequately fulfilled in that case and yet the specified action had not occurred. Now, the question is, what are we to make of this case?

It is open to us, of course, to say that one of the conditions was really *not* fulfilled, even though the normal tests say it was. Here we would be preserving the formula by denying that the case actually provided a counterinstance to it. This is the usual move: the supposed instantiation would simply "dissolve" here and the question of the schema's logical status would not even arise, since one of its antecedent conditions was not regarded as actually fulfilled. But to say this leaves open the possibility that some other such case could provide a counterinstance. We could, on the other hand, say that the case *was* a counterinstance and go on to claim that this constituted, logically, a

Historical Explanation

falsifying instance. Each basic line of retort is equally eligible, and nobody is under compulsion to say either one of these things to the exclusion of the other. Hence, it is rational to say that the formula could be falsified "in the final empirical analysis." If it is, Churchland's point is made: we have here a clear and reasonable general-law interpretation of the formula R'.

I think, however, that the matter is not so simple. There is, admittedly, no logical necessity, no "tie" of entailment, no analytic connection whereby the specified action follows from the "truth" of the premises. Indeed, if there were, our example could not even be imagined. But there is something very curious about this example. It's not that the agent has "done" some action other than the one specified (in the instantiating premises); he has "done" nothing at all. That's just the point. No action was performed; something "happened," you might say, but the agent *did nothing*.

It is important here to be clear on this point: *no action of any sort was performed*. We are not witnessing some action other than A, the action specified, nor are we here considering a case of forbearance (the deliberate not-doing of A); for these would both be instances of action. No, the case we are considering is one where the agent did nothing at all.[2]

It seems to me that the most reasonable construal to place on this case is that it lies *outside* the domain, and hence the purview, of the formula R' altogether. We can view the consequence part of the formula, where it says "he, the agent, does A," as specifying the doing of an action. Whatever comes under this specification, either to instantiate it or not, must be an action. The relevant range of exemplification of "he does A" is the class of actions done. Anything outside this range does not enter in at all. It is not specifiable by reference to R'; it cannot possibly "fit the bill."

Accordingly, we cannot engage the formula with the facts—put it into gear, so to speak—unless there is an action of some sort involved. The formula is simply not employed, it is not used or applied, unless that particular specification is "met" by an action, by the only sort of thing that could have a place in it.

So, the basic requirement for *using* the formula at all is unfulfilled

2. The assassination example is derived from von Wright (see *Explanation and Understanding*, p. 116). It was his point that the erstwhile agent did "literally *nothing*" (p. 117); the term "dissolves" is his also (p. 117).

188

in the example we are considering. The classic case is not a possible counterinstance to the formula R′; rather, it is in a logical disconti-nuity with it.

As long as we specify that no *action* was done, it is simply a logical mistake to try to cover that kind of nonoccurrence (i.e., a nonaction) with a hypothetical formula for action-explanations. Just as we say that there is no explanation of an action unless one has occurred so we can say that there can be no application of a formula for explaining actions to something that is a nonaction.[3] The alleged counterinstance cannot occur here for the simple reason that the formula could not apply to it in the first place. The hypothetical formula is not the right sort of thing to be falsified by the occurrence, or the nonoccurrence, of something that is not an action. If Churchland's argument for a gen-eral-law interpretation of the formula R′ is to be made good, we must deflect consideration back into the class of actions done; for only one of these could count as a possible falsifying instance of the formula in question.

It might appear here, though, that the matter is clear cut. Any oc-currence of an alternative course of action, say a B or a C or a D, or of an action altogether uncontemplated among these, say a Z, in lieu of the agent's doing A would be of the right sort to constitute a possible falsifying counterinstance. That is, it would be where "he does A" specifies *the* action in question.

In order to examine this claim, let us look again at the "assassina-tion" of President Lincoln. As before, we will assume that the ante-cedent conditions are satisfactorily instantiated—at least to the degree that they were in the original example (the so-called classic case). This time, though, we need to vary the scenario somewhat. For the agent is required to do *something*.

---

3. Von Wright makes this point, but in a misleading way, when he says, "It is only when action is already there and a practical argument is constructed to explain or justify it that we have a logically conclusive argument. The necessity of the practical inference schema is, one could say, a necessity conceived *ex post actu*" (*Explanation and Under-standing*, p. 117). This way of putting it is misleading, first, because it suggests that the relationship between the two parts of the schema is temporal rather than conceptual in nature and even that *modus ponens* itself is subject to time. Second, and more impor-tant, it is misleading because it retains, quite inappropriately, the notion of *logical* necessity. For either we have a logical entailment between the two parts of the inference schema or we do not: if "(1)–(7)" *is true* logically entails that "*the agent does* A" *is true* then we do not need the *ex post actu* stipulation. And if (1)–(7) does not logically entail *does* A then adding the stipulation makes no difference as regards *logical* entailment.

Historical Explanation

Now if Booth were to shoot the President, even though not fatally, there would be no problem. This is the action we expected, given the premises. What if he cocked his pistol and then waved the gun to and fro a bit? Again, no problem—if he went ahead to fire it. But suppose he just stood there wobbling the gun about. Well, we could say that he was trying to fire the gun; it's just that he didn't know how, or was funking the job out of nervousness, or the gun was jamming, or something like that. But each of these runs against the initial supposition that the antecedent or premise conditions were *all* satisfactorily instantiated in the case at hand.

So, were we to suppose all these conditions to be nondefectively fulfilled, the wobbling of the gun would have been unexpected, an anomaly of sorts. It could, though, be accounted for within the basic schema as a case of undertaking to shoot: Booth could still be taken as doing something—as setting himself to shoot; there is nothing unnatural or forced in interpreting his action that way.

Suppose though that he pulled out an apple and began to munch it. A macabre incident, much like the sack lunch Kennedy's assassin was said to have eaten during his wait in ambush. But it poses no problem, conceptually, so long as he goes ahead and shoots in time, or tries to. But suppose that *all* he does is stand there eating. Now, surely, this could not count as shooting the President or even as trying to.

Suppose now that Booth did not bother even to eat an apple; he simply turned, without firing a shot, declaimed briefly from Lincoln's box against the iniquities visited upon the South and then jumped to the stage below. (He did jump there after the actual assassination in 1865, and he was an actor.) And, then, after the jump he fled the scene as quickly as he could. Again, we could talk of a loss of nerve or of a momentary mental black out or of his having been seized by some new, grander conception. But this would be to go back on our original assumption that the instantiation of antecedent conditions was nondefective. We could just say, then, that his conduct here was unaccounted for, inexplicable and wholly inconsistent with the premises of our practical inference.

I think, however, that the counterintuitive element in these examples should be factored out somewhat more fully. We might just from the premise of intention alone and the first-hand description of the agent's behavior ("eating an apple") be willing to count the agent's behavior as "aiming at" or "meaning" whatever was intended (the elimination of the President). But we cannot—given *all* the premises, the premise of intention and the means/end belief ("shooting him at the theater tonight is the way to do it") and the holding of normal conditions (Booth brings a loaded gun with him to the theater that night and cocks it upon entering Lincoln's box)—accept that Booth's conduct (eating the apple or declaiming and then jumping and fleeing) was really a form of undertaking to shoot the President.

Accordingly, if we really do let all the premises tell us what the agent is supposed to be doing, then we have to regard some conduct as inconsistent with these premises. What these two examples have in common, then, is that in each case the specified action (shooting the President) was not done but instead another action was (eating the apple, in the one case, declaiming, etc. in the other). And in each case the action performed was inconsistent with the premises (i.e., with the particular instantiation of the antecedent conditions of R') that specified, and led us to expect, the action of shooting the President.

They differ, however, from the earlier example, where Booth was "frozen" in mid-action, and from the "classic case" which that example was meant to illustrate, in which no action of any sort was performed. It is important to retain this particular difference (between no action at all and the doing of an action other than the one specified—where doing such an action is inconsistent with the premises invoked). For if that difference is not retained, then the second case, the one now under consideration, slides away indistinguishably into the first case (the so-called classic case); and nothing more remains to be said.

I am not sure that I can deal with this second case in a wholly satisfactory way. It does seem to me, though, that several persuasive—but not conclusive—considerations can be raised to show that the doing of the *other* action does not constitute a falsifying counterinstance to what the "if . . . then . . ." formula R' is asserting. Let me indicate two such considerations.

The first of these rests on the claim that what was done, Booth's eating the apple or his declaiming from Lincoln's box and then jumping and fleeing, is a nondefective *action*, albeit a different one from the action specified in the premises (in the case at hand: shooting the President). In short, we assume that both the action specified but not done (the shooting) and the action done but not specified (either of the two mentioned here in our example) are actions *in the same sense* and, as

Historical Explanation

such, "full-fledged" actions. Hence, they have *some* schema (call it S) in common; otherwise they could not have been genuinely competitive. (As, for example, Booth's having a seizure would not be regarded as genuinely competitive, in the way that declaiming and then jumping and fleeing would be, with the action of shooting the President specified in the premises.) For, clearly, an event that lies wholly outside the domain of S could not constitute *even possibly* a falsifying counterinstance to S (whatever it is).

Accordingly it is, I would note, difficult to see how Booth's eating the apple or his declaiming, etc. could be denominated *an action*, in the sense required, without allowing that the agent had a relevant purpose and so on. Hence, it is reasonable to believe that either of these conjectured actions, had they been performed, could themselves figure as possible values in satisfaction of the consequence part, "then he does the specified action," of our very general hypothetical formula (R'). Now it is no doubt true that the *factual* premises which could give us the specified action (shooting the President) would not give us the action of eating an apple or that of declaiming, etc. But it is quite reasonable to think, nonetheless, that a *different* set of factual premises, a set not known at present, might yield us an action *other* than shooting the President and might, indeed, yield one of these two.

So we are not committed, in saying that a different action (B) happens in lieu of the one specified (A), to saying that this falsifies the hypothetical formula R'. For to call the doing of B (say declaiming, etc.) an action is, by that very fact, to implicate it in the network of conditions and consequence spelled out in the formula R'. What we are committed to saying is that the *factual instantiation* of the formula which would yield an action A (here shooting the President) is not the one that could yield, say, an action B (here declaiming from the box, etc.).

My point here can be put somewhat differently, and more simply. The set of conditions in the formula R', like the consequence itself, can be indifferently fulfilled by either instantiation: by the one that would give us the action of shooting the President or by the one that gives us the action of Booth's declaiming from Lincoln's box and then jumping and fleeing (or, for that matter, his just eating an apple). The controlling formula itself is perfectly neutral with respect to the doing of the first action or of the second or what have you, although certain of its instantiations, quite clearly, are not. Hence, if this is so, the occurrence of an action other than the one specified cannot be said to disconfirm R'.

So, pending the provision of a new conception of how actions happen (in some schema S different from R'), we are left with the formula R'—so long, that is, as we allow that the formula could cover B (Booth's declaiming, etc.) *as an action*. And, even if this new and different action-framework were to be installed, it also would mark out a common ground between the doing of A (shooting the President) and the doing of B (the declaiming) such that the same relationship between it and B as now obtains would still obtain. Again, B's occurring would not be a falsifying counterinstance to that *new* schema; although it would be, as before, counterinstantial to a certain set of *factual* premises, i.e., that set which would yield an A but not a B.

The consideration I have adduced here does not require me to go back on my earlier argument (in Chapter Nine) that the formula R' is *not* analytic. That formula would be so only if the nonoccurrence of an A was *self-contradictory* over against the claim that the "if . . ." part of the formula had been instantiated by a set of facts which specified the doing of an A. But I have not said about either A or B that the non-doing of that action in the circumstances envisioned is logically impossible. Indeed, if it were, the problem we are discussing—the non-doing of A, where A is specified, and the doing of B instead— could not even arise. All I have argued is that the doing of a B, an action other than A, has to come equally under the formula and, hence, is not a counterinstance to *it*.

This brings me to my second principal consideration: that it is difficult—and, perhaps, impossible—really to conceive the situation in which the occurrence of action B (again let it be Booth's declaiming, etc.) could constitute a falsifying counterinstance to the hypothetical formula R'. To see this let us again start with the supposition that A (as before, the shooting of the President) is the action specified in the premises (i.e., specified by certain particular facts which fulfill the antecedent conditions of R' and which, in so doing, tell us materially what the agent's intention is, his means/end belief, and so on).

Now, clearly, the claim as to falsification depends on saying that A is the action specified and B is not. So we must start from this supposition; otherwise we have no ground for saying that the doing of B could be an infirming or falsifying case *vis-à-vis* the formula R'.

Immediately, though, this raises the question of what is involved in saying that a certain action does count as the specified action, or does not count, as the case may be. Now whatever that standard is, it is by reference to *this*, ultimately, that A (shooting the President), if it were to occur, would be the specified action and B (Booth's declaiming, etc.), if it were to occur, would *not* be the specified action. So, some formula must state the conditions, an instantiation of which gives the specified action that is to occur. Alternatively, it seems clear that if the conditions of this formula had been fulfilled by a *different* set of facts (by B-yielding facts) then B—Booth's declaiming—would be the specified action. So, it just happens that here shooting the President is the action specified and, hence, is the action designated by A *in this particular case*.

Saying all this is required if we are to give any sense to the claim that A is the specified action and B is not, in the example at hand. What follows from this, though, is that the doing of A (shooting the President) and the doing of B (Booth's declaiming, etc.) come equally under the basic "if . . . then . . ." formula (R'). For there is an equal commitment to the *validity* of the formula where one says that the specified action did occur and where one says that an *un*specified action did occur.

Hence, the occurrence of B, as I have described it, could not be a counterinstance to the *formula* at all and, accordingly, could not be a possible falsifying counterinstance to R'. It would, however, be counterinstantial to the citing of certain facts under the formula: to those facts that were A-yielding or to those facts that were not B-yielding. My point, then, is simply that where the formula R' is treated as that by reference to which we do determine ultimately when A is to be counted as the specified action and B is not, in a given case, then it is senseless to claim that the occurrence of an action B, where A is the action specified by the *facts* cited, could conceivably falsify the formula R'. (Cf. the argument of Danto, *Analytical Philosophy of History*, p. 230.)

The only way out of this, it seems to me, is to claim that R' does *not* really specify occurring or not-occurring with respect to any action, that is, when taken in conjunction with a particular factual instantiation of its antecedent conditions. Granting this, however, loosens our grip on the claim that A is the specified action and B is not. For, if this claim about A and B was still made, we would want, then, to ask how, in default of R', one could know *that*. Moreover, granting this defect in R' violates the hypothesis from which we started: that A was the specified action, given a certain instantiation of the "if . . ." conditions of the formula R', and that B was not. In any case, to regain our grip on the claim that A was specified and B was not and to restate, adequately, the hypothesis by which this was so, we would have to move to some new and different basic formula. And the dialectic of my argument would start anew from this point and move to the same conclusion.

The argument here suggests that in order to set the trap against the formula R', in which its falsification will occur, one must do something which in effect guarantees that this prey will never be caught. For in order to set up the possibility of falsifying R' we require the claim that A (here: shooting the President) is the action that should occur, given a certain instantiation of the "if . . ." part of R', and B (here: Booth's declaiming, etc.) is not. But in order to conceive this possibility we require the very formula in question. Hence the occurring of B, in the example we are imagining, does not constitute a falsifying counterinstance to the formula itself: it could not for that formula is presupposed *as true* in the very setting up of the crucial claim whereby B is even to be considered as such an instance.

The point, then, is that the occurrence of B does not falsify the formula; it is not a counterinstance to the formula *per se* and could not be. This conclusion reinforces the one we reached in canvassing an earlier consideration: the conclusion that, since both the actions (shooting the President and the declaiming) were nondefectively actions and actions *in the same sense*, the occurrence of either would come equally under the formula and, hence, could not be a falsifying counterinstance to it.

The occurrence of B (Booth's declaiming, etc.) is, however, inconsistent with a particular *factual instantiation* of R' (it is inconsistent with those material premises that would lead us to expect the action of shooting the President).

Thus it is always open to us to say that the set of facts cited, even if true, is irrelevant to Booth's action of declaiming and then jumping and fleeing (or, for that matter, to his just eating an apple), though they would be relevant to his shooting the President, and that the antecedent conditions of the formula R' with respect to Booth's declaiming (or eating an apple) have not been fulfilled at all. Here it is alleged that some of the conditions required to be fulfilled in order for the formula to be *applied* to an action at all, or to a particular action under a specific description, have not been filled. Hence, this case (where Booth declaims or just eats an apple instead of shooting the President), like the so-called classic case (where no action of any sort happens), is *not* a counterinstance to the basic formula.

This is merely to say that the formula (R') has not been nondefectively applied in either of the key cases at hand. For in the classic case, although there was an instantiation of the necessary antecedent conditions, or "if . . ." part, sufficient to yield the action of shooting the President, no action of any sort occurred. And in the second case, where there was an action done there was not an adequate instantiation by a set of factual premises sufficient to yield that action. In each case, then, the basic formula is defectively fulfilled: in the classic case the failure comes at the "then . . ." or consequent part; in the other case it comes at the "if . . ." or antecedent conditions part. And it follows that we do not have in either case a nondefective application of the formula such that there *could* be a falsifying counterinstance to it.

I am not, of course, saying that the formula R' could be empirically falsified if we did not, perversely or nobly, protect it by refusing to admit certain kinds of facts. I am actually saying the very opposite: rather than conceding the infirming character of certain facts and then refusing to admit them, I am admitting them readily, while denying their infirming character in the first place.

Of course, what I have done with the formula R' is not open to those who want to push a general law interpretation onto the ground of explanatory connection in the case of actions. There is not, in the case of a general law, the sort of logical distance between the statement of the formula and its instantiation that we have with the formula R'. A general law simply *says* that when A happens (when a barium salt, for example, is put into water) then B always happens (the salt dissolves); the nonoccurrence of B, where A has happened, does count as a counterinstance to what the law asserts. (And indeed the "law" I have cited here—in an example suggested by Donald Marquis—is in fact false.) If the nonoccurrence of B, in the situation described, were not counterinstantial, we would not have a general law; for general laws do assert a regularity in the happenings of instances and they are empirically falsifiable. That is just the point: were laws like the formula R' they would not be *empirical* laws; and if the basic

Practical Inference

formula for action-explanations does have the character I have delineated, then it is not a general law.

There is an entirely different framework of thought involved in the case of a general law from what we have in the case of the formula R'. The man who entertains R' is not committed to saying that it is a factual statement which just happens to be true "in the final empirical analysis," nor does he, in a pathological variant of this thesis, just refuse to go to that "final empirical analysis."

We are now in a position, I think, to identify the relevant logical details with respect to R'. Briefly: (a) It is believed that the formula is true. (b) It is not believed, however, that what it asserts is an *analytic* truth. (c) It is believed, then, that its antecedent part could (possibly) be fulfilled as true but its consequent part, "then the agent does a certain specified action," not be fulfilled so. (d) It is not believed, though, that this conjectured occasion could provide a falsifying counterinstance to the formula itself.

The reason for this last point has already been given: the basic formula R' is truly and properly employed, in being applied to a particular set of behavioral circumstances, only when *all* of its elements are fulfilled, only when each of these is satisfied by facts that fit its "places." The whole "if . . . then . . ." formula constitutes *one* statement—or, better, statement form—that embodies "indents" or "specifications" indicating its "eligible filling." An explanatory instantiation, then, is an "application" of this "meaty" hypothetical—conceived here in the role, not of premise, but of inference precept—to the eligible facts.[4]

Hence, with respect to R', it is not so much that the fulfilling of the antecedent conditions is a sufficient condition for the consequence as it is that the fulfilling of the *whole thing* is a sufficient condition for asserting an explanatory connection between the agent's action and the

4. For the logic of my analysis in the first half of this chapter, I am much indebted to von Wright (especially to pp. 115–117 of *Explanation and Understanding*) and to Ryle (especially to pp. 336–339 of " 'If,' 'So,' 'Because' "). I am also indebted to Tim George for his helpful comments on this chapter.

Most of the quoted terms in the paragraph to which this note is attached are drawn from Ryle (see pp. 328, 332–336 of his article) and the phrase "fill the bill" is his as well. Ryle's account also lay behind my earlier distinction (in Chapter Eight) of two basic models for explanation: the Hempelian one, in which explanation is conceived as the logical operation of *deriving* from premises, and the re-enactment one, in which explanation is conceived as the *instantiation* of a principle of inference.

other specified facts. And it is in this rather oblique way that the formula R' conforms to Danto's "semantic criterion": for there is no eligible occasion on which the antecedent conditions are satisfactorily fulfilled that the consequent part is not fulfilled by the action specified.

If one finds these points perplexing, the solution is not to look for further logical quirks of the formula, for yet another logical strategem. On the contrary, the answer is to be found in considering carefully just what it is that we have in the basic formula (R') for action-explanations.

The basic formula exhibits a conception of how actions happen. This formula belongs to the conceptual framework for actions, specifically to that part in which our basic beliefs respecting the happening or the doing of an action are to be found. Accordingly, we can regard it as the foundation of action-explanations; it is a logical feature, whether explicit or not, of the explanation of any particular action.

My claim, in short, is that the formula is a conceptual representation of our understanding of how actions happen. If this claim is correct, then the basic formula would seem to be more appropriately assimilated to a presupposition than to a general law. It is, perhaps, more like "every event has a cause" than it is like the principle of mass-energy conservation. Accordingly, I would suggest that Churchland's assimilation of the formula to a very high order general law, or "deeply entrenched theoretical nomological" as he calls it, is a type mistake. (See his "Logical Character of Action-Explanations," p. 225, for the passage quoted and for the analogy with the conservation principle.)

The point is that the basic schema and its associated hypothetical form (R') have a definite orientation, a particular conceptual setting, that of action. (This should be noted; it is *action*, not intention, that provides the essential location.) Hence, the basic schema is grounded in and cannot be removed from the universe of discourse that it organizes, the universe of action-explanations. Accordingly, one cannot falsify such a schematic principle or, better, one cannot conceive its falsifiability *within* a universe of discourse so long as the principle provides the significant framework for conceiving that universe in the first place. The schema—especially in the version provided by the associated basic formula (R')—provides the paradigm or model of how we conceive actions to happen (at least insofar as they are said to be for

a reason) and our paradigm of what it is to explain actions by reference
to such things as purposes and so on. This being the case, it is not really open to us to think that the occurrence, or nonoccurrence, of a
given action could empirically falsify the conceptual paradigm proper
to action-explanation itself. But, equally, it is not really open to us to
engage this paradigm with the facts of the world unless "action is already there" (in von Wright's phrase, *Explanation and Understanding*, p. 117).

There is, I take it then, an essential difference between conceptual
representations and general laws, a difference that should not be
blurred. It might be to some point then to note the oft-repeated claim
that some laws of nature migrate from being falsifiable empirical hypotheses to being elements in a conceptual framework. I should add
that this distinction seems sharp enough even though we cannot in
every case tell which of these a particular law is. Now what is important to see is that the claim here is not that some general laws are resistant to empirical falsification (for if any one were resistant *in principle*
then it would not be a general law) but, rather, that some natural laws
become resistant to empirical falsification for all practical purposes.

Interestingly, Churchland's argument seems to become incoherent
on precisely this point. He asserts that his L_1 (a formula very like R')
enjoys "nomic status" as "a function of the . . . role it plays" (see
"Logical Character of Action-Explanations," pp. 225–26, esp. p. 226).
But this, of course, is a *non sequitur*. For L_1 can enjoy *nomic* status
only if it is empirically falsifiable in principle, a point essential to
Churchland's claim that it is a general law. Its *role* might make L_1
resistant to falsification for all practical purposes, but that is another
matter; and this alleged resistance to disconfirmation could have bearing on a claim to nomic status, made on behalf of L_1, only where we
had independent grounds for believing that the "law" was possibly falsifiable by reference to matters of empirical fact. On the other hand, if
Churchland's principal reason for assigning nomic status to this "law"
is that it cannot be empirically falsified, that is, given the *role* that it
has, then it may well be that it is not a general law at all. And hence
we should take seriously his suggestion that L_1 is a "conceptual truth"
(p. 226). But this seems difficult, if not impossible, to reconcile with
his explicit claim that L_1 is a general law.

I have suggested one way in which Churchland's position can be
made coherent; we can take him as saying that L_1 is empirically fal-

sifiable in principle but that its role as a deeply embedded element in
our conceptual framework for thinking about and explaining action
protects it, for all practical purposes, from disconfirmation. If that is
not his meaning though, if he really does regard L_1 as a "conceptual
truth" in the sense that it is not in principle empirically falsifiable,
then his argument *is* incoherent. And he will have to find different
categories for developing his account of L_1 than the ones he has used
in his essay.

I have argued, contrary to the claim that L_1 (or R') enjoys "nomic
status," that the formula cannot be empirically falsified—which fits it,
peculiarly well, to play the role it does: that of conceptual foundation
or presupposition of action-explanations. In short, my argument has
been that the formula R' is, as a conceptual representation and in the
role that it does play, simply not of the right sort to be subject to empirical confirmation or disconfirmation in any case.

The fact that the formula is so frequently useful, perhaps even in-
variably applicable with success, in the explanation of actions is no
reason for saying that it is thereby empirically confirmed. It is, however, a good reason for thinking our concept sound and the representation of it accurate. If we were to come to think otherwise, we would
stop applying it altogether, or would restrict its range of application, or
would apply it in a substantially modified form. What happens to a
"bad" conceptual representation is that you stop applying it; but that is
not the same as, or the result of, having falsified it.

At the same time, the claim that the basic formula is a conceptual
representation, hence, logically immune from empirical falsification,
does not require that the formula assert an analytic truth. We do
not—or need not—conceive the elements of the formula, the antecedent part and the consequent part, as being related such that the assertion that the consequent action did not occur is simply self-contradictory, and in that sense inconceivable, in the face of the claim that the
necessary antecedent conditions have been fulfilled.

It may well be true that the relationship between the elements of the
basic formula, between the "if . . ." part and the "then . . ." part, is
established by the way we think. But it does not follow from this, or
from the formula itself, no matter how accurately it does represent
basic beliefs as to how actions are conceived to happen, that the relationship indicated is *analytically* true.

An analytic statement, a "conceptual truth" in that sense, rules out certain things from happening at all. If the antecedent is true then it cannot be that the specified action does not occur: for the occurrence of the action on the occasion in question is *logically entailed* by the truth of the premises. Its not happening on this occasion is logically impossible; hence such a thing is inconceivable *because* self-contradictory. A conceptual representation, a "conceptual truth" in a very different sense, does not rule out the nonoccurrence of the specified action on a given occasion. It is implied merely that we could not understand what did happen on that occasion. We could, quite reasonably, say that an action had taken place (for Booth's declaiming and then jumping and fleeing, for example, does appear to be an action); it is just that we can make no sense of it, given the premises— the instantiation of the "if . . ." part of R' from which we started. If the antecedent is true and the specified action does not happen, then we simply cannot explain *that*. Its not happening is inconceivable because it violates our very conception of how actions do happen. But for all that, it is still possible that it not happen: its happening so is not *logically* impossible.[5]

I think it is important in any theory of explanation to be able to provide an account of the failure to explain, or understand, as well as an account of how one misunderstands. Logically, understanding and misunderstanding are the same. They are of a piece: in each case one provides facts that intelligibly fulfill, in effect, the elements of the basic schema for action-explanations. When the facts are true one understands. When some of them, at least, are false one misunderstands (or misexplains, if you will). But the failure to understand is the inability to provide some of the relevant facts at all. Hence, the failure to

---

5. Norman Malcolm makes roughly the same point I am making when he distinguishes between "two types of *unintelligibility*." The first type is simply logical self-contradiction; the second consists in our having no "thinkable explanation for the falsity of the conclusion"—for it is simply "impossible to *understand* how the conclusion could be false." (See his "Intention and Behavior" [unpublished typescript: forthcoming in published form].)

In my account, though, we are not trying (and failing) to *explain* a mistake that the investigator has made. Nor is it the *falsity* of the conclusion that is puzzling. Rather, it is the occurrence (or nonoccurrence) of a particular action that is puzzling: the occurrence in question is *inexplicable*, in light of the formula R', when we have a particular set of premises which materially instantiate (and nondefectively so, to all appearances) the antecedent conditions of that formula. There is no evident point in speaking of a *false conclusion* for this would suggest that the formula itself was false and *that* would provide an explanation of sorts for the odd occurrence; it would in any case remove all reason for calling such an occurrence inexplicable (or unintelligible) in the first place.

understand is distinct from both understanding and misunderstanding; just as not being able to apply a formula at all, because we cannot get the facts to "fill the bill," is different from applying it, whether correctly or incorrectly.

I would regard the difference between a conceptual representation and an analytic truth, where the former allows for the possibility of the nonoccurrence of the specified action and the latter does not, as marking a point in favor of the conceptual representation interpretation. It seems to me that the analytic version has no real room for failures to explain. It takes up the slack by denying that certain things happened or that certain conditions obtained, even when we have the usual trustworthy evidence that they did happen or did obtain. I would think it altogether better, in the case where the evidence points to conditions obtaining and actions happening, to say that we cannot understand what happened, rather than to say it did not really happen at all, evidence to the contrary.

Yet there are surely some who will balk at my conclusion: the conclusion that the foundation principle of action-explanations is a conceptual representation and that it is, in what it asserts, neither empirically falsifiable nor analytically true. There's something problematic here, they will say. And, even if I point out that the proposition about every event having a cause is equally problematic, in being both conceptual (not empirically falsifiable) and nonanalytic, they will not be assuaged. Indeed, they will say that none of this can be. Why?

The reason is largely a historical one. It will be thought, I am sure, that I have made out R' to be a synthetic a priori proposition. It follows from this that the formula must be universal, necessary, and so on. I am then to be held accountable for something I cannot do, for showing how such propositions are even possible. And, since I cannot do that, or will not do it, my argument might be said, for that very reason, to be open to objection.

I think, however, that this would be an overinterpretation of my argument. I have never used the term "synthetic a priori"; it is a term of art, coined by Kant, and it belongs ultimately to the province of his metaphysics. Now there is, of course, a clear sense in which the formula R' can be regarded as synthetic a priori (as Kant used that term); but the propositions he was talking about under that name all have certain distinctive characteristics: they are somehow operative in all thinking men, in all times and places; they are unchanging and cannot change; they assert some sort of "necessary" relationship; they are inescapable modes of thought.

It is, for example, necessary that men think in terms of causes and effects and hence necessary that, in thinking of an event, they think of it as having a cause. The fact that A is the cause of B is an empirical matter, but that men must think the world under the category of causality is not. It is a priori.

How is it possible that the form for thinking "A is the cause of B" (i.e., the form "every event has a cause") is not an analytic truth and that at the same time it is an a priori necessity for thinking and asserts something necessary? Kant's answer takes us to some transcendental "subject" of experience, to a supra-experiential subject that is rational and obeys the laws of thought for all rational beings. But I have said nothing like this. I have never alleged that the formula R′ is part of the mental furniture of all men, at all times and places, or that it is unchanging. I would be inclined, in fact, to doubt such a claim. Certainly, then, there is no "necessity" for thought in the formula and I am not driven on to account for this necessity. Hence, the question, "How can there be an a priori necessary constraint on thought in a nonanalytic proposition?" is one I am not obliged to answer.

The formula R′ is innocent of all these noumenal affinities; it is simply a statement that is neither empirically falsifiable nor analytically true. There is, nonetheless, an account that can be offered as to why it has this particular logical status.

In this account action-explanations constitute a practice, a language-game (*Sprachspiel*) in Wittgenstein's terms; and the schema, including its associated hypothetical form R′, belongs to the foundation (*Fundament* or *Grund*) of that game. Indeed every system of inquiry has some such foundation, which is from the standpoint of that practice logically ultimate. And these foundations, when stated (as in the basic schema for action-explanations), say something that is neither empirically falsifiable nor analytically true. They are, respecting any given piece of inquiry or explanation within the practice, a priori. [6]

6. In the concluding part of this chapter, my argument draws upon Wittgenstein's *On Certainty*. The editors of this posthumous work have numbered Wittgenstein's entries consecutively as sections. The terms used in the paragraph to which this note attaches can be found in sections 204–205 (*Sprachspiel, Grund*) and 411 (*Fundament*). All my subsequent references in this chapter to Wittgenstein's book *On Certainty* will be

Historical Explanation

The foundation can be said in some sense to organize the language-game; for this reason it is often analogized by Wittgenstein to a rule—as distinct from a move—of the game (see sections 95, 494, 622 in particular). But the notion of a rule is too explicit, too neat. It would be better to say that the foundation of a language-game is not so much a rule, or set of rules, as it is that which *defines* the game, that which gives it its point or character (see section 497).

The foundation sets the kind of moves one can make; it is the form of that world, the limit of that particular game. Just as one judges of the correctness of a given move, by referring to the object of the game (and not vice versa), one distinguishes between correct and incorrect moves in a language-game (between the true and the false or the explanatory and the not explanatory) in the same way.

To know is to make a move in such a game. Knowing involves grounds. To say "I *know* that . . ." is to say, or suggest, that I have proper grounds for my statement: "In these cases, then, one says 'I know' and mentions how one knows, or at least one can do so" (section 484; see also section 550).

Likewise, one could say that Brutus' intention (to save the republican constitution of Rome) *explains* his action (joining Cassius' conspiracy against Caesar). To say that this intention *explains* that action is to have proper grounds for that particular statement. Among these would be evidence that Brutus did this thing and that Brutus had this intention; we would need a setting for all this too, in Caesar's threat to the existing Roman constitution. Suppose we had all these things, would that be enough? No, we would need also the very idea, the groundform, of such an explanation: the idea that intentions (under certain conditions) give rise to actions.

"[T]he concept of knowing is coupled with that of the language-game" (section 560). And we might add, so is the concept of explaining an action.

A particular practical inference has its proper grounds, but this business of citing grounds cannot go on forever. There is an end point which provides grounds but is not itself grounded. This is the difference between a particular practical inference (such as the one we construct to explain Brutus' action) and the schema itself. The ground

given by section number only (in parentheses) in the text. For an expansion of my interpretation of Wittgenstein in this part of the chapter, see my paper "The Problem of the 'Tie' in von Wright's Schema of Practical Inference," esp. sec. 4.

Practical Inference

for saying that *this* intention could explain *that* action is the schema. We could *know* that a particular intention explains a particular action but we could not, if this is the very game-form of action-explanations, be said to know that intentions explain actions. This, rather, is the object of the language-game of explaining; it is *what* we do in the game, not one of the things that we do.

Now the notion of a "foundation" (section 403) or game-form is sometimes correlated by Wittgenstein with "rock bottom" convictions (see sections 246, 248, 512). And his putting of talk of the foundations of a language-game into *epistemic* terms, into terms of conviction and assurance and trust, has given rise to some confusion. (For instances of Wittgenstein's usage see sections 457–458, 499–500, 509, 617.) But I would suggest that when Wittgenstein says, for example, that "absence of doubt belongs to the essence of the language-game" (section 370) he is expressing straightforwardly, the claim that the ground-form—the rules or, better, the object of the game—is simply taken for granted in the playing of the game. (See sections 103, 143, 211, in particular.) There is freedom from doubt there, in the game; but there is no other sense in which the groundform is certain beyond this one. Indeed it would be a deep error to confuse the certainty we have respecting the groundform *in* the game with the form's being true (see sections 308 and 511 in particular; and also section 403).

For that which is logically ultimate in a particular inquiry or universe of discourse is, in a sense, beyond truth and falsity. "If the true is what is grounded, then the ground (*der Grund*) is not *true*, nor yet false" (section 205; see also sections 499–500).

I argued earlier (in Chapter Nine) that the basic schema—or, alternatively, the "if . . . then . . ." formula (R') associated with it—does provide the groundplan of the historians reasoning, both in his explanations and in his use of evidence to verify the explanatory facts he uses. The schema is what he takes for granted in his work. So the question naturally arises whether the foundation for action-explanations, as we have it in the schema of practical inference, is such that it would be equally improper to say either that the schema is (possibly) true or that it is (possibly) false. If neither of these is to be allowed then this would provide a quite interesting reason, albeit a rather drastic one, for saying that such a formula cannot be empirically falsified, since it cannot be false, nor analytically true, since it cannot be true either.

Historical Explanation

Before one attempts to answer this question, however, it should be noted that the claim that the groundform of a practice can be neither true nor false, though often made by Wittgenstein, is qualified by him in a significant way. For we can identify a certain sense in which such a form could be true or false. We can do so, rather roughly, by distinguishing between the *foundation* of a practice (or a language-game) and our description (*Beschreibung*) of this foundation (see esp. sections 56, 82, and 95).

Now a *descriptive* account can be true or false, for it is an attempt to report, more or less accurately, what particular conception of things does organize a given universe of discourse. So, on this reading, the basic schema can be regarded as true or false; for it is simply an attempt to state accurately how we conceive actions to happen. It is, as I suggested earlier, a description—a conceptual representation—of the foundation of one language-game in particular, that of explaining actions. But what of the foundation it describes, can *that* be true or false?

In answer to this question Wittgenstein made his claim that the game-form itself is altogether incapable of taking truth-values. There is, his argument goes, no clear way in which any such groundform could be regarded as true or false. For it is difficult to see what they could be referred to in order to determine their truth-value: as ultimate they presuppose nothing, nothing is logically prior to them; whereas all of our network of knowledge claims, by which we do determine truth or falsity, for example, by going to the facts of the world, already presuppose them (see esp. sections 94, 105). So, clearly, the way in which we could determine a given game-form to be true or false would have to be vastly different from the way in which a statement within the universe of discourse organized by such a game-form would be determined true or false (see here section 88 in particular). Once this is said, there seems to be no other way—at least no obvious or accredited way—to assign them truth-value at all. Indeed it becomes difficult to identify even a sense in which they could be true or false (see esp. sections 188–92).

Hence, to assert the groundform (when put into words, as in the schema) as something that could be true or false, as something we could *know*, is akin to a senseless act (see sections 466–67; and also sections 414, 477). Accordingly, it would be better here to regard the linguistic expression of a game-form, except where it has descriptive force, as a mere utterance (*Äusserung:* see sections 466 and 510). For there is no thought of verification in such an utterance, no knowledge it can yield.

A game-form is the foundation of a *practice*. And within the particular universe of discourse we call action-explanation that foundation governs the explanations we give in the individual case. For these groundforms are not in our collective unconscious or out there somewhere in Plato's heaven, they are *in* the explanatory practices and individual knowledge claims themselves. These game-forms are objective features, though implicit ones, of any going science.

This I take to be the point of Wittgenstein's remark that "the end is not an ungrounded presupposition; it is an ungrounded way of acting" (section 110; see also section 204). These structures in our *praxis*—in our modes of inquiry and of explanation—are neither right nor wrong, true nor false; they just are. (See sections 496 and 559).

We can, of course, put these structures into words, try to formulate and thereby describe them. And such statements can be true or false. These formulations however, though descriptive of objective features of a particular practice, are not reportorial in nature; rather, they are dialectical conclusions to complex arguments. They are, as I have called them, conceptual representations: they represent conceptually, they state what the foundation of a given practice is. Hence, such statements, if true, are not *analytically* true; because there is a clear sense in which what they are asserting is descriptive. But likewise such statements, if false, are not *empirically* false, because equally clearly the method of description here is that of a (partial) rational reconstruction out of the data provided by our language-games. The description of the groundform of a language-game proceeds by reasoned argument to a conclusion respecting what has been assumed in that particular game (see section 411).

One can become conscious of the foundation of a particular practice only by formulating that foundation. Indeed one can discriminate the foundation within the practice only conceptually; for otherwise we would have just the practice itself. The foundation is something that must be argued to: one reasons from the explanatory practices and from the knowledge claims in a given science to the foundation that *must* be ingredient. And this is what is stated in the conceptual representation. In the case of such statements there is no distinction between their truth and their adequate formulation. The foundations of a practice can be known, but only by reason. There is no fact, other than the soundness of the argument involved, that could determine any such statement to be true or false. At best we can be said to have fixed, by reasoning, upon that which is taken as certain in a particular language-game (see section 307).

Here we have come back full circle to the point I noted at the very beginning of this discussion: that the basic schema of practical inference is neither falsifiable by reference to an empirical matter of fact nor true by logical entailment. For it states the groundform of a language-game, that of the explanation of actions. This is, in rough outline, a Wittgensteinian solution to the problem of the logical status of the "tie" that holds between the "agent does A" part and the "because . . ." part within the basic schema of practical inference.

In large measure the principal barrier that would inhibit philosophers from accepting this solution is that at least some of them have tended to keep relatively rigid a distinction which Wittgenstein was inclined to relax. I have in mind here the distinction between the empirical and the logical. To take one example near at hand, both Donagan and Churchland seem to accept, on principle, that a sharp distinction is to be observed here; this would account for the "either-or" way in which each has set the matter up. Donagan, in believing that the formula is not empirically falsifiable, immediately concludes that it is therefore analytic and Churchland, believing that it is not "merely analytic," concludes that it must thereby be a general law of some sort. However, much of Churchland's argument can be viewed as an attempt, never made explicit, to overcome this rigid distinction; and we can take his unarticulated dissatisfaction with the analytic/empirical dichotomy as suggesting in effect that there is another possibility.

It is important not to misconceive what Wittgenstein was saying. He was not saying that empirical statements and logical ones are alike in that statements of each sort can formulate rules of a language-game (which would be much like Plato's claim that men and women are alike in that individuals of each sort can be rulers in the State of the Guardians). Rather, Wittgenstein *suppresses* the distinction between the empirical and the mathematical-logical where a proposition functions as part of the description of the game-form organizing a particular universe of discourse: "everything descriptive of a language-game is part of logic" (section 56). Here logic is whatever describes (or belongs

Practical Inference

descriptively to) the groundform of a language-game. A proposition is "logical" in this sense if "it does describe the conceptual (linguistic) situation" (section 51). Wittgenstein's notion of a *conceptual* statement, then, has to be taken in a very special way.

When a statement belongs descriptively to the game-form, the question does not arise whether it is empirical or logical (that is, logical in the sense denoted by *formal* logic). Indeed, the decision whether a statement is the one of these or the other actually depends on its being a move, rather than a rule-statement, in a particular language-game.

If the Wittgensteinian analysis is followed, the schema (as descriptive of the game-form of action-explanations) could be neither an analytic truth nor an empirically falsifiable statement. Indeed, if we take seriously Wittgenstein's claim that the description of a game-form is never more than partial and approximate (note, for example, sections 103, 559), the schema could, quite obviously, never be a logical entailment. But the more important Wittgensteinian claim here is that, even if the schema could be given an exhaustive and wholly accurate formulation, it would still not state a logical entailment. And if we take seriously the schema's logical role as game-form (conceptually represented) within the language-game of explaining actions, the schema could never within that game be a contingent matter, or be a thing decidable by reference to the kinds of matters which are themselves designated, within the game, as empirical. Wittgenstein's point, then, is that all rule-statements, precisely insofar as they function as descriptive of the groundform of a language-game, are neither empirical nor logical.

One further step, though, remains to be taken. Wittgenstein regarded the groundform of a language-game as consisting of rules, or something like rules. On this view the groundform of a language-game (such as that of action-explanations) is not a proposition, or set of propositions, at all. For it belongs, as a game-form, to an altogether different dimension. A game-form is simply the foundation of a practice; as such it belongs to practice.

The game-form, even when formulated, is not asserted; for, when given linguistic expression, it is, other than being a description of the object or character of the language-game, merely an utterance. And what is expressed in this utterance—the content of the practice itself—can be neither true nor false.

This striking doctrine is much like Collingwood's on absolute presuppositions.[7] And its acceptance would mark off a sharp and deep divide between so-called groundforms (which are *as practices* incapable of being either true or false) and what Kant called "synthetic a priori propositions" (which are *statements* necessarily, but not analytically, true).

Indeed, it would on this view be a mistake even to regard a groundform *qua* groundform as necessary (or as contingent, for that matter). These distinctions—contingent or necessary, true or false, empirical or formal-logical, knowable or not knowable—all belong to the playing of a language-game, to the statements that are moves in the game, and not to those that belong to the game-form.

It is not necessary that a game-form be propounded; its efficacy comes, not from its being true or even from its being conceptually represented, but simply from its ingredience in the practice. What governs an explanation—a particular practical inference—in the individual case is not so much the basic schema as it is that which the schema *describes*. Hence the crucial sense in which the schema is true (i.e., as an accurate description of the groundform) does not give us the crucial sense in which a particular practical inference is governed. What governs the particular inference is simply the way in which the general practice goes on. Thus, when one is said to reason "in accordance with" the principles of practical inference, the controlling idea is not that he uses the schema but, rather, that he conforms to the *practice* of practical inference.

It does not follow from this, however, that we are committed to the practice as a kind of brute ultimate, that we are "locked" into it willynilly, without rhyme or reason. Nor does it follow that a practice is an insulated, self-fulfilling "world" in which one is hermetically sealed off from anything "alien," from what Hegel called "the power of negativity."

For there is a sense in which we can be said to verify a practice. Or, to speak more precisely, there is an equivalent to verification that operates in the case of practices. One might call it authentication or rectification or, if you will, *praxis*-verification. And the fact that it is a form of *self*-rectification within the practice does not detract from the fact that it is a form of verification.

7. Collingwood's account of absolute presuppositions is found principally in Part I of his *Essay on Metaphysics* and in his *Autobiography*. For the point I am referring to, see in particular *Autobiography, pp.* 66–67, and *Metaphysics*, pp. 32–33, 53–54.

Practical Inference

How, then, does one *authenticate* (verify in that sense) the self-contained practice of explaining *the agent does* A by reference to matters that in effect fulfill the conditions of the "if . . ." part of the basic schema? The answer to this question, I suggest, is found in what would cause us to *adjust* the practice. (And in suggesting such an answer I am diverging somewhat from Wittgenstein's own position in this matter.)

We have the premises of a particular practical inference in Booth's intention, in his means/end belief, and so on; we expect him to shoot the President (for this is what he is supposed to do, given these premises). But instead he does something altogether preposterous and unexpectable: he carefully sets his gun up in a nearby potted plant and, appearing to address it, begins to recite in Latin and from memory a complicated but apparently irrelevant passage from Duns Scotus on the "material substantiality" of angels. This is utterly inexplicable. We are incapable of conceiving its actually happening.

Or Booth thought at some deep, subconscious level—we are subsequently told by a psychiatric expert—that eating the apple was the way to kill the President; so he just stood there eating. Would this cause us to adjust the practice? Well, Booth may have meant by his apple eating the shooting of the President; but we do not understand it that way; and we look elsewhere than to practical inference for the explanation of his bizarre conduct. Booth was insane, we say, and we look to another paradigm.

Nonetheless there is, even in these cases, an element of adjustment involved in the practice of practical inference itself. We adjust the practice simply by restricting its range of application, or by declaring some few actions inexplicable, or by turning to other paradigms in certain cases (just as physics turned away at one time from the teleological paradigm to others of its own devising [see section 292]). And, more important, given repeated shocks of the sort encountered in these examples, we might even change the practice itself (which would result in our having a different conceptual representation from that which we currently have in the basic schema).

The crucial point is that inconsistencies at the material level—between what in particular the agent intends, believes respecting means to that end, etc. and what he does—can be identified. And these inconsistencies, simply in virtue of being identified, involve some sort of adjustment in the practice itself. The practice of practical inference, then, is subject to adjustment at every point where we engage in a particular practical inference.

If our explanatory practices should prove inadequate, in any of a variety of ways, then we adjust what we do; and it is through such adjustments in our *praxis* that change can occur in the organizing principles themselves. I am not, of course, suggesting that every adjustment constitutes a change in the practice but, rather, that repeated "shocks"—if they exhibit some sort of pattern—would result in a *general* adjustment, which might take any of several forms. Among these would be an internal alteration in the practice itself: this would count as a change in the ingredient groundform, a change in the very principles of that practice.

For these principles are not shadowy, incipient propositions in the unconscious but objective features of our explanatory practices, features of which we are necessarily unaware *until they are formulated*. And, since they are located where they are, it is possible to change them, by an indirect route, even though we are unaware of their existence. Or, it might be clearer to say, we can cause changes in them, since changes here are not the results of "basic actions," the groundform of a practice not being the sort of thing we can change directly in any case. Rather such change has to "build up" through a series of adjustments and become incorporated into the practice.

The changes in question are indirectly brought about. They are initiated and perhaps can only be initiated by what happens in the individual case, in particular practical inferences, and by the adjustments introduced into the practice itself at each point where an inconsistency has been perceived.

In this way the practice is self-rectifying: it is self-adjusting with respect to inconsistencies that are themselves identified from within the practice. And some of these adjustments may come to constitute changes in the practice itself (changes in its groundform, which will be reflected in changes in the basic schema). For whatever alteration the practice of practical inference has to undergo the schema (which describes that practice) is subject to as well.

On the other hand, there may be no such inconsistencies (or very few of them). Here the effective instantiation of elements in the "if . . ." part gives rise to no unexpected happenings: the particular action that is supposed to happen, given that particular instantiation, *does* happen every time (or almost always).

Practical Inference

In each particular practical inference, there is a "match up" of the various facts on hand: those facts that count as instantiations of the schema "match up" with the available evidence and, where that is so, the action supposed to happen, given the particular premises of our practical inference, does happen. Booth's intention and means/end belief cohere with the action he actually performs (shooting the President) and the evidence we have relied on (in the form of physical artifacts, in what people noted, in what Booth said and did) "matches up" with the details of the particular inference we have constructed.[8]

Where particular inferences are coherent in the way described, given the available evidence, then the practice of practical inference can be said to be (self-) *rectified*—or *praxis*-verified, if you prefer. This is not to say that it is true (for practices are not of that sort) but, rather, that it is sound. It is a coherent practice.

One further conclusion of importance remains to be drawn. I have been arguing throughout this book that an action-explanation that yields understanding is better, as an explanation of action, than one that merely conforms to the schema of practical inference. (Recall here the knife wound example and the argument of Chapter Five.) And this notion of explanatory understanding requires in its turn, I have argued, that the facts that instantiate the schema in any given case be *plausibly* related to one another.

Thus the coherence in question must actually go *three* ways. It is not just that there be coherence within a particular practical inference, such that the action specified in the material premises actually happen, nor additionally just the coherence of the instantiating facts with surrounding evidence, but also a coherence of these facts as intelligibly connected, such that they could be re-enacted: could be followed or "gone through" to get to the action performed. Ultimately it is the coherence of facts in all three dimensions that is properly said to be *praxis*-verifying.

For, if our goal in history and the other human sciences is to combine explanation and understanding, then the practice of providing

---

8. My argument at this point has been influenced by "Determinants of Action," a recent paper by von Wright (forthcoming, to be published in a *Festschrift* for Raymond Klibansky) in which he discussed the problem of *verifying* the explanatory schema itself. The terms "matching" and "coherence" are taken from this paper. It should be recalled as well that "coherence" was one of Collingwood's terms (see *IH*, 245, and Chapter Three of the present book).

such explanations should be one that *integrates* re-enactment and practical inference. And it will be this enlarged congruence, on the various occasions involved, that is ultimately determinative of the soundness of that integrated practice.

Eleven

Other Periods, Other Cultures

I have been arguing for an explanatory model that integrates the themes of re-enactment and practical inference. Specifically, I have tried to show that the conclusions of a satisfactory action-explanation (in which we account for the agent's deed by reference to such things as his motivational background, purpose, means/end belief and so on) are grounded not only in a basic schema of practical inference, which they in effect instantiate, but also in particular generic assertions of intelligible connection.

These general discursive principles, universal statements of two distinct sorts and at two distinct levels, do function, logically, in all such explanations. They are, if not explicitly used, ingredient in any re-enactment. It follows from this that the claim to understand an individual action "by itself" or to understand a deed simply by "discovering" the thought that it "expresses" does not imply that we can dispense with general principles of these sorts.

However, there is a problem with the position I have developed which must be faced: if we argue for the *logically necessary* role of general formulas in re-enactment explanation, then we are led in a logical progression to consider the view that such transhistorical generalizations are *not possible*. This is a view we are already familiar with from our earlier study of Collingwood and it is to this view that we must now turn.

Collingwood's essential argument against the notion of transhistorical generalization is his contention that the development and differentiation of mind in historical process results in a marked heterogeneity over time in the thoughts and deeds of human beings. He apparently thought that persons living at different points in historical process are subjects of wholly different classes of mental predicates, and that we have no ground for claiming an invariance in the phenomena of human thought and action. Relative homogeneity is found only in delimited periods of history, at a given stage in the process. This denial of universal recurrence was the very thing Collingwood set out to establish in his critique of the idea of a science of human nature.

The crucial point is that the actions and thoughts of men at one stage in a historical process are so different from those at another that no transhistorical generalization could be formulated or used. This point comes up in a number of ways in Collingwood's writings. It comes up clearly, to cite one example, in his statement that "the historical as against the natural conditions of man's life differ so much at different times that no argument from analogy will hold" (*IH*, 239). This statement is telling because the same consideration that Collingwood advanced for disallowing all arguments from analogy would also debar all transhistorical generalizations. And the point comes up again in Collingwood's idea of a changing human nature. For here he conceived of a set of thoughts and actions common to men at one time turning into a wholly different set for other men at a later time. Again we have his basis for ruling out transhistorical generalizations in principle.

This notion of historical dissimilarity, conceived in absolute terms, lies behind Collingwood's position on generalization. Collingwood's philosophical anthropology, the process view of mind that he developed, was designed to rule out all transhistorical generalization—and this would include, given the terms of Collingwood's argument, the classificatory headings that figure in general hypotheticals of appropriateness and, as well, the schema of practical inference itself.

Now that I have recalled to mind the relevance of Collingwood's notion of historical process to his remarks about generalization, I want to take this issue further. In particular, I want to determine whether a

Other Periods, Other Cultures

historical understanding of the past (that is, an understanding of the past from the perspective of the present) is possible if the actions and thoughts of persons in the past really are significantly different from those of persons living in another period. For it seems that when we build this condition of dissimilarity into the very concept of the historical existence of man, as Collingwood did in his process view of mind, then the very possibility of historical understanding—whether by reenactment or by reference to universal regularity generalizations—becomes deeply problematical. We can call this problem of compatibility, under the concept of history, between historical processes of change and the historical understanding of the past the problem of other periods.

Interestingly, this problem is structurally identical to a similar problem in anthropology. The subject matter of anthropology has traditionally been conceived as other cultures—cultures different from the anthropologist's own. A primary axiom of anthropology, then, is cultural difference. One implication of this axiom is that we should understand another culture in its otherness, as different from our own. We must know that culture in its own terms, because the very fact that it is different implies that to understand it according to categories drawn from our culture is to have distorted knowledge of it. Hence the axiom of cultural differences leads us to seek internal understanding of other cultures: we should try, as Malinowski put it, "to grasp the native's point of view, his relation to life, to realize *his* vision of *his* world" (*Argonauts of the Western Pacific*, p. 25).

A moment's reflection, though, reveals disturbing implications in the notion of internal understanding of other cultures. For one thing, it is doubtful that ethnocentric distortion can ever be avoided: if thought and knowledge are products of culture, then our own thinking and knowing are products of our culture. And this includes our thinking about other cultures. Hence any understanding we may gain of another culture must stem from our culture, and must inevitably reflect our sense of what is appropriate and our standards for explaining action. Hence, the particular species of understanding "internal" to our culture is "external" to other cultures, simply insofar as they are other. To regard the matter any differently is little more than an exercise in self-deception. And, if we have scant hope of getting out of our own categories of thought, the other half of the process necessary for internal understanding—getting into the categories of another cul-

217

ture—seems equally unattainable. For the very bridges by which we would cross the gap of cultural difference—the various rules of intelligible connection and the very principle of action-explanation itself—are built up in our culture and are not, as such, transcultural. We can at best project our forms of understanding onto alien cultures but this is not the same thing as really understanding, as understanding from within, another culture.

The axiom of cultural difference leads us in conflicting directions. On the one hand it counsels internal understanding to avoid ethnocentric distortion of other cultures; on the other hand it generates a barrage of arguments that such internal understanding is impossible to achieve. So, if the understanding of another culture is conceived, necessarily, as an internal one, then it follows that anthropological understanding is impossible. This in capsule form is what can be called the problem of other cultures. [1]

Several strategies are available for dealing with this problem. One is to accept the axiom of cultural difference and to curtail the applicability of internal understanding by holding that we can achieve it only for those cultures similar to our own. (See Danto, "Other Periods," pp. 571–572 and 575.) Another is to maintain that cultures are not that different after all: that beneath superficial variations lies a solid bedrock of shared traits and characteristic ways of acting which enable men of one culture to understand those of another.

Now, given these strategies for dealing with it, the problem of other cultures begins to cast an interesting shadow on Collingwood's own argument. For his claim that the historian can judge of the appropriateness of actions done in the past, his claim that the historian can connect the deeds and thoughts of past agents simply by making certain calculations of plausibility implies a degree of initial familiarity on the historian's part with these ways of thinking and acting. And this, in turn, suggests a certain uniformity between agents in the past and agents in the present. In short, it seems to me that re-enactment, as Collingwood has described it, would require a much greater similarity between persons at different times than Collingwood's idea of changing human nature would allow. This observation does not "prove"

1. The names of the two problems I have identified are actually the titles of two articles: "The Problem of Other Periods" by A. C. Danto and "The Problem of Other Cultures" by Allan Hanson and myself. I have drawn on both these articles in developing the argument of this chapter.

Other Periods, Other Cultures

that Collingwood's contention respecting historical differences is wrong; it certainly does not establish Hume's doctrine of "a great uniformity among the actions of men." But it does indicate, I think, a sort of unresolved and largely unnoticed tension between Collingwood's idea of a radical difference among agents at various times in history, as we find it expressed in his notion of changing human nature, and his idea of explanatory re-enactment. The most obvious rejoinder to the question I have raised, then, would seem to be that the two ideas are simply incompatible.

In this same vein, but approaching the question of compatibility from a somewhat different direction, Walsh comments,

When it is said that human nature changes from age to age, are we meant to conclude that there is *no* identity between past and present . . . but that the two are sheerly different? And if we are (as Collingwood himself suggested in his more skeptical moments) does not that rule out the possibility of any intelligent understanding of the past? If men in ancient Greece or the Middle Ages, for example, had nothing in common with men in the world today, how could we hope to make anything of their experiences? An attempt to do so would be like trying to read a cypher text of which it was laid down in advance that the solution must elude us. [*Introduction to Philosophy of History*, p. 68; see also pp. 33–34]

I think an extension of the argument which I have been developing in this book would tend to support the misgivings Walsh has expressed. For acknowledgment of the indispensable logical role of general discursive principles in historical explanation would provide a ground for saying that any theory of history that rules out transhistorical generalizations in principle and thereby makes the use or presupposition of general principles (of appropriateness or of practical inference) systematically impossible is incompatible with the very existence of historical understanding, whether by re-enactment or by any other "method." The claim that we cannot have transhistorical concepts and general formulas, which are needed to subsume the deeds of the past under general classificatory headings and to connect the elements of the actions of past agents by means of generic assertions of appropriateness, would rule out any historical understanding of the past *ab initio*.

Now it might be retorted that Collingwood's conception of historical process does not force this conclusion. For, after all, Collingwood did contend that there were regular patterns of thought and behavior com-

Historical Explanation

mon to men at any given stage in historical process and this does afford grounds for using generalizations—albeit historically delimited ones. What Collingwood was arguing is simply that the generalizations applicable to men at one time could not be transferred to the understanding of actions at another time. This principle of nontransfer goes both ways along the lines of temporal sequence, so that it also prohibits any present from applying *its* generalizations to any past. But since it does not prohibit the application of generalizations *per se* to any historical group, and since my earlier argument required only that deeds be brought under generalizations, it is not clear that a case has been made for the necessary role of transhistorical generalizations.

But this retort does not take us very far. For the point still holds, after all this has been said, that an investigator could not bring even the general categories we find in the basic schema of practical inference to his study of deeds done in the past. If all transhistorical general formulas were to be ruled out in principle, then the investigator would be debarred from any effective use of such notions as purpose, situation-conception, means/end belief and so on, in his attempt to understand past actions. Since the principle of practical inference would itself have to be set aside as inapplicable, he would not even have a clear sense of how these notions could be applied to agents in the past. Nor would he know what was to count as an explanation of anything they did. Indeed he would simply be unable to understand or to explain a past action *as an action* at all. And there would be no available way to re-enact a past action or to follow one—at least of the sort Collingwood had in mind—without employing, or presupposing, these crucial general categories and relationships. In short, we could have no history of the past except a natural history, one where the language of events has wholly superseded that of actions. The practice of explaining actions done in the past, then, would have dropped out.

It is not even clear, now, that we can state the grounds on which Collingwood sought to debar all transhistorical generalizations in the first place: for his principal contention was that the thoughts and actions of agents in one period are markedly dissimilar from those of agents in another period, due to the development and differentiation of mind (that is, mind-as-thought) in historical process. But to make this contention is to say that the crucial difference is one that holds between thoughts and actions, that the things said to differ do differ *as* deeds, purposes, beliefs, and so on. However, if the transhistorical gulf

220

Other Periods, Other Cultures

is too great to be bridged even by the schema itself then Collingwood's way of making his point is no longer conceivable, no longer something that can be intelligibly said. Past and present would differ as wholly different *kinds* of things and not just as periods in which thoughts and actions differed qualitatively. And so-called cultures would differ so radically that it would not be possible to have, merely, the problem of other cultures: for they would not differ as cultures but, rather, as something else.

Nor would the matter be substantially improved were we to move to the second main level in the logical structure of re-enactment explanations, to the level of generic assertions of appropriateness. For the investigator could not use the rules of intelligible connection available to him in the understanding of present-day actions to justify the connective reasoning involved in his explanations of actions done in the past. His present-day categories are necessarily empty as regards the past. We would have a wholly incongruous situation: one where the only rules of appropriateness by which the past could be understood would not be available to the investigator, since he is *ex hypothesi* not a man of the past, and where the only ones available to him could not be used, for *ex hypothesi* they are inapplicable.

So we do not change things, really, in pointing out that Collingwood's position does not rule out generalization *per se*, for this clearly is not enough. His contention does rule out transhistorical general principles and this, as I have tried to indicate, is the very crux of the issue. The result of holding to Collingwood's position, even where we do allow for local generalizations, would still be that *historical* knowledge is impossible; for persons alive at one time are effectively cut off from any understanding of the men and deeds at another time. If an age could be understood only by using classificatory headings and rules of appropriateness that are peculiar and uniquely applicable to persons alive at that time, then a knowledge of any past by any present is inconceivable. We could have no histories for the simple reason that we could have no historians.

I see no acceptable intermediate ground. Either we assert that the relevant general elements are delimited not only in scope but also in accessibility to a period in the past or we assert that they are the generalizations we bring, from our understanding of actions in the present, to the study of the past. The only resolution to this, in my view, is to allow that the general categories (action-universals—purposes, beliefs, deeds, and so on—under generic *material* descriptions) and the principles (the schema of practical inference and the rules of appropriateness) by which we organize the study of the past are the same as those by which we understand human action in the present. And this is simply to say that these principles must have transhistorical application.

Explanation by re-enactment requires the very transhistorical generalizations which, on the process view of mind developed in Collingwood's critique, are ruled out in principle as impossible. And the only position on historical knowledge consistent with the implications of the philosophical anthropology of this critique would seem to be a thorough-going skepticism, at least, as regards the possibility of re-enactment.[2]

But at this point we should take care. I have been arguing that Collingwood cannot have *both* his claim to radical dissimilarity between different periods and a viable account of historical explanation: the argument was based on showing that historical understanding requires transhistorical application of the discursive principles ingredient in a re-enactment. However, it is not clear that we can really preserve this notion of historical understanding from the corrosive effects of Collingwood's process view of mind. It could well turn out that skepticism *is* the proper solution to the problem of other periods. It may be that the facts of historical difference (or cultural difference) are such that transhistorical discursive principles, in particular those that assert intelligibility of connection, are *not* possible. So this is a point that still needs to be addressed.

I would begin by allowing that what Collingwood had to say about the development and differentiation of human action and thought is, for the most part, arguable. I do not think we could deny his emphasis on the difference between deeds and thoughts in different historical ages. What I would question is not the fact of relative heterogeneity in different times, a consideration which is validly raised against Hume's

2. Collingwood did not, in my opinion, hold the view that human nature changes as a prelude to or symptom of "skepticism," contrary to what Walsh suggests (*Introduction to Philosophy of History*, p. 68); rather, this doctrine undergirds Collingwood's rather ambitious historicism and governs much of his argument for re-enactment, and none of this is skeptical either in intent or in execution. That his views may have had, undiscerned by him, skeptical *implications*—which is what I have alleged—is quite another matter.

doctrine of relative homogeneity, but the argument Collingwood developed on the basis of this fact.

It is no simple matter to say that the difference is too great to allow for transhistorical generalizations, for one has to apply a certain amount of logical pressure to the admitted facts of difference and, I might add, to the notion of a general principle. When we say that there is a difference in the phenomena of thought and action at different historical times, do we mean to say just that the total ensemble of phenomena at various times is different? Or do we mean to say as well that the phenomena are different in kind? And if we do mean precisely the latter claim, how could we convincingly establish it? And, more to the point, how are we ever to decide that the difference is great enough to warrant Collingwood's contention about transhistorical generalizations?

But I see no point in pursuing this line of questioning. It would be very difficult to decide for or against Collingwood's assertion. Rather than undertake a minute examination of the phenomena of history, a task which would prove both tedious and unrewarding, I suggest that we approach Collingwood's contention from another direction. I think the best strategy for dealing with the problem of other periods is to determine the logical moves whereby it has become a problem and to dissolve the problem by taking a different series of logical steps. In short, the solution to our problem will really depend on how we set it up: given one frame of reference, we might be inclined to agree with Collingwood; but, given another, we might not.

Whether or not there are transhistorical general principles that can cover phenomena at diverse times depends on the sort of descriptions we employ. Any given set of phenomena can be described using only historically determinate and particularized terms or it can be described using general classificatory headings. In matters of description, unlike explanation, there is no uniquely preferred level at which we are to work. For example, the phenomena of Athenian political life can be described in the time-bound vocabulary of talk about the *polis* (*archon, demokratia, ostrakon,* etc.) or in time-free and general terms. And we can replace terms at one level with terms at the other, but at each level we are providing a description of these phenomena. If this is so, we can say that the question of the possibility of transhistorical generalization is really connected with the question of how historical phenomena—deeds and thoughts—are described.

Historical Explanation

Any question about historical phenomena, as it bears on their qualitative differences, presupposes a certain level in our descriptive language. Transhistorical general principles will be possible only at a certain level of language use. (See Danto, *Analytical Philosophy of History*, p. 218.) And this, in a rough way, gives the line of solution to our problem: generalizations are relativized, not to phenomena, but to our descriptions of phenomena. So if we shift our focus from phenomena *per se* to the *description* of phenomena, we are in a position to deal with the conceptual issue raised in relating historical process to transhistorical generalization.

The terms that figure in a transhistorical general principle—in the schema of practical inference or in any given rule of appropriateness—do not designate particular objects. They are applicable to all times because they are time-free, because they are not tied to any special set of temporally delimited phenomena. Hence, the use of transhistorical discursive principles in an explanation of specific phenomena is compatible with qualitative differences in phenomena over time. In other words, these principles can have transhistorical application; they can, and do, cover phenomena occurring at various times in history despite admitted qualitative dissimilarities in these phenomena. This view will allow us to take account of Collingwood's contention about difference, for that contention really requires only that the generalizations we formulate to explain phenomena must allow for heterogeneity in the phenomena covered.[3]

There is nothing in the concept of transhistorical generalizations that would prevent this. It all depends, as I have said, on how we formulate them. And I would claim that the transhistorical general principles discussed in this essay, the schema of practical inference and the various generic assertions of appropriateness, can cover heterogeneous instances. This is so because the terms that occur in these

3. Cf. Nagel's remark, "It is obvious that, if a law in any domain of inquiry is to cover a wide range of phenomena exhibiting admittedly relevant and important differences, the formulation of the law must ignore these differences, so that the terms employed in the formulation make no explicit mention of traits specific to the phenomena occurring in special circumstances. Such a formulation can sometimes be achieved by using variables [general classificatory headings], . . . the application of the law to particular situations being mediated by assigning to the variables constant values [particularized and historically determinate descriptions of phenomena] which may vary from situation to situation" (*The Structure of Science*, p. 463; see also pp. 462–464). In the analysis I am offering, the terms in brackets would be substituted for the corresponding terms used by Nagel in the passage quoted.

general formulas can have nonhomogeneous phenomena as their extensions.[4]

Indeed, this is obviously so in the case of R, the basic schema, but it is also the case, though less obviously, with rules of appropriateness. For example, the general headings which figure, logically, in an explanation of the Romans' exposure of newborn infants could also function in the explanation of other attempts to control the numbers of population at other times and, more important, of attempts at control that differed qualitatively from that of the Romans. A mere look at the relevant deliberations of Vatican II or at a women's liberation book like *Our Bodies, Ourselves* should be sufficient to indicate the range of diverse attitudes, all nonetheless describable as purposes, which could be covered by the single heading "attempting to limit the number of population" (or, for that matter, the range of different *deeds* which could be brought under the one heading "practicing birth control"). And a similar point could be made about the explanatory categories which were brought to bear on Caesar's invasion of Britain (where his purpose was described as "attempting to conquer," etc.).

My contention is that the same general classificatory heading can cover qualitatively distinct phenomena. A whole range of qualitatively distinct phenomena, thoughts or actions under different particular descriptions, can be covered and explained by the same general heading. It is possible to frame general categories which do not indicate univocally one specific kind of action or thought but which, rather, are satisfied by a variety of particular descriptions. These general categories and resultant formulas are in Ryle's language highly determinable rather than determinate, many-track rather than single-track.[5]

We are now ready to consider a point which was touched on earlier and which can occasion some confusion: Collingwood's contention that human actions are always delimited in scope of occurrence to a particular age. It might be thought that the use of *general* categories or

4. This point is made by Danto; he says, "The law *L*—and a great many, if not all the laws which are elements of explanations in history—covers a class of instances which is both *open* and *non-homogeneous*. This is so because the descriptions which serve as *explanata* have open and non-homogeneous classes of events as their extensions" (*Analytical Philosophy of History*, p. 225). My argument in this part of the present chapter draws on points made in Danto's book on pp. 225–231 and 242–244. (See also his *Analytical Philosophy of Action*, esp. pp. 100–101 and 113.)

5. See *Concept of Mind*, pp. 43–44 and 118 in particular. Hempel's notion of "broadly dispositional" (see "Rational Action," esp. pp. 13–15) would also be serviceable here.

formulas would imply their nondelimitation. But I think the claim that the general elements we bring to the study of the past are transhistorical does not require that the phenomena we explain by reference to them be distributed over all time. It is, on the contrary, quite conceivable that the phenomena we bring under these transhistorical elements, in order to explain them, are historically delimited in their occurrence.

For example, confronted with an instance of the widespread practice in Greek and Roman times of leaving newborn infants out to die, the investigator would begin by consciously classifying this phenomenon. He would try to determine the kind of thing that it was; he would, presumably, describe it as an act of "exposing" a newborn baby to the elements. But he could equally well describe it as a case of preventing, or eliminating, live births. And then he would try to connect this deed, as described, with the thoughts of an agent, with, for example, the relevant purpose "controlling the numbers of their population." Again, with the purpose he would consciously classify it not only as a purpose but as the particular kind that it was. But, though the general heading "preventing or eliminating live births" is transhistorical, its use in an explanation of the Romans' action does not entail that infants have been exposed at all times in history.[6]

Under a particularized description, e.g., the one given in the explanandum, phenomena can be historically peculiar. And a summative generalization formulated about these phenomena can be historically delimited. But this is in no way incompatible with the idea that the terms which figure in our explanatory apparatus—not just at the level of the categories in the basic schema itself but also at the level of generic assertions of appropriateness—are transhistorical.

When we say that a general principle is transhistorical, the force of this qualifying adjective is not simply that the principle, as formulated, has universal scope but also that it has transhistorical application. It does cover, or can be shown to cover, phenomena occurring at different times in history. But it does not follow from this that a given subset of these phenomena, actions and thoughts under a peculiar and particularized description, need be so distributed.

These considerations allow us to take account of a fundamental point made in Collingwood's argument: that the phenomena of his-

6. The example used in this paragraph is Collingwood's (see *IH*, 239–240) but the logical moral is quite different from the one he drew.

tory, the deeds and thought of agents, are historically delimited. But it is also true that, if the delimitation of phenomena is compatible with the nondelimitation of explanatory categories, then we have no ground for arguing from the fact of delimitation to the conclusion that explanatory general principles cannot be transhistorical.

Let us widen the range of discussion to consider one further point raised by Collingwood. For Collingwood also argued, consistent with his position that generalizations in history are always restricted to their period of origin, that the general principles framed to cover present-day phenomena could not be used to cover the phenomena of the past: past phenomena are, from the perspective of the present, novel and unprecedented. (See *IH*, 239–240.)

Collingwood's point is of considerable methodological importance. And since I have argued that our knowledge of action done in the past is an extension of our knowledge of actions done in the present, this admissibility of phenomena from the past to the class of instances covered by generalizations framed with respect to phenomena in the present is crucial. For if we allow—as I think we must—that the phenomena of the past will be unlike the phenomena with which the historian is familiar, then the general formulas that the historian brings to the past from the study of actions in the present must be capable of covering new and different phenomena. Otherwise he could not use these formulas in an attempt to understand the past, and barring their use, we would have to say that the past could not be made intelligible.

But it seems to me that the same considerations which allowed us to include heterogeneous phenomena under the same general principle would also allow us to include novel phenomena from the past. For novelty is, after all, a species of difference. A generalization, if properly formulated, could *in principle* accommodate phenomena, in the class of instances covered, which are markedly different from hitherto included instances and, indeed, are novel with respect to the historian's possible experience of present-day thought and action.

In short, the logical problem posed by Collingwood's point can be handled by what I earlier called the multi-track "dispositional" character of transhistorical generalizations. To say that a general category or formula is "many-track," determinable rather than determinate, is to say that it rides loose on the class of instances covered. The claim that the class of instances subsumed under a general classificatory heading is heterogeneous and that the heading is transhistorical entails that the class of instances be regarded as open-ended. If this is so, we can meet Collingwood's contention that the generalizations framed so as to cover present-day phenomena could not be used to cover the novel phenomena of the past.

This line of argument brings us back to a point raised earlier by Walsh against Collingwood. Walsh suggests that, if we are to have the possibility of historical knowledge, we must assume an identity between past and present. But this identity need not exist, as we have seen, at the level of phenomena. Indeed, there is a good case for doubting the notion of a homogeneity in phenomena over historical time. The identity Walsh speaks of must exist, however, at the conceptual level. The necessary identity consists in this: the same general schema of practical inference, the same action-universals (purposes, beliefs, deeds under generic material descriptions), the same rules of appropriateness which function in our explanations of present-day actions must be brought to our understanding of actions done in the past. The weak point in Walsh's analysis is that he fails to stipulate the level at which likeness can be said, or expected, to hold. It seems to me that Walsh has conflated the phenomenal with the categorial and has argued, proceeding on the implicit assumption of a one-to-one univocal relationship between general elements and instances, that likeness in the explanatory concepts applied to different times must entail a corresponding identity in the phenomena which occur at different times.[7]

But I do think that there is something fundamentally rightminded about Walsh's approach. He has correctly emphasized that our understanding of actions done in the past is an extension of our understanding of actions done in the present. Rather than say with Collingwood that "all knowledge of mind is historical" I would say that all historical knowledge of human thought and action logically presupposes this present-day understanding.

There is a sense in which the content of our understanding is fixed before we turn to the past. But I would not suggest that we can learn

---

7. Walsh has substantially amended his position in a subsequent essay ("The Constancy of Human Nature"). There Walsh argues that the *one* constant is "the form of practical thinking" or "general schema of the practical syllogism," as he also calls it (see pp. 282–283, 285; also pp. 286, 288; and also "Vico's Ideal Eternal History," p. 151). Here Walsh does make the distinction I have outlined and does stipulate that the required universality is to hold at the categorial or "formal" level.

nothing from a study of the past. For we can learn about the past in its details and this knowledge will affect, indeed partially constitute, our descriptions of the present and even of the future. And we can learn about the different ways in which our categories of present-day understanding can be exemplified. In going to the past, we "unpack" unexpected data from our concepts. History is the science of perspective, of scope, of development, of the unanticipated; and, as such, it is one of the primary avatars of realistic thinking. Like any other discipline which aspires to the status of a science, history finds things out; it expands our knowledge. And, like art, it expands our experience.

There is, then, a sense in which we come to acquire new knowledge in the study of the past. There is even a sense in which we revise the generalizations which we bring, implicitly, to the study of the past. We revise them, not so much in reformulating them, as in recognizing that descriptions of particular phenomena which we had not hitherto had occasion to put under these generalizations can be put under them. The revision comes in the class of instances which we are able to subsume under a certain heading and in the classes of instances which we are able to connect through certain rules of appropriateness. These revisions will come, no doubt, because we encounter new and different phenomena in history—different, that is, from what we possibly could have encountered in our present-day experiences. But the fact of novelty does not mean that we cannot use transhistorical generalizations; so long as the class of instances covered by any given general principle is open-ended, then a logical problem in dealing with novelty does not arise. In the course of any historical investigation, we may have to revise the respective classes of instances covered by the general elements we bring to that inquiry, but we do not, in the nature of the matter, dispense with such transhistorical categories and formulas altogether. We could not and still expect to understand what we were investigating.

I would not claim that no problem is posed by novelty. There may well be—in fact, I am sure there are—novel phenomena exhibitied in history which we do not understand. There are also, no doubt, some which we misunderstand by subsuming them under the wrong general categories. I can provide no guidelines for dealing with this problem. But I would still maintain, against Collingwood's analysis, that when we do understand, or claim to understand, novel phenomena from the past, we do so by subsuming them under general formulas, under formulas which are applied to the understanding of actions done in the historian's own day.

My argument up to now may have suggested that the historian "builds up" his explanatory categories from *personal* experience of actions done in his own day and then applies these to his study of the past. I hasten to say that I do not want to leave any such impression. As Danto says, "There is a social inheritance here, and the bulk of the generalizations we employ have been built up over the generations and have been built into the concepts we most of us employ most of the time in organizing experience and explaining how things happen" (*Analytical Philosophy of History*, p. 242). This way of putting the matter seems to me the correct one; I do not think that my remarks in this chapter are in any way incompatible with it.

My point is that, regardless of how or when the historian's generalizations are built up, they must cover both actions done in the present and actions done in the past. It is in this sense that they have transhistorical application. At the same time, I would want to emphasize that our understanding of the present has temporal priority; that our understanding of the past presupposes explanatory categories which we first learn to use in application to the present; and that in no case does our understanding of the past "outrun" the conceptual apparatus involved in our understanding of the present.

This particular emphasis can easily become distorted, especially under the pressure exerted by the problem of other periods, into the claim that we must and inevitably do impose our conceptual apparatus on the period or culture that we are studying. I do not doubt that it is difficult to avoid doing this, but I do not think that the compulsion is a *logical* one. The point I was making should not be recast as suggesting a radical distinction between different frames of reference, such as the difference between seeing the universe in terms of the Ptolemaic system versus the Copernican system, or between seeing an alien period or culture in "its own terms" versus "our terms." Indeed, if we have ultimately to choose between these latter alternatives, then the problem of other periods has not really been resolved.

The intended point of my emphasis can be clarified and its exact tendency gauged more accurately if we allow for a distinction between the *actual* order of our understanding and its *logical* order. The *actual* order is as I have described it: there is a sort of export-import relationship between our present-day understanding of actions and our understanding of actions done in the past. For "the intelligibility of anything new said or done does depend in a certain way on what has already been said or done and understood" (Winch, "Understanding a Primitive Society," p. 316). And here it is appropriately emphasized that our " 'stock' of descriptions" must constantly be extended and modified, with respect both to what particular classificatory headings we are using and to what *kinds* of instances are to be subsumed under them. (See Winch, pp. 316–318).

But in the *logical* order of our understanding, the matter stands somewhat differently. When we bring the deeds and attitudes of another period under such headings as "practicing birth control" or "attempting to limit the number of their population," these headings and the rules of appropriateness that link them do not, logically at least, belong to *our* conceptual apparatus as opposed to *theirs*. Indeed, they may not reproduce much, if anything, that is familiarly said or thought in either society. Rather, these rules ought to be regarded as impersonal, cross-cultural formulas which just happen to unpack, given a certain language, into a particular preferred "stock of descriptions" and covered instances. (See Walsh, "Constancy of Human Nature," pp. 287–288.) Each such rule of appropriateness is, logically speaking, a *family* of rules, each one of which is to be conceived as a different use or exemplification of the rule itself. (See here the parallel argument of N. R. Hanson regarding laws of nature: *Patterns of Discovery*, esp. p. 98; also pp. 99–118.)

To put the point more precisely, each such rule is a *member* of a family of rules. Now each of these rules does arise in its own particular cultural milieu and has thereby its own peculiar formulation and its own preferred "stock" of covered instances. What makes for the "family" character of these rules is that the "stock" of covered instances is *extended*, in the case of one rule, to include instances that were originally part of the preferred "stock" of the *other* rule. And this extending of instances can go both ways; indeed it can go both ways from many different directions. So, different rules with different original extensions get locked in together through the (partial) overlap of their covered instances and in that way become familiarized to one another.

This practice of bridging from both ends to create a family of rules is very like what I described earlier as "filling in," only this time the "filling in" is conceived as *reciprocal*. It results from the linkage of different rules through the interpenetration of what were originally different "stocks" of covered instances.

There need not be, and probably is not, an ideal rule which, if formulated, would bring together and make explicit what these rules have in common. Rather, what does stand between and bridge two cultures is the practice of bringing together mutually alien rules by extending their "stock" of covered instances so that these stocks interpenetrate. And this domestication of different rules to one another is very like the procedure of establishing intelligibility between two phenomena by "filling in"—a procedure which in effect involved their being redescribed.

A particular rule of intelligibility ought not, on this showing, to be regarded as a way of translating the detail of another culture into *our* categories: for the way we talk and think constitutes but one of the styles that can be accommodated within a given family of rules. And just as this family is culturally neutral with respect to the detailed kinds of instances that can ultimately be accommodated under it, so it is logically neutral with respect to the cultures and "forms of life" themselves. It is the property of no one society or period.

Past and *present* are relative terms: what has been present becomes past and the past has been studied by many different presents. Our culture has no privileged status, for it will be the past studied by some future period and it is now an alien culture to other cultures in our time. I am not, of course, suggesting that a society is never guilty of seeing other periods and other cultures in its *own* terms. But I am suggesting that there is a perspective available in which genuine cross-cultural understanding is possible.

That we are so often troubled by a concern not to impose our categories on other periods and other cultures is, I think, revealing. In part it stems from our awareness that imposition is possible. But it also stems, paradoxically, from a sense that such imposition is not necessary. Most of all, though, it represents a kind of "optical illusion": in bridging the space between past and present it is *we* who do the work. History is always written in the present; just as anthropology is always done by *another* culture, one different from the culture under study.

The work of creating a family of rules is always, or almost always, the work of the investigators. Even so, it can be done. But to do so we must conceive our explanatory practices in a certain way. We may even have to change them. So it is well that we are concerned not to impose our categories on other periods and other cultures.

Accordingly, rather than say that we project our cultural perspective via a rule of appropriateness onto another culture or period, we might do better to say that the formula itself is projectible in two different directions, to cover *our* thought and conduct and that of the society under investigation. Hence, the oft-repeated claim that we understand other periods or cultures by "analogy" with our own is misleading: there is no analogy between surgical abortion, exposure of infants, and the late-marriage and landholding practices of the Irish; but they can all be brought under the same heading, that of "practicing birth control," and under a single rule of appropriateness. It is not the "likeness" of these things that governs our bringing them together but, rather, the fact that they can all be brought together under one *rule*, which happens to have these disparate things among its extension, as part of its stock of covered instances.

Now the rule has this character, not because these things were part of its original extension, but because explanatory practice can assimilate instances from other stocks and thereby assimilate rules, from other periods (or other cultures) and from our own, to one another. It is in this way, by assimilating instances and thence rules to one another, that transhistorical, or cross-cultural, understanding is possible. We can conceive our understanding of another period or culture as, in a sense, an internal one insofar as it is mediated by what I have been calling a family of rules.[8]

But is this really an *internal* understanding? There are many ways, it should be clear, in which it is not. I am not suggesting that the investigator can experience in himself the inner side—the fugitive thoughts, the conviction of beliefs, the naturalness of behavior—the feeling of living as a participant in the other culture. The investigator is not required to integrate his descriptive material with any sort of "sympathic" element (the term is from Danto's "Problem of Other

8. Note Jarvie's remark: "It becomes my counter-contention that we *cannot but* approach alien societies with preconceptions formed in our society; we therefore look at other societies in terms of ours, and as a first approximation try to understand them on analogy with us" (*Concepts and Society*, p. 38; see also pp. 40 and 66). My argument is intended to take account of points urged by Jarvie and at the same time to show that the *imposition* of our standards of intelligibility is not a logical necessity in the understanding of other cultures.

Periods," p. 571). For the investigator is not attempting to duplicate or to acquire the interior dimension of life in the other culture. He is not going to share their beliefs, or their social horizons, or their view of the world.

Nor does the notion of internal understanding which I am developing require that the investigator's rules (of intelligibility) in some way reproduce the rules that persons in other cultures have formulated, or that they could articulate upon request. Indeed, sometimes there is no rule, at least none that the participants have been able to put into words. But in this regard the investigator stands no differently to other periods and other cultures than he stands to his own—and, hence, than any indigenous investigator would stand to *his* native period or culture. So, if no one native to a particular period or culture could formulate the rule (though the participants there did seem to be following one—at least to the extent that they could say whether or not something was being done correctly [9]), then all anyone could offer would be a construction (in the form of a rule-statement) which more or less accurately formulates certain objective features in that society. And where a variety of such formulations are workable, then each would be acceptable. For in no event is the historian or anthropologist engaged in the spurious task of attempting to recapitulate in his own mind the deeply buried subconscious cognition of participants.

Rather, this whole business of duplicating or sharing or recapitulating—whether the duplication is said to be of native feelings or beliefs or rules (either articulated or seemingly unexpressible)—is beside the point. What I have called internal understanding is not conceived as the duplication of anything in the native mind or culture at all. On the contrary, the model of internal understanding I am advocating involves the assimilation of native rules (or rule constructions, as the case may be) and not their duplication.

By assimilating instances from other "stocks" we are able to draw rules together, from other periods and other cultures and from our own, and thereby assimilate them to one another. The understanding so achieved is internal because it allows us to use their rule *as a rule of intelligibility*; for it, as assimilated to a rule (of intelligibility) from our society, is conceived as a different way of formulating that rule—as a redescription of it. (And, of course, the reverse is true as well.) And

9. See Winch, *Idea of a Social Science*, p. 64.

the understanding is internal because it allows us to bring *their* actions, intentions, beliefs and so on—when assimilated to our "stock" of instances—under a rule of intelligibility which, in principle, both investigator and participant can use. Or it might be more precise to say that the understanding is internal inasmuch as it is possible to bring their actions, intentions, beliefs, etc. and our own under the same family of rules.

The core of this theory of understanding is not some putative communion of private experiences or beliefs (based ultimately on an inner-outer distinction) but rather the *practice* of what I have called assimilation. Assimilation so conceived is not a matter of duplication: for it requires not only that the one set of rules remain distinct from the other but also that the difference in their formulation be retained as well.

We do not, of course, have to accept their rule of intelligibility (nor they ours); it is required merely that we be able to follow it (and they ours). Nor must one share the belief or engage in the action that has been assimilated to his "stock" of instances—in fact even with this stock one need only be familiar, though not necessarily through active participation. For what is at issue is not the advisability of behaving or believing in a certain way but, instead, the intelligibility of it. And this is something that is to be determined by assimilating instances to instances, rules to rules.

This practice of assimilating allows us to follow, in the sense of make intelligible, the material connections between particular actions, intentions, beliefs, etc. of agents in another culture. Indeed the practice of so assimilating *is* the following of those connections and, hence, is to count as internal understanding.[10]

On my view, then, we can achieve an internal understanding of other periods and other cultures. We have it when the participants can tell us the rules, can state the rationale or principles of intelligibility inherent in their actions, and we can follow—can take account of—

---

10. I think much confusion in this matter has been engendered by the tendency to put the issue in terms of *rationality* rather than in terms of intelligibility. (See, for example, the essay by Jarvie, "Understanding and Explanation in Sociology and Social Anthropology," esp. pp. 231, 238–239.) I remain unconvinced that explanatory reasoning *per se* really requires the use of any prescriptive norms of rationality, a point I have already argued in Chapter Six. I think, as well, that a distinction should be drawn between (morally) evaluating another period or culture and understanding it. (See here the very lucid argument by Allan Hanson, *Meaning in Culture*, esp. ch. 2.)

their behavior in those terms. And "when the natives cannot articulate the rules they follow, we [construct] formulations or statements of them, . . . statements which we evaluate by their ability to account for or predict behavior which natives accept as appropriate." (See Allan Hanson, *Meaning in Culture*, p. 65, for the point made and for the passage quoted in this paragraph; see also "Problem of Other Cultures," sec. 4, esp. pp. 203–204.)

There is, however, a sense of internal understanding that is easily confused with the one I have developed. Accordingly, in concluding this chapter I want to draw out this other sense and to indicate in what way my sense of internal understanding will correspond to it—or not correspond, as the case may be. I have in mind here the distinction between the internal understanding appropriate to an investigator, which is what I have been discussing, and that appropriate to a participant.

The main point of difference seemingly comes in this: the investigator's understanding, as I have outlined it, consists in the application of explicit rule-statements. These are devices which aid the historian or the anthropologist in learning to "get around" in the culture or period under study; and they are as well, as we have seen, his principal way of teaching students and readers about that culture or period. But because the investigator's experience of knowing how to operate in that culture, or period, involves the conscious application of rule-statements in areas where the participants do not use explicit rules at all, or sometimes in areas where they cannot even articulate rules for their behavior, the investigator's way of doing things in that culture is not wholly congruent with the participant's. And therefore investigator's understanding cannot be termed *internal* in the same way that participant's understanding can be.

Yet there is nothing to prevent the investigator from achieving the kind of understanding appropriate to the participant. The investigator's rule-statements are tools or codes which enable him (or anyone) to select the proper behavior in a variety of particular circumstances. This selection can be a very complex and difficult task—which is precisely why such rules are so often necessary for an outsider. However, through long residence or scholarly immersion in the society under study he begins to be able to select appropriate behavior "automatically," without applying the rules.

The investigator is engaged in a learning process much like learning to speak a foreign language or to play a new game. At first there is constant repetition of rules in order to produce utterances or movements in accordance with them. After time and practice one masters the skill: one can use the language or swing the raquet effortlessly and effectively with no more need for rule-reciting. And if one is not involved in teaching others, it is possible to speak the language fluently or to play the game expertly through continued use after having *forgotten* the rules one so laboriously followed when first learning.

The participant (the native, the man of the period) knows his kinship terminology, theory of disease and curing, and whole world view so well that he applies them effortlessly, automatically. Having learned them from childhood, and probably by example, he may *never* have followed explicit rules at all in becoming skilled in their use. The investigator is both a novice and an outsider: he requires the help of rules. But he need not remain that way; he may learn those things so well that he can dispense with rules. And if he is not concerned with teaching anyone else, he could easily forget the rules. There is nothing, logically, that prohibits him from going native.

When he has learned the native world view and practices so well that he can "get around" in that culture without relying on rules in places where natives have no explicit rules, then he has attained a participant's know-how—the internal understanding appropriate to a participant—and he does in fact duplicate the participants' ways, doing neither more nor less than they do. But so long as one must rely on rules in cases where participants do not, his understanding to that extent is not wholly participatory. And by extension, understanding would be wholly nonparticipatory, where rule statements could be accurately cited but in no wise applied. This would be like the case of a student who could recite the rules of French grammar perfectly well but who could neither speak nor write nor understand the language. This is the situation of many of the investigator's readers and students. They have only the rules but not the practices; in this sense, they have an *external* understanding for they lack the understanding appropriate to a participant.

The relationship of investigator's understanding to participant's understanding, when put in terms characteristic of the latter (in terms of *know-how*), can be represented, then, as a sort of continuum. At one end is rules-only understanding; at the other is full participant's understanding, or native-level proficiency. Investigator's understanding marks out a zone somewhere between these poles, usually falling well short of the pole of full proficiency. In some cases the investigator's know how will take a rather active form (he will speak or read the language indigenous to the period or culture under study). And in other cases it may be of a somewhat more passive sort; he may not be able to swing his raquet with the best of them but he will be able to follow the game as expertly as the rest of them: he will be able to tell the correct moves—the appropriate responses—as judged by native standards. Nonetheless, there is no sharp dichotomy between different *kinds* of understanding, but simply different degrees of proficiency in "getting around" *like a participant* in another culture or another period. And this difference is largely a difference in the degree to which explicit rules are needed or used.[11]

But this latter difference is more deeply embedded than might at first be apparent. For the difference between, on the one hand, merely having accurate rules (and being able to apply them) and, on the other, having the activity or skill that the rules only state has tended to become the principal difference between investigator's understanding and participant's. And the reason for this is not that the kind of understanding to be met with on each hand is radically dissimilar, for arguably the difference in question could be overcome; rather it is that this particular difference is required by the role of investigator.

Investigator's understanding serves the end of scientific knowledge and, accordingly, requires explicit narratives and rules. And the interest in such things is precisely what characterizes the investigator *qua* investigator and precisely what marks off investigator's understanding (as understanding by reference to rules) from participant's understanding (as know-how, with full native proficiency as its upper limit).

I say "mark off" but the point is that this interest has actually tended to *fix* the difference between investigative and participatory understanding: so that the differences in proficiency, which are largely a matter of the degree to which explicit rules are needed and used, have stabilized at roughly this point. The characteristic interest of the investigator in rules has arrested his know-how, keeping it within the zone where rules are always going to be needed and used and, thence, for-

11. In the concluding part of this chapter, where I have made a distinction between investigator's and participant's understanding, I have drawn, often verbatim, upon the argument of "The Problem of Other Cultures" (esp. sec. 5).

ever short of full native proficiency. For him to act otherwise would be to step out of character.

If my brief account here is substantially correct then we should not be surprised to find that the notion of internal understanding is subject to a certain ambiguity and has, as a result, been subjected to a certain dialectical pressure. For it is possible to identify internal understanding with participant's understanding, including thereby those respects in which the latter is peculiarly to be distinguished from investigator's understanding. Thus it has been argued that investigator's understanding is not *the same* as participant's and, accordingly, must fall short of genuine internal understanding. (See Danto, "Problem of Other Periods," pp. 574–576 [point 2].) But equally, the argument continues, if this defect could be repaired, if the goal of a fully *internal* understanding could ever be achieved, then the investigator would cease to be an investigator and become instead just a participant, thereby exchanging one world (the present, his own culture) for another (another period, another culture) with no resultant gain in (investigative) understanding. Indeed, what would result here would not, and could not, count as scientific understanding. As Danto says, "So were *Verstehen* to succeed, it would fail, for instead of exchanging, as it were, one psyche for another, one would instead exchange one world for another. And the problem of understanding the Other would remain" ("Historical Language and Historical Reality," p. 257; see also pp. 255–256 and "Problem of Other Periods," pp. 576–577 [point 3]).

In either case, Danto's argument concludes, we would fail to have internal understanding; for what we had would fail either to be internal or, if internal, to be understanding of the investigative sort. With my analysis, however, it is possible to avoid the toils of this argument and still to have a tolerably full notion of internal understanding. I grant the point that investigator's understanding is not the same as participant's; but in being *know-how* it is *like* participant's understanding, differing in degree but not in kind from it. (This is at least an arguable point in my view.) And the difference allowed for is traceable to that which grounds the principal distinction of investigator from participant: to the investigator's characteristic focus on explicit narratives and rules. Thus, in my account, investigative understanding as know-how is sufficiently like participant's understanding to count as *internal* (in

the sense emphasized by Danto, where he identifies internal understanding with participant's understanding) and is, as understanding by
reference to rules, sufficiently like scientific knowledge to count as *understanding* in that sense. I think this account provides a kind of answer, then, to Danto's argument against the possibility of a *verstehende*
internal understanding.

My analysis has also served to reveal a curious asymmetry between
explanation and understanding in the human sciences. Explanation
(in the form of practical inference) is a one-dimensional thing; it is
something an investigator does. But understanding, as I have described
it, has more than just this one dimension. It is an investigator's thing
(as understanding by reference to rules) but it can also be put to use as
know-how. And here, ranging from the ability to reach the same
conclusions and the same prescriptions for action as natives would in
the same circumstances up to full proficiency in the skills and activities of other periods and other cultures, it is a participant's thing.

This asymmetry bears on my general argument in this book, in particular on the attempt to integrate the themes of re-enactment and
practical inference within a single model of explanation. If understanding does operate in both dimensions, then it should be possible to
exploit this protean character and put its greater scope to advantage.
(And here I am restricting my point just to understanding in the
narrower sense discussed throughout this book—as understanding that
makes intelligible the material connections between particular deeds
and intentions of the agent, etc.—and to that kind of understanding
when employed transhistorically or cross-culturally.) Specifically, re-
enactive or investigator's understanding (as understanding through the
assimilation of instances under a family of rules) should be translatable
in principle into participant's understanding (or know-how). And this
fact has important ramifications for what was called (in the previous
chapter) *praxis*-verification. For the ability to translate the family of
rules used in the understanding of another period, or another culture,
into but some of the multifarious abilities of participants, at an appre-
ciable degree of proficiency, would afford an indirect but nonetheless
valuable and revealing confirmation of the soundness of the explanatory *praxis* itself. Hence, "getting around" as a participant in another
period (which is probably not possible) or in another culture (which
probably is) would constitute a further test of "coherence" for this
praxis.

Twelve

Conclusion

In a sense, the argument of the previous chapter has served to turn Collingwood's critique on its head. Rather than taking the basic contention of the critique as a ground for rejecting transhistorical generalizations, we can take it as setting a requirement for them. If Collingwood is right about historical difference, then we have an argument for saying that the generalizations used in history must be capable of covering nonhomogeneous phenomena. Conceived this way, Collingwood's critique does not rule out transhistorical generalizations; rather, it provides a criterion to which they must adhere. Here we treat Collingwood's critique as a prolegomenon to a view of generalizations different from that developed by Hume and Walsh and Hempel. Collingwood's critique gives the reason why we cannot have generalizations predicated on the assumption of relative homogeneity in historical phenomena, the reason why we cannot use generalizations which are capable of covering only homogeneous or "like" instances.

It is unlikely, for reasons Collingwood has given, that a transhistorical generalization could ever be formulated which did not exhibit qualitative difference in the instances covered. The typical case of explanatory generalization in history is one in which the members of the class subsumed under that generalization will not be homogeneous. In reaching these conclusions we seem to have accorded a substantial validity to the argument of Collingwood's critique. For we have accepted his idea that we can have no transhistorical general principles which apply to phenomena *under particularized descriptions*: particular actions, deeds and thoughts under historically determinate descriptions, cannot readily be brought under generalizations that have universal scope and validity.

If we take Collingwood's critique at this level, the level of phenomena under historically (or culturally) particularized descriptions, then it would appear that his argument against transhistorical generalizations is basically sound. But we need not remain at this level. For, though deeds (and purposes and motivation backgrounds, etc.) may be historically peculiar and distinctive under some descriptions, this fact does not provide, inherently, an obstacle to the formulation and use of comprehensive transhistorical general principles. As I have shown, we can cover a historical event with a general formula if we first bring it under a general classificatory heading; at this level transhistorical general principles are applicable to the phenomena of human thought and action.

The conditions formulated in the basic schema of practical inference and the action-universals which figure as terms in generic assertions of appropriateness are general in the sense required. Hence, discursive formulas of these two sorts can, I argued, have universal application even though there may be no universally recurrent phenomena and despite the fact that there are admitted qualitative dissimilarities in the phenomena, of different times or cultures, which such formulas have to cover.

It was precisely on the basis provided by this notion of transhistorical generalization that I was able to develop the "assimilationist" account of internal understanding, of other periods and other cultures, which was put forward in the concluding part of the previous chapter. In principle, the generic assertions of intelligible connection on the part of the investigator can be extended, by virtue of the "many-track" or "highly determinable" character of the terms which normally figure in them, to include instances strikingly different in kind from those in the original "stock" of covered instances. Thus, by assimilating qualitatively dissimilar instances under a single rule, it is possible to draw together generic assertions of appropriateness (or material rules of intelligibility, as they have also been called) from markedly different cul-

Conclusion

tural settings and to assimilate *these* rules to one another within a single family of such rules.

If the way of conceiving transhistorical or cross-cultural understanding that I outlined in the previous chapter is accepted, we must say, on reflection, that much has been conceded to the argument of Collingwood's critique of the idea of a science of human nature. And we may counter the philosophy of human nature, in its doctrine of relative historical and cultural homogeneity, with the much sounder view of relative historical and cultural heterogeneity.

I do not think, in short, that the various arguments I have advanced against Collingwood reinstate in effect the analysis put forward in the philosophy of human nature. For the intellectual baggage required by this analysis is formidable indeed. Nor does Hume's claim that "Human Nature is the only science of man," insofar as it points to an intrinsic relation between the uniformity philosophy and the human sciences, seem to have been borne out in the very considerable development of these sciences since his time. And, indeed, in the account of historical explanation I have been developing in this book the uniformity conception of human nature does not figure. In my view that conception is not internally connected to the idea of the social sciences: the science of man is not necessarily or essentially a science of human nature.

Certainly, though, this does not dispose of the matter entirely. For there are philosophers who, even though they are unwilling to accept the whole apparatus of the uniformity conception or to adopt the Hume-Mill program for reconstructing the human sciences on the basis of that conception, would argue that the *principle* of a science of human nature should be maintained. Thus, we find W. H. Walsh asserting,

> [T]here is also for each [historian] a fundamental set of judgments on which all his thinking rests. These judgments concern human nature: they are judgments about the characteristic responses human beings make to the various challenges set them in the course of their lives, whether by the natural conditions in which they live or by their fellow human beings. . . . That the body of propositions as a whole is extremely important is shown by the reflection that it is in the light of his conception of human nature that the historian must finally decide what to accept as fact and how to understand what he does accept. What he takes to be credible depends on what he conceives to be humanly possible, and it is with this that the judgments here in question are

concerned. The science of human nature is thus the discipline which is basic
for every branch of history. [*Introduction to Philosophy of History*, pp. 64–65;
see also pp. 25, 69]

Walsh's argument is that certain general propositions about human
behavior, statements about what is humanly possible or credible, are
presupposed by historians. It is in this sense that one of the existing
social science disciplines, history, is essentially connected to the
science of human nature. Though I am in substantial agreement with
Walsh's position, I am inclined to think that he has overstated the
matter when he calls the body of these presuppositions a science. I
wonder, in addition, whether Walsh has really made a case for saying
that history depends on such a science.

When Walsh speaks of a "fundamental set of judgments" he seems
to be asserting that there are some general propositions which must
apply to men at all times. These constitute, he claims, a set of propositions upon which all historians could, or should, be able to agree.
(See *Introduction to Philosophy of History*, pp. 115–116.) Walsh ties
this set of propositions in with what he calls "an objective historical
consciousness" (p. 116). It would seem, if Walsh's idea of "a fundamental science of human nature" (p. 115) is practicable, that there
is or is going to be an identifiable body of truths, a fund of preformulated general propositions, which the historian can take to his work of
understanding the past. That Walsh envisions something of this sort is
clear from his remark that "we need to bring to it [the study of the
past] certain pre-existing beliefs about the nature of man" (p. 69). And
the same would be needed, presumably, for the study of other cultures
as well.

All these commitments would appear, then, to be involved in what
Walsh *means* by a basic science of human nature. What I find dis-
quieting in Walsh's analysis is precisely this idea of a fund of preformulated general propositions, potentially the basis of an objective historical consciousness, upon which history is said to depend.

It seems to me that the historian, insofar as he does bring general
propositions to bear, does not draw on a fund of such propositions. His
explanatory judgments may rest on certain beliefs; but these need not
first be formulated in a set of propositions, which the historian then
takes to his study of the past. To call the historian's presuppositions a
science is to suggest that these presuppositions are more articulate and

Conclusion

systematic and experimentally grounded than is probably the case. Moreover, even if all the general maxims of appropriateness which historians do use, either implicitly or explicitly, were stated and collected together, I doubt that many of them would be propositions which *must* apply to men at all times. Accordingly, I see no reason for saying that such a body could come to have the status of an agreed-upon canon, an objective historical consciousness, from which historians would be able to draw.

The body of historical presuppositions, often vague and largely unformulated, is not as it stands a fundamental science of human nature. Even if these presuppositions were made explicit, the resulting set of propositions would not, in all likelihood, constitute the basis for an objective historical consciousness. It seems then that, whatever name we may give the ground of the historian's deliberations about plausibility, the term "science of human nature" raises expectations that are probably incapable of fulfillment.

It is interesting to note that Walsh, at the conclusion of his argument, asserts something very akin to what I have just said. He concedes that a science of human nature, in the sense he has specified, does not now exist; and he allows that for now it "must remain no more than a pious aspiration," the realization of which is problematical. (See *Introduction to Philosophy of History*, pp. 115–116). If this is so, I find Walsh's way of putting the case for the dependence of history on a fundamental science of human nature paradoxical indeed. For surely, history cannot be said to depend on or presuppose, in any recognizable sense, a science that does not even exist and may never exist. It would be more plausible to say that history does *not* depend on a science of human nature, in the sense in which Walsh uses this term.

I should add that Walsh has qualified his own argument, subsequently, in two other important respects.

In a later paper "The Constancy of Human Nature" he virtually repudiates the whole idea of "characteristic responses"—such as "the truth that men who undergo great physical privations are for the most part lacking in mental energy"—which had played such a central role in the argument of his book. (See esp. *Introduction to Philosophy of History*, pp. 64–65.) In the paper he alleges that few reliable generalizations can be made even about hungry or thirsty men and suggests that even in the area of sex there are few responses "characteristic" of men or women in all times and places. (See also Walsh, "Causation of Ideas," esp. pp. 195–196.) Indeed he and I agreed, in a discussion once, that perhaps the one truly characteristic response would be that of persons placed in a smother chamber—and this uniform response would be more nearly a piece of reflex behavior than it would be any sort of decided action.

In the third edition of his book, he has added a concluding footnote which says, "The argument of this section [i.e., pp. 114–116] is, I fear, seriously confused. Historians certainly need to refer in their work to what is thought normal or appropriate as well as to what regularly occurs; but the thought in question is that of the persons of whom they write, not their own. Hence the problem of a uniform historical consciousness, as presented here, does not arise" (p. 116n).[1]

I would add that it is no simple matter really to see things as appropriate or normal from the point of view of those whom the historian or the anthropologist studies. But this point need not detain us, for it was canvassed in considerable detail in the previous chapter. I am much more concerned to keep in view the prospect—held out by Walsh and then, ultimately, dismissed—of an *objective* science of history based on a uniform historical consciousness.

Such an idea, attractive though it is, has not been suggested by my analysis. What I have been contending does not imply that there is one particular set of appropriateness generalizations upon which historians should agree as the basis for their study of the past. In fact, I think it worthwhile to stress that the generalizations presupposed will probably vary from one age to another, and even from one historian to another. I have contended only that rules of appropriateness—without specifying any ones in particular—do play a logically indispensable role in the explanatory accounts given by historians and that these generalizations must have transhistorical application. Much more important in this respect, though, is the schema of practical inference itself; for it does provide an objective framework for the explanatory practices of historians. Without it there would be no universe of discourse for historians at all and no real sense in which historical inquiry could be called a science, or even a discipline. What I have said

1. See also Walsh, "Causation of Ideas," pp. 193–194. Perhaps the most ambitious attempt to found historical explanation on such a notion of appropriateness (where appropriateness is determined, it should be noted, from the *agent's* point of view) is Gardiner's essay "Concept of Man," esp. pp. 18–21, 26–27.

Conclusion

then does provide for objectivity of a sort, though not for objectivity in the strong sense Walsh had in mind (that of a uniform historical consciousness). My account provides, instead, merely for the possibility of a reflective consensus in the discipline of history. It does allow for an interchange or communication among historians on the subject of their explanatory preconceptions, and it does make a relative consensus on the appropriateness generalizations used an achievable goal.

It is important to see in this connection, moreover, that the consensus so achieved will not, once we get beyond the basic schema itself, be grounded simply in the beliefs and predilections of the particular historians involved. Indeed, to reduce the notion of consensus to a mere agreement in beliefs (for example, to a widely received or accepted body of material rules of intelligibility, supposing these to have been made explicit) goes against an argument I conducted earlier (in Chapter Seven). Rather, we need to include in our picture of reflective consensus, as a part of the backdrop, an important truth condition that *any* generic assertion of appropriateness must satisfy: the condition that its elements (arbitrarily designated, say, by Q and R) are so related that a regularity generalization could be formulated (as $p[R, Q] > 0$) and that such a generalization, though most likely a "loose" one, would satisfy the matrix of probabilistic relevance relationships discussed in that chapter.

I think we now have the makings for an acceptable notion of reflective consensus among historians—acceptable at least insofar as we are concerned with explaining actions done for a reason, with explanations that account for a given deed by referring to the agent's purpose, motivational background, means/end belief, and so on. (i) The groundform of this practice, the practice of practical inference, would be outlined in the basic schema. (ii) Within this framework, particular practical inferences would be conducted, each one of which could be represented as a particular set of generic assertions of appropriateness. (iii) The assertibility of the members of each set (that is, the assertibility and hence acceptibility of the particular rules of intelligibility employed therein) would be subject to the proviso that the mutual relevance of the elements (say, Q and R) involved in each such rule could be established by probabilistic reasoning.

In these three points we have the basis for a discipline, if not a science, of history. And on this basis the historian should be able to hold to a middle ground between objectivity in a strong but unattainable sense (that of uniform historical consciousness), on the one side, and a subjectivity that precludes appeal to any objective standards, on the other.

At one time I was prepared to stop with this. I see now, though, that this conception of history could be objected to as needlessly parochial. For, apparently, it does not take account of the fact that the discipline of history is itself transhistorical. This objection, of course, is not meant to suggest that historians, social scientists, philosophers (or some reasonable facsimile) could be found in all societies. But it does seem evident that there have been historians in *other periods*, for example, the Greek or the medieval, though perhaps not among the Incas; and historians in *other cultures*, for example, the Oriental societies, though perhaps not among some of the tribes in Africa. Certainly, then, we should not close our eyes to the fact that there has been an interest, on the part of persons from other periods and other cultures, in the explaining of human actions.

I think we must take account of this objection. For though we do not seek a uniform historical consciousness we do seek principles of history with adequate scope. And where the practice of history can be discerned in other periods and other cultures we must define a reflective consensus among historians which can itself be transhistorical. So the problem becomes to extend the reflective consensus which exists in principle for historians today to historians in other periods and in other cultures.

At first glance this does not appear to be a problem of any great size. We simply take the "assimilationist" account of transhistorical understanding developed in the previous chapter and apply it to the special case of *historians* in other periods and other cultures. Since there is no special difficulty posed by the fact that we want to grapple onto the rules used by historians of another period, or culture, in their practice of explaining actions (as distinct, say, from rules used by priests or by practitioners of healing or by chiefs or by farmers to do the things they do) and since what I have described represents no special departure from acceptable canons of historical inquiry, there would appear to be no issue of principle here at all. Hence, there appears to be no special problem.

Now I do think the assimilationist account provides part of the answer to the problem. And I think it also helps us see more clearly why Walsh's idea of preformulated principles of intelligibility ("pre-existing

Conclusion

beliefs" as he called them) will not do in the special case of understanding other periods or other cultures (where the stress is on the
other). If assimilation is as I have described it, there is an important
reason why *some* of its rules can never be formulated in advance. (Specifically those rules, from the other culture, that we grapple onto.) For
these can become rules of intelligibility for us only after the fact, only
after they have been assimilated to our rules of intelligibility and after
we have learned to use them as rules of intelligibility in that way, as
reformulations of rules already indigenous to our practice.

What we can achieve, as the intended result of the practice of assimilation, is internal understanding of actions performed in another
period, or in another culture. We are concerned in such cases merely
to follow the rules of intelligibility of that time or place; we need only
be able to use these rules, when assimilated to our own, as rules of intelligibility (of appropriateness, of plausible connection). We do not,
however, have to accept these rules as rules of intelligibility, except insofar as they are that by reference to our rules of intelligibility.

But when we talk of a transhistorical reflective consensus among
historians, one that transcends differences between periods or between
cultures, we must be in a position to credit the practice of history as it
exists in other periods or other cultures. If we set a relative consensus
on appropriateness generalizations as an achievable goal and want this
consensus to be a genuinely transhistorical one, then we must be able
to *accept* some of the rules of historians in other perods and other cultures into the consensus. The consensus is, however, also billed as a
reflective one. And this requires that the rules of intelligibility from
other places and times not be accepted as a matter of parliamentary
courtesy or of international goodwill; rather they must be acceptable
solely *as rules of intelligibility.*

The practice of assimilation does provide for internal understanding;
but it does not provide for asserting a rule of intelligibility (from another period or culture) as a rule of intelligibility except derivatively, as
assimilated to our rule of intelligibility within a particular family of
such rules. This is why the assimilationist account, though it may provide part—even a major part—of the answer to our problem, cannot
be taken as the single-dose solution.

It is no easy matter to "see what intelligibility amounts to in the life
of the society we are investigating" (Winch, "Understanding a Primitive Society," p. 317). And, in particular, it is no easy matter to assert

a rule of intelligibility (from another culture or time) as an *acceptable* rule, to assert it *as a rule of intelligibility*. The problem of extending reflective historical consensus to include rules from other periods and other cultures, then, is precisely the problem of asserting such rules as rules of intelligibility.

This is a more difficult problem than at first it appeared to be, but I think some additional headway towards solving it can yet be found in the argument I have put forward. I mentioned earlier that a rule of intelligibility can legitimately be asserted, as stating an intelligible connection, only if it could be supported by probabilistic reasoning. This necessary condition seems to me to provide the key we are seeking.

Just as we can learn to *use* a rule of intelligibility from another culture, and to use it as a rule of intelligibility, by assimilating it to our rule; so we can also be in position to *assert* it *as a rule of intelligibility* on condition that it could be backed up by probabilistic reasoning. It would appear that a reflective historical consensus could exist, one that transcends differences in periods and cultures. Its basis is provided by combining the assimilationist account of internal understanding (developed in Chapter Eleven) with the notion of probabilistic support (developed in Chapter Seven).

Now the second of these two component accounts, which specifies a necessary condition of *asserting* intelligible connection, requires merely that there *exist* a certain relationship between two factors (Q and R, arbitrarily designated). But we can show that this condition is met in a given case by actually *producing* the regularity generalization which has been presumed. Of course, this generalization (formulated as $p[R, Q] > o$) would have to be able to satisfy a matrix of probabilistic relevance relations. But this latter point presents no insuperable difficulty, since the notion of satisfying was itself made relative to the fact of existing cultural and historical differences, insofar as these could be recognized. Hence this requirement should be read as saying that the generalization in question must satisfy the matrix, given the *epistemic* situation of the historian and when due account is taken of the constraints on his understanding afforded by the kinds of experience available to him, either directly or evidentially, and by his "picture of life" formed thereby.

The only real difference between the case discussed in Chapter Seven and the one now under consideration is that the historian here is himself a man of another period, or culture. And our focus is on the

Conclusion

rule of intelligibility that *he* uses in his historical investigations—and, hence, on a rule that belongs not to our time or place but to another.

However, though the rule of intelligible (or appropriate or plausible) connection is not indigenous to our culture, it nonetheless is a rule of intelligibility and has been recognized as such. Hence, the same necessary condition (of asserting intelligible connection) obtains, and should obtain, in either of these cases: it is required equally of all generic assertions of appropriateness (of ours and of those from other periods and other cultures) that they be able to meet the test of probabilistic support. And where there is doubt as to a particular rule of intelligibility, a doubt that could attach to any generic assertion of appropriateness, the same test is actually employed: we show that a particular discursive principle can legitimately be asserted as a rule of intelligibility by showing that it satisfies a matrix of probabilistic relevance relations.

Of course, the elements (deeds, purposes, means/end beliefs, and so on) in a generic assertion of appropriateness, from another period or culture, might sometimes have to be redescribed in order for the requisite probabilistic backing to be achieved. In this respect, though, that rule is no different from any other rule of intelligibility. It is even possible that the redescription might be offered by someone other than the historian in question, even by someone from a period or culture different from his own. But so long as these redescriptions are culturally available to the historian and to others from his period or culture—in the significant sense that intelligibility (for them!) is preserved in the new generic material descriptions used—then no difficulty in principle is occasioned by the fact of redescription. For we can still say we are dealing with rules which make for intelligibility in that period or culture. And the point remains that any such rule, in order really to count as a rule of intelligibility, must be able to pass the test of probabilistic relevance.

It seems, then, that my general line of analysis does afford a solution of sorts to the problem raised. For it does make possible the inclusion of rules of intelligibility drawn from other periods and other cultures. Indeed, the standard that underwrites our rules of intelligibility, as rules that legitimately assert an intelligible or plausible connection, and hence warrants their inclusion, would underwrite the eligible rules drawn from any place or time.

Unlike mere internal understanding, the combination of the assimilationist account with the criterion of probabilistic support provides the wherewithal to accept the rules of intelligibility of other periods and other cultures. The first—the assimilationist account of internal understanding—allows us to discern the "thought" of appropriate connection that exists on the part of persons in another period, or culture. It allows us to use the rule of intelligibility or appropriateness, as a rule of intelligibility, insofar as it is assimilated to our rule within a single family of such rules. And the second—the account of establishing probabilistic relevance—allows us to affirm that what is said in such a rule to be intelligibly or plausibly connected is so connected. It enables us to assert the rule—on its own, so to speak—as a rule of appropriateness.

Hence I would want to say of this elusive but estimable goal, transhistorical reflective consensus, what Walsh said of his now banished idea of a uniform historical consciousness (his putative "fundamental science of human nature"): that it is "possible in principle." [2] There is no inherent barrier, no issue of principle, which would prevent the inclusion of rules of intelligibility from other periods and other cultures within the reflective consensus of historians. I do not think this puts history one step further on the way to being a science, at least of the "covering law" sort; but it does help establish history's credentials as a human science, as a disciplined mode of inquiry into human things on grounds that could be commended *in principle* to reflective men in differing times and cultures. And this notion of a transhistorical reflective consensus is not so much an act of piety as it is an intellectual debt we owe to the idea of a science of human nature.

I have tried in the argument of this book to bring the science of human nature and historicism and, more particularly, the "covering law" and *verstehen* positions together on a middle ground. My aim has been to find what is of value in each and, by taking account of their positive elements, to develop a mediating position between them.

Analytic philosophy of history, despite its considerable sophistication and indisputable contributions, has tended up to now to reflect rather than to overcome this historic dichotomy. My book, if it has been true to its aim, has achieved a coherent moderating position be-

2. See Walsh, *Introduction to Philosophy of History*, p. 68. In developing the argument of this chapter I have been influenced as well by points made by Danto (see his *Analytical Philosophy of Action*, esp. p. 113) and by Winch ("Understanding a Primitive Society," esp. pp. 317–318).

Conclusion

tween these two fundamental and often opposed lines of thought. I would not claim that truth in philosophy lies always in the mean. But I do believe that philosophy of history, in order to achieve a constructive philosophy for the present, can best proceed by reconciling the disharmonies in its own past.

Bibliography of Works Cited

Books

Atkinson, R. F. *Knowledge and Explanation in History: An Introduction*. (Forthcoming from Cornell University Press.)

Berlin, Isaiah. *Historical Inevitability*. Auguste Comte Memorial Trust Lecture No. 1. London: Oxford University Press, 1954.

Bloch, Marc L. B. *Feudal Society*. Translated by L. A. Manyon. Chicago: University of Chicago Press, 1968. (First published in French in two volumes, the second of which appeared in 1940; the English translation first published in 1961: Routledge & Kegan Paul.)

Collingwood, Robin G. *An Autobiography*. Oxford: Oxford University Press, 1939.

——. *An Essay on Metaphysics*. Oxford: Oxford University Press, 1940.

——. *The Idea of History*. Edited with an introduction by T. M. Knox. New York: Oxford University Press, 1956. (First published in 1946: Oxford, Oxford University Press.)

——. *The New Leviathan*. Oxford: Oxford University Press, 1942.

——. *The Principles of Art*. New York: Oxford University Press, 1958. (First published in 1938: Oxford, Oxford University Press.)

Note: Where more than one source is listed, the citation in my text or notes comes from the entry marked with the asterisk, unless specifically indicated otherwise.

Bibliography

——, and J. N. L. Myres. *Roman Britain and the English Settlements*. Vol. I of *The Oxford History of England*. Oxford: Oxford University Press, 1936. (2d ed., 1937.)

Danto, Arthur C. *Analytical Philosophy of Action*. Cambridge: Cambridge University Press, 1973.

——. *Analytical Philosophy of History*. Cambridge: Cambridge University Press, 1965.

——. *Analytical Philosophy of Knowledge*. Cambridge: Cambridge University Press, 1968.

——. *What Philosophy Is: A Guide to the Elements*. New York: Harper & Row, 1968.

Deane, Herbert A. *The Political and Social Ideas of St. Augustine*. New York: Columbia University Press, 1963.

Dilthey, Wilhelm. *Pattern and Meaning in History*. Edited and translated by H. P. Rickman. New York: Harper & Row, 1961.

Donagan, Alan H. *The Later Philosophy of R. G. Collingwood*. Oxford: Oxford University Press, 1962.

Dray, William H. *Laws and Explanation in History*. London: Oxford University Press, 1957.

——. *Philosophy of History*. Foundations of Philosophy Series. Englewood Cliffs, N.J.: Prentice-Hall, 1964.

Gardiner, Patrick L. *The Nature of Historical Explanation*. Oxford: Oxford University Press, 1952.

——, ed. *The Philosophy of History*. Oxford Readings in Philosophy Series. London: Oxford University Press, 1974.

——, ed. *Theories of History*. Glencoe, Ill.: Free Press, 1959.

Hanson, F. Allan. *Meaning in Culture*. London: Routledge & Kegan Paul, 1975.

Hanson, Norwood R. *Patterns of Discovery*. Cambridge: Cambridge University Press, 1959.

Hodges, Herbert A. *The Philosophy of Wilhelm Dilthey*. London: Routledge & Kegan Paul, 1952.

Hume, David. *An Inquiry Concerning Human Understanding*. Edited by C. W. Hendel. New York: Liberal Arts Press, 1955. (Note: this edition includes Hume's "An Abstract of a Treatise of Human Nature.")

——. *A Treatise of Human Nature*. Edited by L. A. Selby-Bigge. Oxford: Oxford University Press, impression of 1958. (First published in the Selby-Bigge edition, by Oxford University Press, 1888.)

Jarvie, I. C. *Concepts and Society*. London: Routledge & Kegan Paul, 1972.

Johnson, Deborah G. "Legal Responsibility, Legal Liability and the Explanation of Action." Ph.D. dissertation, The University of Kansas, Lawrence, 1976.

Bibliography

Kluback, W. *Wilhelm Dilthey's Philosophy of History.* New York: Columbia University Press, 1956.

Krausz, Michael, ed. *Critical Essays on the Philosophy of R. G. Collingwood.* Oxford: Clarendon Press, 1972.

Louch, A. R. *Explanation and Human Action.* Oxford: Basil Blackwell, 1966.

Malinowski, B. *Argonauts of the Western Pacific.* London: Routledge & Kegan Paul, 1922.

Mill, John Stuart. *A System of Logic.* 8th ed. London: Longmans, Green, 1952.

Mink, L. O. *Mind, History and Dialectic: The Philosophy of R. G. Collingwood.* Bloomington: Indiana University Press, 1969.

Nagel, Ernest. *The Structure of Science.* London: Routledge & Kegan Paul, 1961.

Newman, Fred D. *Explanation by Description.* The Hague: Mouton, 1968.

Popper, Karl R. *The Open Society and Its Enemies.* Princeton: Princeton University Press, 1950.

——. *The Poverty of Historicism.* Boston: Beacon Press, 1957.

Rubinoff, Lionel. *Collingwood and the Reform of Metaphysics: A Study in the Philosophy of Mind.* Toronto: University of Toronto Press, 1970.

Ryle, Gilbert. *The Concept of Mind.* New York: Barnes & Noble, 1949.

Taylor, Charles. *The Explanation of Behaviour.* London: Routledge & Kegan Paul, 1964.

von Wright, Georg Henrik. *Causality and Determinism.* New York: Columbia University Press, 1974.

——. *Explanation and Understanding.* Ithaca, N.Y.: Cornell University Press, 1971.

——. *The Varieties of Goodness.* London: Routledge & Kegan Paul, 1963.

Walsh, William H. *An Introduction to Philosophy of History.* 3d ed. London: Hutchinson University Library, 1967.* (1st ed., 1951; 2d ed., 1958.)

White, Morton G. *Foundations of Historical Knowledge.* New York: Harper & Row, 1965.

Winch, Peter. *The Idea of a Social Science.* London: Routledge & Kegan Paul, 1958.

Wittgenstein, Ludwig. *On Certainty.* Edited by G. E. M. Anscombe and G. H. von Wright; translated by D. Paul and G. E. M. Anscombe. New York: Harper & Row, 1972.

Articles

Berlin, Isaiah. "The Concept of Scientific History." In W. H. Dray, ed., *Philosophical Analysis and History.* New York: Harper & Row, 1966, pp.

Bibliography

5–53.* (Originally published: "History and Theory: The Concept of Scientific History," *History and Theory*, 1 [1960], 1–31.)

Bricke, John. "Emotion and Thought in Hume's *Treatise.*" *Canadian Journal of Philosophy*, suppl. vol. 1, Pt. I (1974), pp. 53–71.

——. "Hume's Associationist Psychology." *Journal of the History of the Behavioral Sciences*, 10 (1974), 397–409.

Cebik, L. B. "Collingwood: Action, Re-enactment, and Evidence." *Philosophical Forum*, 2 (1970), 68–90.

Churchland, P. M. "The Logical Character of Action-Explanations." *Philosophical Review*, 79 (1970), 214–236.

Danto, Arthur C. "Causation and Basic Actions: A Reply *en passant* to Professor Margolis." *Inquiry*, 13 (1970), 108–125.

——. "Historical Language and Historical Reality." *Review of Metaphysics*, 27 (1973), 219–259.

——. "The Problem of Other Periods." *Journal of Philosophy*, 63 (1966), 566–577.

Davidson, Donald. "Actions, Reasons, and Causes." *Journal of Philosophy*, 60 (1963), 685–700.

——. "Causal Relations." In E. Sosa, ed., *Causation and Conditionals*. London: Oxford University Press, 1975, pp. 82–94.* (Originally published: *Journal of Philosophy*, 64 [1967], 691–703.)

Donagan, Alan H. "Alternative Historical Explanations and Their Verification." *Monist*, 53 (1969), 58–89.

——. "Comment" (on the article "Imperfect Rationality" by Watkins). In R. Borger and F. Cioffi, eds., *Explanation in the Behavioural Sciences*. Cambridge: Cambridge University Press, 1970, pp. 218–227.

——. "Explanation in History." In P. L. Gardiner, ed., *Theories of History*. Glencoe, Ill.: Free Press, 1959, pp. 428–443.* (Originally published: *Mind*, 66 [1957], 145–164.)

——. "The Popper-Hempel Theory Reconsidered." In W. H. Dray, ed., *Philosophical Analysis and History*. New York: Harper & Row, 1966, pp. 127–159.* (Originally published as "Historical Explanation: The Popper-Hempel Theory Reconsidered," *History and Theory*, 4 [1964], 3–26.)

Dray, William H. "The Historical Explanation of Actions Reconsidered." In Sidney Hook, ed., *Philosophy and History*. New York: New York University Press, 1963, pp. 105–135.

——. "Singular Hypotheticals and Historical Explanation." In L. Gross, ed., *Sociological Theory: Inquiries and Paradigms*. New York: Harper & Row, 1967, pp. 181–203.

Gardiner, Patrick L. "The Concept of Man as Presupposed by the Historical Studies." In *The Proper Study*. Vol. IV of *The Royal Institute of Philosophy Lectures*. London: Macmillan, 1973, pp. 14–31.

258

Bibliography

——. "Historical Understanding and the Empiricist Tradition." In B. Williams and A. Montefiori, eds., *British Analytical Philosophy*. London: Routledge & Kegan Paul, 1966, pp. 267–284.

——. "The 'Objects' of Historical Knowledge." *Philosophy*, 27 (1952), 211–220.

Gellner, Ernest. "Holism versus Individualism in History and Sociology." In P. L. Gardiner, ed., *Theories of History*. Glencoe, Ill.: Free Press, 1959, pp. 489–503.* (Originally published as "Explanations in History," in *Proceedings of the Aristotelian Society*, Suppl. vol. 30 [1956], pp. 157–176.)

Hanson, F. Allan, and Rex Martin. "The Problem of Other Cultures." *Philosophy of the Social Sciences*, 3 (1973), 191–208.

Hempel, Carl G. "Aspects of Scientific Explanation." In C. G. Hempel, *Aspects of Scientific Explanation and Other Essays in the Philosophy of Science*. New York: Free Press, 1965, pp. 331–496.

——. "Deductive Nomological vs. Statistical Explanation." In Herbert Feigl and G. Maxwell, eds., *Minnesota Studies in the Philosophy of Science*, vol. III. Minneapolis: University of Minnesota Press, 1962, pp. 98–169.

——. "Explanation in Science and in History." In W. H. Dray, ed., *Philosophical Analysis and History*. New York: Harper & Row, 1966, pp. 95–126.* (Originally published in Robert G. Colodney, ed., *Frontiers of Science and Philosophy*. Pittsburgh: University of Pittsburgh Press, 1962, pp. 9–33.)

——. "The Function of General Laws in History." In P. L. Gardiner, ed., *Theories of History*. Glencoe, Ill.: Free Press, 1959, pp. 344–356.* (Originally published: *Journal of Philosophy*, 39 [1942], 35–48.)

——. "The Logic of Functional Analysis." In C. G. Hempel, *Aspects of Scientific Explanation and Other Essays in the Philosophy of Science*. New York: Free Press, 1965, pp. 297–330.* (Originally published in L. Gross, ed., *Symposium on Sociological Theory*. New York: Harper & Row, 1959, pp. 271–307.

——. "Rational Action." *Proceedings and Addresses of the American Philosophical Association*, vol. 35. Yellow Springs, Ohio: Antioch Press, 1962, pp. 5–23.

——. "Reasons and Covering Laws in Historical Explanation." In Sidney Hook, ed., *Philosophy and History*. New York: New York University Press, 1963, pp. 143–163.

——, and P. Oppenheim. "Studies in the Logic of Explanation." *Philosophy of Science*, 15 (1948), 135–175.

Jarvie, I. C. "Understanding and Explanation in Sociology and Social Anthropology." In R. Borger and F. Cioffi, eds., *Explanation in the Behavioural Sciences*. Cambridge: Cambridge University Press, 1970, pp. 231–248.

Knox, T. M. "Editor's Preface." In Robin G. Collingwood, *The Idea of History*. New York: Oxford University Press, 1956, pp. v–xxiv.

Bibliography

Kroeber, A. L. "The Superorganic." *American Anthropologist*, 19 (1917), 163–213.

Landesman, Charles A. "Actions as Universals: An Inquiry into the Metaphysics of Action." *American Philosophical Quarterly*, 6 (1969), 247–252.

Leach, J. J. "Discussion: Dray on Rational Explanation." *Philosophy of Science*, 33 (1966), 61–69.

———. "The Logic of the Situation." *Philosophy of Science*, 35 (1968), 258–273.

Malcolm, Norman. "Intention and Belief." In P. A. Schilpp, ed., *The Philosophy of Georg Henrik von Wright*. The Library of Living Philosophers series (forthcoming).

Marquis, Donald. "Historical Explanation: A Reconsideration of the New Popper-Hempel Theory." *Southwestern Journal of Philosophy*, 4 (1973), 101–108.

Martin, M. "Situational Logic and Covering Law Explanations." *Inquiry*, 11 (1968), 388–399.

Martin, Rex. "Explanation and Understanding in History." In Juha Manninen and Raimo Tuomela, eds., *Essays on Explanation and Understanding*. Synthese Library 72. Dordrecht, Holland: Reidel, 1976, pp. 305–334.

———. "The Problem of the 'Tie' in von Wright's Schema of Practical Inference: A Wittgensteinian Solution." In J. Hintikka, ed., *Essays on Wittgenstein in Honour of G. H. von Wright. Acta Philosophica Fennica*, 28 (1976), 326–363.

Mink, L. O. "Collingwood's Historicism: A Dialectic of Process." In M. Krausz, ed., *Critical Essays on the Philosophy of R. G. Collingwood*. Oxford: Clarendon Press, 1972, pp. 154–178.

Niiniluoto, Ilkka. "Inductive Explanation, Propensity, and Action." In Juha Manninen and Raimo Tuomela, eds., *Essays on Explanation and Understanding*. Synthese Library 72. Dordrecht, Holland: Reidel, 1976, pp. 335–368.

Olafson, Frederick A. "Narrative History and the Concept of Action." *History and Theory*, 9 (1970), 265–289.

Rotenstreich, Nathan. "History and Time: A Critical Examination of R. G. Collingwood's Doctrine." *Scripta Hierosolymitana*, 6 (1960), 41–103.

Ryle, Gilbert. " 'If,' 'So,' and 'Because.' " In Max Black, ed., *Philosophical Analysis: A Collection of Essays*. Ithaca, N.Y.: Cornell University Press, 1950, pp. 323–340.

Salmon, Wesley C. "Statistical Explanation." In R. G. Colodny, ed., *The Nature and Function of Scientific Theories*. Pittsburgh: University of Pittsburgh Press, 1970, pp. 173–231.

Bibliography

Scriven, Michael. "Truisms as the Grounds for Historical Explanations." In Patrick L. Gardiner, ed., *Theories of History*. Glencoe, Ill.: Free Press, 1959, pp. 443–475.

Stoutland, F. "The Logical Connection Argument." In N. Rescher, ed., *Studies in the Theory of Knowledge*. American Philosophical Quarterly Monograph Series, no. 4. Oxford: Basil Blackwell in cooperation with the University of Pittsburgh, 1970, pp. 117–129.

Taylor, Charles. "Explaining Action." *Inquiry*, 13 (1970), 54–89.

Tuomela, Raimo. "Explanation and Understanding of Human Behavior." In Juha Manninen and Raimo Tuomela, eds., *Essays on Explanation and Understanding*. Synthese Library 72. Dordrecht, Holland: Reidel, 1976, pp. 183–205.

———. "Purposive Causation of Action." In R. Cohen and Marx Wartofsky, eds., *Boston Studies in the Philosophy of Science*, vol. XXXI. Dordrecht, Holland: Reidel, 1977 (forthcoming).

von Wright, Georg Henrik. "On So-called Practical Inference." *Acta Sociologica*, 15 (1972), 39–53.

———. "On the Logic and Epistemology of the Causal Relation." In E. Sosa, ed., *Causation and Conditionals*. London: Oxford University Press, 1975, pp. 95–113.* (Originally published in P. Suppes, *et al.*, eds., *Logic, Methodology and Philosophy of Science*, vol. IV. Amsterdam: North-Holland, 1973, pp. 293–312.

———. "Replies." In Juha Manninen and Raimo Tuomela, eds., *Essays on Explanation and Understanding*. Synthese Library 72. Dordrecht, Holland: Reidel, 1976, pp. 371–413.

———. "The Determinants of Action." In Klibansky *Festschrift* (forthcoming).

Walsh, William H. "The Causation of Ideas." *History and Theory*, 14 (1975), 186–199.

———. "The Constancy of Human Nature." In H. D. Lewis, ed., *Contemporary British Philosophy*. Fourth series. London: Allen & Unwin, 1976, pp. 274–291.

———. "The Logical Status of Vico's Ideal Eternal History." In Giorgio Tagliacozzo and Donald P. Verene, eds., *Giambattista Vico's Science of Humanity*. Baltimore: Johns Hopkins University Press, 1976, pp. 141–153.

Watkins, J. W. N. "Imperfect Rationality." In R. Borger and F. Cioffi, eds., *Explanation in the Behavioural Sciences*. Cambridge: Cambridge University Press, 1970, pp. 167–217, and "Reply" (to A. H. Donagan), pp. 228–230.

Wertz, Spencer K. "Hume, History, and Human Nature." *Journal of the History of Ideas*, 36 (1975), 481–496.

Winch, Peter "Understanding a Primitive Society." *American Philosophical Quarterly*, 1 (1964), 307–324.

Bibliography

Wittgenstein, Ludwig. "Remarks on Frazer's 'Golden Bough.' " Translated by
A. C. Miles and R. Rhees with an introduction (pp. 18–28) by zr. Rhees.
Human World, 1 (1971), 18–41.* (Originally published in German:
Synthese, 17 [1967], 233–253.)

Reviews of Books

Passmore, John. Review of W. H. Dray's *Laws and Explanation in History*.
In *Australian Journal of Politics and History*, 4 (1958), 269–276.
Scriven, Michael. Review of A. C. Danto's *Analytical Philosophy of History*.
In *Journal of Philosophy*, 63 (1966), 500–504.
Strawson, P. F. Review of W. H. Dray's *Laws and Explanation in History*. In
Mind, 68 (1959), 265–268.

Index

263

Index

Index

Index

Index

Science of Human Nature (*cont.*)
  Walsh, W. H., 219, 243–246, 252 (*criticism*, 228, 241, 244–249)
Scriven, Michael, 90n, 114, 116n, 125n, 148n, 149n
Situational-motivation, 33, 66–69, 72, 91; *see also* Explanatory adequacy
Socialist, bank-bombing (example), 83–84, 88
Stoutland, F., 165, 176n
Strawson, P. F., 118n

Taylor, Charles, 165n, 176n
Toynbee, Arnold J., 30
Transhistorical general principles, the possibility of, 215–219, 222–231, 241–243
  transhistorical application, necessity for, 220–222, 230, 246
Triangle of explanation, 72–74, 91–92, 99–100, 112–114, 130, 153
  pictured, 69, 149

Understanding:
  concept of, 94–95
  cross-cultural, 229–243, 247–252
  Danto, criticism of, 239–240
  and explanation, 43, 90, 240
  investigative, 233–240
  and misunderstanding (and failure to understand), 201–202, 229
  see also Re-enactment, general concept of, *and* Schema for action-explanations
Uniformity conception of human nature, 31, 38, 243, 252; *see also* Hume, David, *and* Mill, J. S.
Universal regularities (in mind and behavior), 18–21; *see also* Collingwood, R. G., transhistorical difference

Validation, *see* Re-enactment, general concept of, *and* Schema for action-explanations
Verification
  entailment relationship, distinct from, 179
  the logic of, 174–175, 178–179, 205
  the practice of (in history), 178–179
  praxis-verification, 210–213, 240
Von Wright, Georg Henrik, 22, 81n, 95–97, 152n, 186, 189n, 197n, 199, 204n, 213n
  material invalidity, 92–94
  means/end relationship, 85–90, 94
  normal conditions, 85–87
  schema for action-explanations, entailment status ascribed to, 170–173 (*criticism*, 174–175)
  understanding (as a semantic category), 94–95
  verification argument, 170–173 (*criticism*, 174–175)

Waismann, F., 94
Walsh, William H., 13, 14n, 17n, 22, 30, 48–49, 52n, 58n, 116n, 222n, 231
  science of human nature, 219, 243–246, 252 (*criticism*, 228, 241, 244–249)
Watkins, J. W. N., 117n
Wertz, Spencer K., 23n
White, Morton G., 17n, 22, 101n, 106, 118n, 136
  existential regularism, 138–141, 144, 155, 163 (*criticism*, 140–145)
  one-instance laws, problem of, 155
Winch, Peter, 231, 234n, 249, 252n
Wittgenstein, Ludwig, 90n, 137n
  on language games, 203–209, 211

267

Library of Congress Cataloging in Publication Data
(For library cataloging purposes only)

Martin, Rex.
  Historical explanation.

  (Contemporary philosophy)
  Bibliography: p. 255
  Includes index.
    1. History—Philosophy. I. Title. II. Series.
D16.9.M279   901   77-3121
ISBN 0-8014-1084-3